Japanese History & Culture from Ancient to Modern Times
Seven Basic Bibliographies

JAPANESE HISTORY & CULTURE FROM ANCIENT TO MODERN TIMES:

Seven Basic Bibliographies

JOHN W. DOWER

ᴍᴍ Markus Wiener Publishing
ᴡᴡ New York

220305

A NOTE ON THE TITLE & HALF-TITLE DESIGNS

The designs used on the title and half-title pages are Japanese *mon* or crests. The basic square design motif is known as the "mesh" (*meyui*, literally "eye tie"), and derives from procedures used in an expensive traditional dyeing process to create a dappled effect. An almost identical variant on the same square pattern is the "nail puller" (*kuginuki*), based on an old carpenter's tool and carrying connotations of deriving leverage and strength from small sources.

Published 1986 by Markus Wiener Publishing, Inc.

For information write to:
Markus Wiener Publishing, Inc.
2901 Broadway, Suite 107
New York, NY 10025

Library of Congress Cataloging-in-Publication Data

Dower, John W.

Japanese history and culture from ancient to modern times.

Bibliography: p.
   1. Japan -- History -- Bibliography. I. Title.

Z3306.D69 1986   [DS835] 016.952 86-15836

ISBN 0-910 129-36-3 (paper)
ISBN 0-910 129-20-7 (cloth)

Printed in the United States of America.

CONTENTS

PREFACE

As a graduate student in the late 1960s, I recall being impressed by the passing comment of a senior scholar. Until recently, he said, he had been pretty much able to keep abreast of Western scholarship about the Far East, but that was becoming more difficult. Today, almost twenty years later, we can only marvel at a time when it was possible for academics to still dream about being conversant with the gamut of scholarly writings about China and Japan. In the Japan field, the articles and books that have been published since the 1950s in English alone are so numerous, in fact, that even the bibliographers appear to have abandoned hope of keeping up.

How else can one account for the fact that even now the best known general bibliographic surveys of Western writings about Japanese history and culture still date from between the 1950s and early 1970s? The pioneer Harvard listing by Hugh Borton and his colleagues appeared in 1954. Bernard Silberman's useful annotated bibliography was published in 1962. Naomi Fukuda's union catalog of Western books on Japan is dated 1968, and the two multi-volume cumulative bibliographies covering all Asia issued by the Association of Asian Studies cover publications through 1970. Most of the more recent bibliographic guides to scholarship on Japan have been of a specialized, attenuated, or annual nature--valuable indeed, but still making it necessary for a generation of students, teachers, and scholars to compile their own working bibliographies.

This present publication is the unexpected offspring of such a private endeavor, having its origin in personal bibliographies compiled over the years to guide students into the flourishing but poorly marked terrain of historical studies of Japan. History is the most catholic and generous of scholarly fields--bridging the humanities and social sciences, as it necessarily does, and weaving together such diverse concerns as personality and economic forces, ideologies and institutions, the gentle arts and the exercise of unbridled violence. The bibliographies of Japanese history offered here are thus multidisciplinary in content and wide-ranging in their topical as well as chronological focus. At the same time, they inevitably reflect personal pedagogic concerns, and the criteria of selection and organization require explanation.

1. Every effort has been made to maintain and enhance the practical, "working" nature of this guide. Thus, the classroom origins of the volume have been preserved in a manner that will enable teachers to lift out parts of the whole as basic reading lists for the most common survey courses pertaining to Japan: the ancient and medieval periods to 1600; early modern and modern Japan (1600-1945); diplomacy, imperialism, and war from the 1850s to 1945; and the Allied occupation of Japan (1945-1952). In addition, each of these major bibliographies is broken down into numerous topical sections to facilitate quick identification of specific concerns, and cumbersome cross-referencing has been kept to an absolute minimum by repeating the same reference wherever it is topically pertinent.

2. Entries under every section or subsection tend to be clustered in ways that are internally logical. Grand overviews are listed together, for example, as are articles and books focusing on essentially the same subject. Where chronology is relevant within any section, references dealing with earlier events naturally precede those concerning later periods. Subjective evaluation undeniably colors such organization to a minor degree, and even whimsy may come into play on occasion. To anyone immersed in history, however, it is much more rational and convenient to have sources grouped in accordance with thematic affinity, as opposed to purely mechanical conventions such as authors in alphabetical order. The bibliography is designed to keep jumping around to a minimum.

3. The difficulty of Oriental languages always is evoked as one of the greatest barriers to Western comprehension of the East, and no one can deny the importance of understanding other peoples through their native tongue. At the same time, however, it must be noted that much of the "primary" record through which we can better understand Japanese history is accessible in English. The great classics of ancient and medieval literature are now available in excellent translations; the minor classics are gradually finding their translators;

v

and translation of modern Japanese literature has become a small cottage industry. Most of the basic legal codes and "house laws" from early times on have been rendered into English, as has a great variety of religious texts. In the modern period, the Japanese themselves produced literally millions of pages in Western languages in the form of books, magazines, newspapers, yearbooks, documents submitted to international organizations, and sheer propaganda. Their diplomatic exchanges with foreign nations beginning in the mid-nineteenth century, along with the voluminous reports of British and American diplomats concerned with Japan, are now widely accessible. The crisis years between World War One and World War Two saw Japan, China, and the Western nations produce a veritable deluge of English-language material. This wide range of "primary" materials in English is of immense value to students, teachers, and scholars alike, and special care has been taken to introduce the most important of such sources here for every period of Japanese history. For 1931 to 1945, a separate bibliography is devoted exclusively to such materials.

4. On more technical matters, it should be noted that Japanese as well as Western authors of cited English-language publications are listed with given name first and surname second, thus keeping the treatment of authors' names consistent throughout. It has not been possible to place macrons over the "long" vowels in Japanese names.

5. The bibliographies are generally up-to-date through 1985, and include materials scheduled for publication early in 1986. Special effort has been made to itemize not only articles from the basic scholarly journals that deal with Japan, but also especially useful essays that appear in edited volumes. Selectivity--and plain oversight--are naturally most conspicuous at the article and essay level, and worthy scholarly contributions have undoubtedly been overlooked. I can only hope their number is relatively small and their authors will be understanding. In passing, I might note that the selective process has extended to exclusion of some of my own publications.

Over the course of the years I have shared bibliographies with William Wray and learned of many sources from him that might otherwise have been neglected. Carol Gluck, James O'Brien, and Martin Collcutt kindly read portions of earlier drafts of this volume and offered helpful addenda. Julie Bogle not only typed the ever expanding draft of the manuscript, but also provided invaluable library assistance in clarifying and correcting imprecise references. Lee Tablewski assisted in the final design of the manuscript, and Markus Wiener, the publisher, tolerated innumerable revisions with unfailing patience. My thanks to these individuals and others who contributed to this compilation.

I presume this will be the last of the survey bibliographies of Japanese history and culture to emanate from file cards in a private study. Certainly I hope that is the case, for like anyone in the Japan field I look forward to the day when we will have available a multi-volume and truly comprehensive computer-based bibliography of writings on Japan in Western languages. Until then, it will be gratifying if this guide enables other teachers and researchers to "keep up" with greater ease--and, at the same time, suggests some useful ways to organize our thinking about Japan.

JOHN W. DOWER

Madison, Wisconsin
March 11, 1986

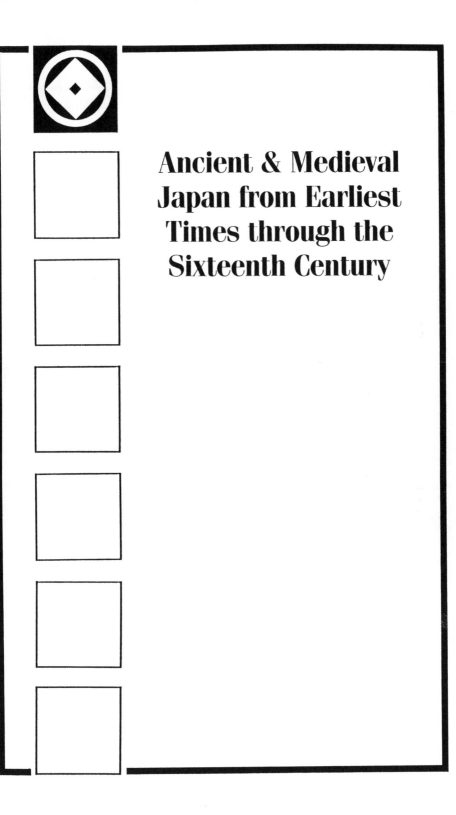

Ancient & Medieval Japan from Earliest Times through the Sixteenth Century

ANCIENT & MEDIEVAL JAPAN

FROM EARLIEST TIMES THROUGH THE SIXTEENTH CENTURY

GENERAL WORKS: HISTORICAL OVERVIEWS

KODANSHA ENCYCLOPEDIA OF JAPAN. 1983: Kodansha. Eight volumes plus Index volume. Contains over 10,000 articles, including major essays (with bibliographic references) by contemporary scholars on all aspects of Japanese history and culture. See especially the long "History of Japan" entry in volume 3.

Ryusaku Tsunoda, Wm. Theodore DeBary & Donald Keene, eds. SOURCES OF JAPANESE TRADITION. 1958: Columbia University Press.

David J. Lu, ed. SOURCES OF JAPANESE HISTORY. Volume 1. 1974: McGraw-Hill.

George B. Sansom. JAPAN: A SHORT CULTURAL HISTORY. Revised edition. 1943: Appleton. The classic English- language study of premodern Japanese culture.

_____. A HISTORY OF JAPAN TO 1334. 1958: Stanford University Press.

_____. A HISTORY OF JAPAN, 1334-1615. 1961: Stanford University Press.

_____. A HISTORY OF JAPAN, 1615-1867. 1963: Stanford University Press.

John W. Hall. JAPAN: FROM PREHISTORY TO MODERN TIMES. 1970: Delacorte.

_____. GOVERNMENT AND LOCAL POWER IN JAPAN, 500 TO 1700: A STUDY BASED ON BIZEN PROVINCE. 1966: Princeton University Press.

Edwin O. Reischauer. JAPAN: THE STORY OF A NATION. 3rd edition. 1984: Knopf. Revision of the author's JAPAN, PAST AND PRESENT. Strongest on the modern period.

_____ & John K. Fairbank. EAST ASIA: THE GREAT TRADITION. 1960: Houghton Mifflin.

John K. Fairbank, Edwin O. Reischauer & Albert M. Craig. EAST ASIA: TRADITION AND TRANSFORMATION. 1973: Houghton Mifflin. Abridged version of preceding work, plus chapters on the modern period.

Edwin O. Reischauer & Albert M. Craig. JAPAN: TRADITION AND TRANSFORMATION. 1978: Houghton Mifflin. Contains same abridged chapters on premodern Japan as preceding work.

Mikiso Hane. JAPAN: A HISTORICAL SURVEY. 1972: Scribner's.

Arthur E. Tiedemann, ed. AN INTRODUCTION TO JAPANESE CIVILIZATION. 1974: Heath. Both chronological and topical essays by leading scholars.

Conrad Totman. JAPAN BEFORE PERRY: A BRIEF SYNTHESIS. 1981: University of California Press.

H. Paul Varley. JAPANESE CULTURE: A SHORT HISTORY. 3rd edition. 1984: University of Hawaii Press.

Robert S. Ellwood, Jr. AN INVITATION TO JAPANESE CIVILIZATION. 1980: Wadsworth.

James Murdoch. A HISTORY OF JAPAN. 3 volumes. 1923-1926; reprinted 1949, 1964: Ungar. Outdated, but occasionally useful for detail.

Mitsusada Inoue. INTRODUCTION TO JAPANESE HISTORY BEFORE THE MEIJI RESTORATION. 1962: Kokusai Bunka Shinkokai.

Takeo Yazaki. SOCIAL CHANGE AND THE CITY IN JAPAN: FROM EARLIEST TIMES THROUGH THE INDUSTRIAL REVOLUTION. 1968: Japan Publications.

Yosaburo Takekoshi. ECONOMIC ASPECTS OF THE HISTORY OF THE CIVILIZATION OF JAPAN. 3 volumes. 1930: Macmillan. Poorly presented, but contains interesting detail.

GENERAL WORKS : HISTORICAL OVERVIEWS--II

Ryosuke Ishii. A HISTORY OF POLITICAL INSTITUTIONS IN JAPAN. C. Kiley, transl. 1980: University of Tokyo Press.

Hyoe Murakami, ed. GREAT HISTORICAL FIGURES OF JAPAN. 1978: Japan Culture Institute.

GENERAL WORKS: SOCIO-CULTURAL & INTELLECTUAL OVERVIEWS

Kurt Singer. MIRROR, SWORD AND JEWEL: THE GEOMETRY OF JAPANESE LIFE. 1981: Kodansha International.

Ruth F. Benedict. THE CHRYSANTHEMUM AND THE SWORD: PATTERNS OF JAPANESE CULTURE. 1946: Houghton Mifflin. A famous and controversial analysis, based on wartime studies by the U. S. Office of War Information.

Yasusuke Murakami. "*Ie* Society as a Pattern of Civilization," *Journal of Japanese Studies* 10.2 (1984), 279-363. See also commentaries on this article in *Journal of Japanese Studies* 11.1.

Robert J. Smith. JAPANESE SOCIETY: TRADITION, SELF, AND THE SOCIAL ORDER. 1984: Cambridge University Press.

_____ & Richard K. Beardsley. JAPANESE CULTURE: ITS DEVELOPMENT AND CHARACTERISTICS. 1962: Aldine.

Takie Sugiyama Lebra. JAPANESE PATTERNS OF BEHAVIOR. 1976: University of Hawaii Press.

_____ & William P. Lebra, eds. JAPANESE CULTURE AND BEHAVIOR: SELECTED READINGS. 1974: University of Hawaii Press.

John W. Hall & Richard K. Beardsley, eds. TWELVE DOORS TO JAPAN. 1965: McGraw-Hill. Disciplinary approaches to Japan.

Eiichiro Ishida. JAPANESE CULTURE: A STUDY OF ORIGINS AND CHARACTERISTICS. Teruko Kachi, transl. 1974: University of Hawaii Press.

Edwin O. Reischauer. THE JAPANESE. 1977: Belknap.

Harumi Befu. JAPAN: AN ANTHROPOLOGICAL INTRODUCTION. 1971: Chandler.

Bernard S. Silberman, ed. JAPANESE CHARACTER AND CULTURE: A BOOK OF SELECTED READINGS. 1962: University of Arizona Press.

Hyoe Murakami & Edward G. Seidensticker, eds. GUIDES TO JAPANESE CULTURE. 1977: Japan Culture Institute.

Nyozekan Hasegawa. THE JAPANESE CHARACTER: A CULTURAL PROFILE. 1965: Kodansha International.

Charles A. Moore, ed. THE JAPANESE MIND: ESSENTIALS OF JAPANESE PHILOSOPHY AND CULTURE. 1967: University of Hawaii Press.

Hajime Nakamura. WAYS OF THINKING OF EASTERN PEOPLES: INDIA, CHINA, TIBET, JAPAN. 1964: University of Hawaii Press.

David Pollack. THE FRACTURE OF MEANING: THE JAPANESE SYNTHESIS OF CHINA FROM THE EIGHTH THROUGH THE EIGHTEENTH CENTURIES. 1986: Princeton University Press.

Ivan Morris. THE NOBILITY OF FAILURE: TRAGIC HEROES IN THE HISTORY OF JAPAN. 1976: Holt, Rinehart & Winston.

Masayoshi Sugimoto & David L. Swain. SCIENCE AND CULTURE IN TRADITIONAL JAPAN, A.D. 600-1854. 1978: Massachusetts Institute of Technology Press.

Hideomi Tuge. HISTORICAL DEVELOPMENT OF SCIENCE AND TECHNOLOGY IN JAPAN. 1968: Kokusai Bunka Shinkokai.

Shigeru Nakayama. A HISTORY OF JAPANESE ASTRONOMY. 1969: Harvard University Press.

GODS & HEROES: THE MYTHIC WORLD

KOJIKI ("Records of Ancient Matters," A.D. 712)

* Donald L. Philippi, transl. *KOJIKI:* A JAPANESE CLASSIC. 1968: University of Tokyo Press.

* Basil Hall Chamberlain, transl. *KOJIKI,* OR RECORDS OF ANCIENT MATTERS. 1932: Routledge & Kegan Paul. Originally published 1882 as supplement to *Transactions, Asiatic Society of Japan.*

NIHONGI (or NIHON SHOKI: "Chronicles of Japan," A.D. 720)

* William G. Aston, transl. *NIHONGI,* CHRONICLES OF JAPAN FROM THE EARLIEST TIMES TO A.D. 697. 1896; reprinted 1956: Allen & Unwin.

Masaharu Anesaki. "Japanese Mythology," in Louis H. Gray, ed. MYTHOLOGY OF ALL RACES (1964: Cooper Square), volume 8, 205-400.

E. Dale Saunders. "Japanese Mythology," in Samuel Noah Kramer, ed. MYTHOLOGIES OF THE ANCIENT WORLD (1961: Doubleday), 409-442.

Post Wheeler. THE SACRED SCRIPTURES OF THE JAPANESE. 1952: Schuman.

Joseph Campbell. THE MASKS OF GOD: ORIENTAL MYTHOLOGY. 1962: Viking.

Taryo Obayashi. "The Origins of Japanese Mythology," *Acta Asiatica* 31 (1977), 1-23.

_____. "Origins of Japanese Mythology," in Joseph Pittau, ed. FOLK CULTURES OF JAPAN AND EAST ASIA. (1966: Monumenta Nipponica Monographs), 1-15.

_____. "The Origin of the Universe, 1," *The East* 12.1 (1976), 8-15.

_____. "The Origin of the Universe, 2," *The East* 12.2 (1976), 9-13.

_____. "The Structure of the Pantheon and the Concept of Sin in Ancient Japan," *Diogenes* 98 (1977), 117-132.

Joseph M. Kitagawa. "Prehistoric Background of Japanese Religion," *History of Religions* 2 (1963), 292-328.

_____. "The Japanese *Kokutai* (National Community) in Myth and History,"*History of Religions* 13 (1973), 209-226.

_____. "A Past of Things Present: Notes on Major Motifs of Early Japanese Religions," *History of Religions* 20 (1980), 27-42.

Atsuhiko Yoshida. "Japanese Mythology and the Indo-European Trifunctional System," *Diogenes* 98 (1977), 93-116.

Daniel C. Holtom. "The Storm God Theme in Japanese Mythology," *Sociologius* 6.1 (1956), 44-56.

Cornelius Ouwehand. "Some Notes on the God Susa-no-o," *Monumenta Nipponica* 14. 3-4 (1958-1959), 384-407.

Manabu Waida. "Sacred Kingship in Early Japan: A Historical Introduction," *History of Religions* 15 (1976), 319-342.

Y.T. Hosoi. "The Sacred Tree in Japanese Prehistory," *History of Religions* 16 (1976), 95-119.

John C. Pelzel. "Human Nature in the Japanese Myths," in Albert C. Craig & Donald Shivley, eds. PERSONALITY IN JAPANESE HISTORY (1970: University of California Press), 29-59.

Donald L. Philippi, transl. SONGS OF GODS, SONGS OF HUMANS: THE EPIC TRADITION OF THE AINU. 1979: Princeton University Press.

Joseph M. Kitagawa. "Ainu Myths," in Joseph M. Kitagawa & Charles H. Long, eds. MYTHS AND SYMBOLS: STUDIES IN HONOR OF MIRCEA ELIADE (1969: University of Chicago Press), 309-323

Gordon T. Bowles. "Origin of Japanese People," KODANSHA ENCYCLOPEDIA OF JAPAN 4: 33-35.

"Symposium: Japanese Origins," *Journal of Japanese Studies* 2.2 (1976), 295-436. Essays by Roy Andrew Miller, Bruno Levin, and Shichiro Murayama on historical linguistics, and by Richard Pearson on archeological finds.

Roy Andrew Miller. "The Relevance of Historical Linguistics for Japanese Studies," *Journal of Japanese Studies* 2.2 (1976), 335-388.

_____. ORIGINS OF THE JAPANESE LANGUAGE. 1980: University of Washington Press.

_____. THE JAPANESE LANGUAGE. 1967: University of Chicago Press.

_____. "The Origins of Japanese," *Monumenta Nipponica* 29.1 (1974), 93-102. Review of Murayama Shichiro & Obayashi Taryo, *Nihongo no Kigen*, 1973.

Bruno Lewin. "Japanese and Korean: The Problems and History of a Linguistic Comparison," *Journal of Japanese Studies* 2.2 (1976), 389-412.

Shichiro Murayama. "The Malayo-Polynesian Component in the Japanese Language," *Journal of Japanese Studies* 2.2 (1976), 413-436.

Lajos Kazar. "Uralic-Japanese Language Comparison," *Ural-Altaishe Jahrbucker* 48-49 (1976), 127-150.

Susumu Ono. THE ORIGIN OF THE JAPANESE LANGUAGE. 1970: Kokusai Bunka Shinkokai. Criticized in R.A. Miller review, *Monumenta Nipponica* 26. 3-4 (1971), 455-469.

Isao Komatsu. THE JAPANESE PEOPLE: ORIGINS OF THE PEOPLE AND THE LANGUAGE. 1962: Kokusai Bunka Shinkokai.

Peter Bleed. "Prehistory," KODANSHA ENCYCLOPEDIA OF JAPAN 3: 158-160.

C. Melvin Aikens & Takayasu Higuchi. PREHISTORY OF JAPAN. 1981: Academic.

Fumiko Ikawa-Smith. EARLY PALEOLITHIC OF SOUTH AND EAST ASIA. 1974: Mouton.

Chester S. Chard. NORTHEAST ASIA IN PREHISTORY. 1974: University of Wisconsin Press.

Jonathan Edward Kidder, Jr. JAPAN BEFORE BUDDHISM. 2nd edition. 1959: Thames & Hudson.

_____. ANCIENT JAPAN. 1965: John Day.

_____. THE BIRTH OF JAPANESE ART. 1965: Praeger.

_____. "Jomon Culture," KODANSHA ENCYCLOPEDIA OF JAPAN 4: 72-74.

_____. PREHISTORIC JAPANESE ARTS: JOMON POTTERY. 1968: Kodansha International.

_____. THE JOMON POTTERY OF JAPAN. 1957: Artibus Asiae.

9

Vadime Elisseeff. ANCIENT CIVILIZATIONS: JAPAN. 1974: Barrie & Jenkins. Translated from the French.

Richard Pearson. "The Contribution of Archeology to Japanese Studies," *Journal of Japanese Studies* 2.2 (1976), 305-327.

_____. "Paleo-environment and Human Settlement in Japan and Korea," *Science* 197 (1977), 1239-1245.

Mizuno Yu. "The Origins of the Japanese Race," *The East* 10.4 (1974), 37-44.

Charles T. Keally. "The Earliest Cultures in Japan," *Monumenta Nipponica* 27.2 (1972), 143-148.

Sosuke Sugihara & Mitsumori Tozawa. "Pre-ceramic Age in Japan," *Acta Asiatica* 1 (1960), 1-28.

Harumi Befu & Chester S. Chard. "Preceramic Cultures in Japan," *American Anthropologist* 62.4 (1960), 815-849.

Richard E. Morlar. "Chronometric Dating in Japan," *Arctic Anthropology* 14.2 (1967), 180-212.

C. G. Turner. "Dental Evidence of the Origins of the Ainu and Japanese," *Science* 193 (1976), 911-913.

Richard K. Beardsley. "Japan Before History: A Survey of the Archeological Record," *Far Eastern Quarterly* 14 (1955), 317-346. Reprinted in John A. Harrison, ed. JAPAN (1972: University of Arizona Press), 149-178.

Johannes Maringer. "Clay Figurines of the Jomon Period: A Contribution to the History of Ancient Religion in Japan," *History of Religions* 14 (1974), 129-139.

Peter Bleed. "Yayoi Cultures of Japan," *Arctic Anthropology* 9.2 (1972), 1-20.

Erika Kancho. "Japan: A Review of Yayoi Burial Practices," *Asian Perspectives* 9 (1966), 1-26.

PROTOHISTORY: THE GREAT TOMBS & THE INVASION CONTROVERSY

Primary Sources

R. Tsunoda & L. Carrington Goodrich, transl. JAPAN IN THE CHINESE DYNASTIC HISTORIES: LATER HAN THROUGH MING DYNASTIES. 1951: P. D. & Ione Perkins.

KOJIKI ("Records of Ancient Matters," A.D. 712)

* Donald L. Philippi, transl. *KOJIKI:* A JAPANESE CLASSIC. 1968: University of Tokyo Press.

* Basil Chamberlain, transl. *KOJIKI,* OR RECORDS OF ANCIENT MATTERS. 1932: Routledge & Kegan Paul.

NIHONGI (or NIHON SHOKI: "Chronicles of Japan," A.D. 720)

* William G. Aston, transl. *NIHONGI,* CHRONICLES OF JAPAN FROM THE EARLIEST TIMES TO A.D. 697. 1896; reprinted 1956: Allen & Unwin.

SHOKU NIHONGI (official historical sequel to NIHONGI, covering years 697-791)

* J.B. Snellen, transl. "*SHOKU NIHONGI,* Chronicles of Japan, Continued, A.D. 697-791," *Transactions, Asiatic Society of Japan,* 2nd series, 11 (1934), 151-239; 14 (1937), 209-278.

FUDOKI (8th-century local records)

* Michiko Yamaguchi Aoki. *IZUMO FUDOKI.* 1971: Monumenta Nipponica Monographs.

* Atsuharu Sakai. "The *Hitachi Fudoki* or Records of Customs and Land of Hitachi," *Cultural Nippon* 8.2 (1940), 145-185; 8.3 (1940), 109-156; and 8.4 (1940), 137-186.

TAKAHASHI UJIBUMI (local chronicle, A.D. 792)

* Douglas Edward Mills. "The *Takahasi uzibumi,*" *Bulletin of the School of Oriental and African Studies* 16.1 (1954), 113-133.

The Great Tombs

Gina Lee Barnes. "Kofun (Tomb Mounds)," KODANSHA ENCYCLOPEDIA OF JAPAN 4: 244-246.

"Studies on Ancient Japanese History." Special Issue of *Acta Asiatica* 31 (1977). Includes articles on mythology, tombs, Yamato state & Korea, and Ritsuryo legal structure.

Ken Amakasu. "The Significance of the Formation and Distribution of *Kofun,*" *Acta Asiatica* 31 (1977), 24-50.

Sokichi Tsuda. "On the Stages of the Formation of Japan as a Nation, and the Origin of Belief in the Perpetuity of the Imperial Family," *Philosophical Studies of Japan* 4 (1963), 49-78.

Hiroshi Mizuo. "Patterns of Kofun Culture," *Japan Quarterly* 16.1 (1969), 71-77.

Jonathan Edward Kidder, Jr. EARLY JAPANESE ART: THE GREAT TOMBS AND TREASURES. 1964: Thames & Hudson.

_____. EARLY BUDDHIST JAPAN. 1972: Thames & Hudson.

11

PROTOHISTORY: THE GREAT TOMBS & THE INVASION CONTROVERSY--II

_____. "The Newly Discovered Takamatsuzuka Tomb," *Monumenta Nipponica* 27.3 (1972), 245-251.

Shichiro Murayama & Roy Andrew Miller. "The Inariyama Tumulus Sword Inscription," *Journal of Japanese Studies* 5.2 (1979), 405-438.

The "Conquistador" Thesis & the Invasion Controversy

Namio Egami. "Mounted Nomadic Peoples," in Hyoe Murakami & Edward Seidensticker, eds. GUIDES TO JAPANESE CULTURE (1977: Japan Culture Institute), 130-134.

_____. "Light on Japanese Cultural Origins from Historical Archeology and Legend," in Robert J. Smith & Richard K. Beardsley, eds. JAPANESE CULTURE: ITS DEVELOPMENT AND CHARACTERISTICS (1962: Aldine), 11-16.

_____. "The Formation of the People and the Origin of the State in Japan," *Memoirs of the Toyo Bunko* 23 (1964), 35-70.

_____. THE BEGINNINGS OF JAPANESE ART. 1973: Weatherhill.

[Namio Egami] See summary in Ledyard, *Journal of Japanese Studies* 1.2 (1975), especially p. 222 (the "8 points").

[Namio Egami] For summary and discussion of the invasion thesis, see Eiichiro Ishida, JAPANESE CULTURE: A STUDY OF ORIGINS AND CHARACTERISTICS (1974: University of Hawaii Press), 86-88.

Gari Ledyard. "Horse-Rider Theory," KODANSHA ENCYCLOPEDIA OF JAPAN 3: 229-230.

_____. "Galloping Along with the Horseriders: Looking for the Founders of Japan," *Journal of Japanese Studies* 1.2 (1975), 217-254.

John H. Douglas. "The Horsemen of Yamato," *Science News* 113.22 (1978), 364-366.

Walter Edwards. "Event and Process in the Founding of Japan: The Horserider Theory in Archeological Perspective," *Journal of Japanese Studies* 9.2 (1983), 265-295.

PROTOHISTORY: EMERGENCE OF THE IMPERIAL STATE

John W. Hall. GOVERNMENT AND LOCAL POWER IN JAPAN, 500-1700: A STUDY BASED ON BIZEN
PROVINCE. 1966: Princeton University Press.

George B. Sansom. A HISTORY OF JAPAN TO 1334. 1958: Stanford University Press.

Robert Karl Reischauer. EARLY JAPANESE HISTORY (c. 40 B.C.-A.D. 1169). 2 volumes. 1937: Princeton
University Press. An adaptation of Katsumi Kuroita, *Kotei Kokushi no Kenkyu* (1931).

The Korean Influence

Gari Ledyard. "Yamatai," KODANSHA ENCYCLOPEDIA OF JAPAN 8: 305-307.

Benjamin H. Hazard. "Korea and Japan, Premodern Relations (to 1875)," KODANSHA ENCYCLOPEDIA OF
JAPAN 4: 276-279.

Kunio Hirano. "The Yamato State and Korea in the Fourth and Fifth Centuries," *Acta Asiatica* 31 (1977), 51-82.

James K. Ash. "Korea in the Making of the Early Japanese State," *Journal of Social Sciences and Humanities*
(1971).

Yasukazu Suematsu. "Japan's Relations with the Asian Continent and the Korean Peninsular (Before 950 A.D.),"
Cahiers d'histoire Mondiale (Journal of World History) 4.3 (1958), 671-687.

George B. Sansom. "An Outline of Recent Japanese Archeological Research in Korea in its Bearing Upon Early
Japanese History," *Transactions, Asiatic Society of Japan*, 2nd series, 6 (1929), 5-19.

KODANSHA ENCYCLOPEDIA OF JAPAN. See also entries on "Hata Family," "Kaya (Mimana)," "Kikajin," and
"Wani."

Yamato State / Ritsuryo

Cornelius J. Kiley. "State and Dynasty in Archaic Yamato," *Journal of Asian Studies* 33.1 (1973), 25-49.

_____. "Uji and Kabane in Ancient Japan," *Monumenta Nipponica* 32.3 (1977), 365-376.

_____. "Uji-Kabane System," KODANSHA ENCYCLOPEDIA OF JAPAN 8: 131-137.

_____. "Ritsuryo System," KODANSHA ENCYCLOPEDIA OF JAPAN 6: 322-332.

Mitsusada Inoue. "The Ritsuryo System in Japan," *Acta Asiatica* 31 (1977), 83-112.

Alan L. Miller. "Ritsuryo Japan: The State as Liturgical Community," *History of Religions* 11 (1971), 98-121.

John Young. THE LOCATION OF YAMATAI: A CASE STUDY IN JAPANESE HISTORIOGRAPHY, 720-1945.
1957: Johns Hopkins.

John A. Harrison. NEW LIGHT ON EARLY AND MEDIEVAL JAPANESE HISTORIOGRAPHY. 1960: University of
Florida Press.

Richard J. Miller. ANCIENT JAPANESE NOBILITY: THE KABANE RANKING SYSTEM. 1974: University of
California Press.

13

PROTOHISTORY: EMERGENCE OF THE IMPERIAL STATE--II

_____. "A Study of the Development of a Centralized Japanese Government Prior to the Taika Reform (A.D. 645)." 1953: Ph.D. dissertation in History, University of California.

_____. JAPAN'S FIRST BUREAUCRACY: A STUDY OF EIGHTH-CENTURY GOVERNMENT. 1978: *Cornell University East Asia Papers.*

J. I. Crump. "Borrowed T'ang Titles and Offices in the Yoro Code," *Occasional Papers of the Center for Japanese Studies, University of Michigan* 2 (1952), 35-58.

George B. Sansom. "Early Japanese Law and Administration," *Transactions, Asiatic Society of Japan*, 2nd series, 9 (1932), 67-110 & 11 (1934), 117-150.

J. Edward Kidder. "Asuka History (mid-6th century to 710)," KODANSHA ENCYCLOPEDIA OF JAPAN 3: 161-163.

E. Patricia Tsurumi. "The Male Present Versus the Female Past: Historians and Japan's Ancient Female Emperors," *Bulletin of Concerned Asian Scholars* 14.4 (1983), 71-75.

Ancient Economy

Dana Robert Morris. "Peasant Economy in Early Japan, 650-950." 1980: Ph.D. dissertation in History, University of California.

William Wayne Farris. POPULATION, DISEASE AND LAND IN EARLY JAPAN, 645-900. 1985: Harvard-Yenching Institute Monograph Series.

Kozo Yamamura. "The Decline of the Ritsuryo System: Hypotheses on Economic and Institutional Change," *Journal of Japanese Studies* 1.1 (1974), 3-38.

Ancient Cities

Paul Wheatley & Thomas See. FROM COURT TO CAPITAL: A TENTATIVE INTERPRETATION OF THE ORIGINS OF THE JAPANESE URBAN TRADITION. 1978: University of Chicago Press. See also the review by R.A. Miller in *Journal of Japanese Studies* 5.1 (1979), 211-234.

Takeo Yazaki. SOCIAL CHANGE AND THE CITY IN JAPAN: FROM EARLIEST TIMES THROUGH THE INDUSTRIAL REVOLUTION. 1968: Japan Publications.

Richard A. Ponsonby-Fane. IMPERIAL CITIES: THE CAPITALS OF JAPAN FROM THE OLDEST TIMES UNTIL 1229. 1979 reprint by University Publications of America of 2 long essays published prior to World War Two: "Ancient Capitals and Palaces of Japan" and "The Capital and Palace of Heian."

THE COURTLY SOCIETY OF THE NARA (710-794) & HEIAN (794-1185) PERIODS: SECONDARY SOURCES

George B. Sansom. A HISTORY OF JAPAN TO 1334. 1958: Stanford University Press.

_____. JAPAN: A SHORT CULTURAL HISTORY. Revised edition. 1943: Appleton. See especially pp. 107-184 ("Nara"), and 185-269 ("The Heian Period").

Ivan J. Morris. THE WORLD OF THE SHINING PRINCE: COURT LIFE IN ANCIENT JAPAN. 1960: Oxford University Press.

Rizo Takeuchi. "Nara History (710-794)," KODANSHA ENCYCLOPEDIA OF JAPAN 3: 163-165.

G. Cameron Hurst III. "Heian History (794-1185)," KODANSHA ENCYCLOPEDIA OF JAPAN 3: 165-169.

_____. "Regency Government," KODANSHA ENCYCLOPEDIA OF JAPAN 6: 286-288.

H. Paul Varley. "The Age of the Court Nobles," in Arthur Tiedemann, ed. AN INTRODUCTION TO JAPANESE CIVILIZATION (1974: Heath), 33-59.

Robert K. Reischauer. EARLY JAPANESE HISTORY (c. 40 B.C.-A.D. 1167). 2 volumes. 1937: Princeton University Press.

John W. Hall & Jeffrey P. Mass, eds. MEDIEVAL JAPAN: ESSAYS IN INSTITUTIONAL HISTORY. 1974: Yale University Press. See especially pp. 3-124, containing five essays on "Court and *Shoen* in Heian Japan."

John W. Hall. "Kyoto As Historical Background," in Hall & Mass, MEDIEVAL JAPAN (1974: Yale University Press), 3-38.

G. Cameron Hurst III. "The Structure of the Heian Court: Some Thoughts on the Nature of 'Familial Authority' in Heian Japan," in Hall & Mass, MEDIEVAL JAPAN (1974: Yale University Press), 39-59.

_____. "The Development of the *Insei:* A Problem in Japanese History and Historiography," in Hall & Mass, MEDIEVAL JAPAN (1974: Yale University Press), 60-90.

_____. "*Insei,*" KODANSHA ENCYCLOPEDIA OF JAPAN 3: 314-315.

_____. "The Reign of Go-Sanjo and the Revival of Imperial Power," *Monumenta Nipponica* 27.1 (1972), 65-84.

_____. *INSEI:* ABDICATED SOVEREIGNS IN THE POLITICS OF LATE HEIAN JAPAN, 1086-1185. 1976: Columbia University Press.

Richard Ponsonby-Fane. KYOTO THE OLD CAPITAL OF JAPAN (794-1869). 1956 reprint of 1931 work: Ponsonby Memorial Society.

_____. THE FORTUNES OF THE EMPERORS: STUDIES IN REVOLUTION, EXILE, ABDICATION, USURPATION, AND DEPOSITION IN ANCIENT JAPAN. 1979 reprint of 6 articles published prior to World War Two: University Publications of America.

Rose Hempel. THE GOLDEN AGE OF JAPAN, 794-1192. 1983: Rizzoli. A translation of *Japan zur Heian Zeit.*

Ross Bender. "The Hachiman Cult and the Dokyo Incident," *Monumenta Nipponica* 34.2 (1979), 125-154.

Shigeki Kaizuka. "Confucianism in Ancient Japan," *Cahiers d'histoire Mondiale* (*Journal of World History*) 5.1 (1959), 41-58.

Robert Borgen. "The Japanese Mission to China, 801-806," *Monumenta Nipponica* 37.1 (1982), 1-28.

THE COURTLY SOCIETY OF THE NARA (710-794) & HEIAN (794-1185) PERIODS: SECONDARY SOURCES--II

_____. SUGAWARA NO MICHIZANE AND THE EARLY HEIAN COURT. 1986: Harvard East Asian Monographs.

Ivan Morris. "The Deity of Failures," in his THE NOBILITY OF FAILURE (1976: Holt, Rinehart & Winston), 41-66. About Sugawara no Michizane, who died in 903 and was "deified" in 987.

_____. "Women of Ancient Japan: Heian Ladies," *History Today* 13.3 (1963), 160-168.

_____. "Marriage in the World of Genji," *Asia* 11 (1968), 54-77.

William McCullough. "Japanese Marriage Institutions of the Heian Period," *Harvard Journal of Asiatic Studies* 27 (1967), 103-167. Takes issue with Ivan Morris.

_____. "Spirit Possession in the Heian Period," in The Japan P. E. N. Club, ed. STUDIES ON JAPANESE CULTURE, volume 1 (1973: The Japan P. E. N. Club), 91-98.

Helen McCullough. "Social and Psychological Aspects of Heian Ritual and Ceremony," in The Japan P. E. N. Club, ed. STUDIES ON JAPANESE CULTURE, volume 2 (1973: The Japan P. E. N. Club), 275-279.

G. Cameron Hurst III. "Michinaga's Maladies," *Monumenta Nipponica* 34.1 (1979), 101-112.

Donald Keene. "Feminine Sensibility in the Heian Era," in his LANDSCAPES AND PORTRAITS: APPRECIATIONS OF JAPANESE CULTURE (1971: Kodansha International), 11-25.

Andrew Pekarik, ed. UKIFUNE: LOVE IN THE TALE OF GENJI. 1982: Columbia University Press.

Edwin A. Cranston. "The Dark Path: Images of Longing in Japanese Love Poetry," *Harvard Journal of Asiatic Studies* 35 (1975), 60-100.

Janet Walker. "Conventions of Love Poetry in Japan and the West," *Journal of the Association of Teachers of Japanese* 14.1 (1977), 31-65.

Kenneth Rexroth & Ikuko Atsumi, transl. THE BURNING HEART: WOMEN POETS OF JAPAN. 1976: Seabury.

D. E. Mills. "Popular Elements in Heian Literature," *Journal Newsletter of the Association of Teachers of Japanese* 3.3 (1966).

THE COURTLY SOCIETY IN ITS OWN WORDS: PROSE & POETRY IN TRANSLATION

MANYOSHU (mid 8th-century poetic anthology)

* Nippon Gakujutsu Shinkokai (Japan Society for the Promotion of Scientific Research), comp. *MANYOSHU:* ONE THOUSAND POEMS. 1965: Columbia University Press.

* Ian Hideo Levy, transl. THE TEN THOUSAND LEAVES: A TRANSLATION OF *MAN'YOSHU*, JAPAN'S PREMIER ANTHOLOGY OF CLASSICAL POETRY. 1981: University of Tokyo Press & Princeton University Press. A projected 4-volume translation.

* Edwin A. Cranston. "The Ramifying Vein: An Impression of Leaves--A Review of Levy's Translation of the *Man'yoshu,*" *Journal of Japanese Studies* 9.1 (1983), 97-138.

* _____. "*Man'yoshu,*" KODANSHA ENCYCLOPEDIA OF JAPAN 5: 102-111.

* Ian Hideo Levy. HITOMARO AND THE BIRTH OF JAPANESE LYRICISM. 1984: Princeton University Press.

* Paula Doe. A WARBLER'S SONG IN THE DUSK: THE LIFE AND WORK OF OTOMO YAKAMOCHI (718-785). 1982: University of California Press.

KINKAFU (collection of Japanese songs dated 981)

* Noah S. Branner, "The *Kinkafu* Collection," *Monumenta Nipponica* 23.3-4 (1968), 229-320.

Donald L. Philippi, transl. THIS WINE OF PEACE, THIS WINE OF LAUGHTER--A COMPLETE ANTHOLOGY OF JAPAN'S EARLIEST SONGS. 1968: Grossman.

Burton Watson, transl. JAPANESE LITERATURE IN CHINESE. 2 volumes. 1975: Columbia University Press.

Robert H. Brower & Earl Miner. JAPANESE COURT POETRY. 1961: Stanford University Press.

Elizabeth Markham, transl. *SAIBARA:* JAPANESE COURT SONGS OF THE HEIAN PERIOD. 1983: Cambridge University Press.

NIHON RYOIKI (Buddhist stories from the 5th to 9th centuries)

* Kyoko Motomochi Nakamura, transl. MIRACULOUS STORIES FROM THE JAPANESE BUDDHIST TRADITION: THE *NIHON RYOIKI* OF THE MONK KYOKAI. 1973: Harvard University Press.

DAINIHONKOKU HOKEKYOKENKI (129 Buddhist tales collected in the 11th century)

* Yoshiko K. Dykstra, transl. MIRACULOUS TALES OF THE LOTUS SUTRA FROM ANCIENT JAPAN: THE *DAINIHONKOKU HOKEKYOKENKI* OF PRIEST CHINGEN. 1983: University of Hawaii Press.

THE COURTLY SOCIETY IN ITS OWN WORDS: PROSE & POETRY IN TRANSLATION--II

KOKINSHU (early 10th-century "official" poetic anthology; more formally known as KOKIN WAKASHU)

* Laurel Resplica Rodd & Mary Catherine Henkenius, transl. *KOKINSHU:* A COLLECTION OF POEMS ANCIENT AND MODERN. 1984: Princeton University Press.

* Helen McCullough, transl. *KOKIN WAKASHU:* THE FIRST IMPERIAL ANTHOLOGY OF JAPANESE POETRY, WITH *TOSA NIKKI* AND *SHINSEN WAKA*. 1985: Stanford University Press.

* _____. BROCADE BY NIGHT: *KOKIN WAKASHU* AND THE COURT STYLE IN JAPANESE CLASSICAL POETRY. 1985: Stanford University Press.

ISE MONOGATARI

* Helen McCullough, transl. TALES OF ISE: LYRICAL EPISODES FROM TENTH-CENTURY JAPAN. 1968: Stanford University Press.

* Fritz Vos. A STUDY OF THE *ISE-MONOGATARI,* WITH THE TEXT ACCORDING TO THE *DEN-TEIKA-NIPPON* AND AN ANNOTATED TRANSLATION. 2 volumes. 1957: Mouton.

* H. Jay Harris, transl. THE TALES OF ISE. 1972: Tuttle.

TOSA NIKKI (by Ki no Tsurayuki, ca. 935)

* Earl Miner, transl. JAPANESE POETIC DIARIES. 1969: University of California Press.

* Helen McCullough, transl. *KOKIN WAKASHU:* THE FIRST IMPERIAL ANTHOLOGY OF JAPANESE POETRY, WITH *TOSA NIKKI* AND *SHINSEN WAKA*. 1985: Stanford University Press.

TAKETORI MONOGATARI (mid-10th century)

* Donald Keene, transl. "*Taketori Monogatari* (Tale of the Bamboo Cutter)," *Monumenta Nipponica* 11.1 (1955), 1-28.

YAMATO MONOGATARI (10th century)

* Mildred Tahara, transl. TALES OF YAMATO: A TENTH-CENTURY POEM-TALE. 1980: University of Hawaii Press.

SHOMONKI (Japan's earliest war chronicle, concerning events culminating in 940)

* Judith N. Rabinovitch, transl. *SHOMONKI:* THE STORY OF MASAKADO'S REBELLION. 1986: Monumenta Nipponica Monographs.

* Guiliana Stramigioli. "Preliminary Notes on the *Masakado-ki* and the Taira no Masakado Story," *Monumenta Nipponica* 28.3 (1973), 261-294.

THE COURTLY SOCIETY IN ITS OWN WORDS: PROSE & POETRY IN TRANSLATION--III

KAGERO NIKKI (ca. 974, covering the previous two decades)

* Edward C. Seidensticker, transl. THE GOSSAMER YEARS: A DIARY BY A NOBLEWOMAN OF HEIAN JAPAN. 1964: Tuttle.

OCHIKUBO MONOGATARI (ca. 980)

* Wilfrid Whitehouse, transl. *OCHIKUBO MONOGATARI,* OR THE TALE OF THE LADY OCHIKUBO: A TENTH-CENTURY JAPANESE NOVEL. 1965: Hokuseido.

GENJI MONOGATARI (by Murasaki Shikibu, ca. 1006)

* Arthur Waley, transl. THE TALE OF GENJI. 1960: Random House.

* E. Seidensticker, transl. THE TALE OF GENJI. 1976: Knopf. See reviews by Edwin Cranston in *Journal of Japanese Studies* 4.1 (1978), 1-26, and Helen McCullough in *Monumenta Nipponica* 32.1 (1977), 93-110.

* _____. GENJI DAYS. 1978: Kodansha International. A diary kept by Seidensticker while he was translating Lady Murasaki's classic work.

* Andrew Pekarik, ed. UKIFUNE: LOVE IN THE TALE OF GENJI. 1982: Columbia University Press.

* Marian Ury. "The Real Murasaki," *Monumenta Nipponica* 38.2 (1983), 175-190.

* David Pollack. "The Informing Image: 'China' in *Genji Monogatari,*" *Monumenta Nipponica* 38.4 (1983), 359-376.

* Ivan Morris, ed. and transl. THE TALE OF GENJI SCROLL. 1971: Kodansha International.

* Miyeko Murase. ICONOGRAPHY OF THE TALE OF GENJI: *GENJI MONOGATARI EKOTOBA.* 1984: Weatherhill.

MURASAKI SHIKIBU NIKKI (Diary of Lady Murasaki, ca. 1010)

* Richard Bowring. MURASAKI SHIKIBU: HER DIARY AND POETIC MEMOIRS: A TRANSLATION AND STUDY. 1982: Princeton University Press.

MAKURA NO SOSHI (by Sei Shonagon, early 11th century)

* Ivan Morris, transl. and ed. THE PILLOW BOOK OF SEI SHONAGON. 2 volumes. 1967: Columbia University Press.

* Arthur Waley, transl. THE PILLOW BOOK OF SEI SHONAGON. 1953: Grove.

IZUMI SHIKIBU NIKKI (early 11th century)

* Edwin Cranston, transl. THE IZUMI SHIKIBU DIARY. 1969: Harvard University Press.

19

THE COURTLY SOCIETY IN ITS OWN WORDS: PROSE & POETRY IN TRANSLATION--IV

* Earl Miner, transl. JAPANESE POETIC DIARIES. 1969: California University Press.

* Janet A. Walker. "The *Izumi Shikibu Nikki* As a Work of Courtly Literature," *The Literary Review* 23.4 (1980), 463-480.

OKAGAMI ("history" covering years 850-1025)

* Helen Craig McCullough, transl. *OKAGAMI:* THE GREAT MIRROR. 1980: Princeton University Press & University of Tokyo Press.

* Joseph K. Yamagiwa, transl. THE *OKAGAMI:* A JAPANESE HISTORICAL TALE. 1967: Allen & Unwin.

* _____ & Edwin O. Reischauer. TRANSLATIONS FROM EARLY JAPANESE LITERATURE (1951: Harvard University Press), 271-374.

EIGA MONOGATARI ("history" of the great Fujiwara leader Michinaga)

* Helen Craig McCullough & William H. McCullough, transl. A TALE OF FLOWERING FORTUNES. 2 volumes. 1979: Stanford University Press.

* Karen Brazell. "Three Tales of Michinaga," *Journal of Japanese Studies* 10.1 (1984), 185-196.

SANUKI NO SUKE NIKKI (ca. 1010)

* Jennifer Brewster, transl. THE EMPEROR HORIKAWA DIARY. 1977: University of Hawaii Press.

SARASHINA NIKKI (ca. 1059)

* Ivan Morris, transl. AS I CROSSED A BRIDGE OF DREAMS: RECOLLECTIONS OF A WOMAN IN ELEVENTH- CENTURY JAPAN. 1971: Dial.

HAMAMATSU CHUNAGON MONOGATARI (11th century)

* Thomas H. Rohlich, transl. A TALE OF ELEVENTH-CENTURY JAPAN: *HAMAMATSU CHUNAGON MONOGATARI.* 1983: Princeton University Press.

MUTSU WAKI (account of mid 11th-century military campaign; predecessor of the "war chronicles" of the feudal period)

* Helen C. McCullough, transl. "A Tale of Mutsu," *Harvard Journal of Asiatic Studies* 25 (1964-1965), 178-211.

TSUTSUMI CHUNAGON MONOGATARI (10 stories, attributed largely to 11th and 12th centuries)

* Robert L. Backus, transl. THE RIVERSIDE COUNSELOR'S STORIES: VERNACULAR FICTION OF LATE HEIAN JAPAN. 1985: Stanford University Press.

THE COURTLY SOCIETY IN ITS OWN WORDS: PROSE & POETRY IN
   TRANSLATION--V

* Umeyo Hirano, transl. THE *TSUTSUMI CHUNAGON MONOGATARI:* A COLLECTION OF 11TH
  CENTURY SHORT STORIES OF JAPAN. 1976: Hokuseido.

* Edwin O. Reischauer & Joseph Yamagiwa, transl. TRANSLATIONS FROM EARLY JAPANESE
  LITERATURE (1951: Harvard University Press), 137-267.

* Oscar Benl. *"Tsutsumi Chunagon Monogatari," Monumenta Nipponica* 3.1 (1940), 144-164.

* Arthur Waley, transl. THE LADY WHO LOVED INSECTS. 1929: Blackmore.

TORIKAEBAYA MONOGATARI (12th century)

* Rosette F. Willig, transl. THE CHANGELINGS: A CLASSICAL JAPANESE COURT TALE. 1983:
  Stanford University Press.

KONJAKU MONOGATARI (collection of 1,080 stories from China, India, and Japan; early 12th century)

* Marian Ury, transl. TALES OF TIMES NOW PAST: SIXTY-TWO STORIES FROM A MEDIEVAL
  JAPANESE COLLECTION. 1979: University of California Press.

* Susan Wilber Jones, transl. AGES AGO: THIRTY-SEVEN TALES FROM THE *KONJAKU
  MONOGATARI* COLLECTION. 1959: Harvard University Press.

* Robert H. Brower. "The *Konzyaku Monogatarisyu:* An Historical and Critical Introduction, with
  Annotated Translations of Seventy-Eight Tales." 1952: Ph.D. dissertation in History, University
  of Michigan.

* W. Michael Kelsey. *KONJAKU MONOGATARI-SHU.* 1982: Twayne.

KENREIMON'IN UKYO NO DAIBU SHU (early 13th century)

* Phillip Tudor Harries, transl. THE POETIC MEMOIRS OF LADY DAIBU. 1980: Stanford University
  Press.

21

FEUDAL JAPAN & THE WARRIOR SOCIETY: Overviews

Peter Duus. JAPANESE FEUDALISM. 1969: Knopf.

_____. "Feudalism," KODANSHA ENCYCLOPEDIA OF JAPAN 3: 263-267.

Edwin O. Reischauer. "Japanese Feudalism," in Rushton Coulborn, ed. FEUDALISM IN HISTORY (1956: Princeton University Press), 26-48.

H. Paul Varley. "The Age of the Military Houses," in Arthur Tiedemann, ed. AN INTRODUCTION TO JAPANESE CIVILIZATION (1974: Heath), 61-95.

Jeffrey P. Mass & William B. Hauser, eds. THE BAKUFU IN JAPANESE HISTORY. 1986: Stanford University Press.

John W. Hall. GOVERNMENT AND LOCAL POWER IN JAPAN, 500-1700: A STUDY BASED ON BIZEN PROVINCE. 1966: Princeton University Press.

_____. "Feudalism in Japan--A Reassessment," *Comparative Studies in Science and History* 5.1 (1962). Reprinted in John W. Hall & Marius B. Jansen, eds. STUDIES IN THE INSTITUTIONAL HISTORY OF EARLY MODERN JAPAN (1968: Princeton University Press), 15-51.

Ryosuke Ishii. "Japanese Feudalism," *Acta Asiatica* 35 (1978), 1-29.

Motohisa Yasuda. "History of the Studies of the Formation of Japanese *Hoken* System (Feudalism)," *Acta Asiatica* 8 (1965), 74-100.

Conrad Totman. "English Language Studies of Medieval Japan: An Assessment," *Journal of Asian Studies* 38.3 (1979), 541-551.

Archibald Lewis. KNIGHTS AND SAMURAI: FEUDALISM IN NORTHERN FRANCE AND JAPAN. 1974: Harper.

Louis Frederic. DAILY LIFE IN JAPAN IN THE AGE OF THE SAMURAI, 1185-1603. 1972: Praeger.

Keiji Nagahara. "The Medieval Origins of the *Eta-Hinin*," *Journal of Japanese Studies* 5.2 (1979), 385-403.

22

FEUDAL JAPAN & THE WARRIOR SOCIETY: The Kamakura Period (1185-1333)

Minoru Shinoda. "Kamakura History (1185-1333)," KODANSHA ENCYCLOPEDIA OF JAPAN 3: 169-172.

_____. THE FOUNDING OF THE KAMAKURA SHOGUNATE, 1180-1185--WITH SELECTED TRANSLATIONS FROM THE *AZUMA KAGAMI*. 1960: Columbia University Press. See especially 15-39 and 136-144 for a concise overview of the origins of warrior government.

George B. Sansom. A HISTORY OF JAPAN TO 1334. 1958: Stanford University Press.

Keiji Nagahara. "The Social Structure of Early Medieval Japan," *Hitotsubashi Journal of Economics* 1 (1960), 90-97.

John W. Hall & Jeffrey P. Mass, eds. MEDIEVAL JAPAN: ESSAYS IN INSTITUTIONAL HISTORY. 1974: Yale University Press. Reviewed by Keiji Nagahara in *Journal of Japanese Studies* 1.2 (1975), 437-445.

Jeffrey P. Mass. WARRIOR GOVERNMENT IN EARLY MEDIEVAL JAPAN: A STUDY OF THE KAMAKURA BAKUFU, SHUGO & JITO. 1974: Stanford University Press. Reviewed by Kozo Yamamura in *Journal of Japanese Studies* 1.2 (1975), 451-459.

_____. THE DEVELOPMENT OF KAMAKURA RULE, 1180-1250: A HISTORY WITH DOCUMENTS. 1979: Stanford University Press. Reviewed by Dan F. Henderson in *Journal of Japanese Studies* 9.2 (1983), 367-373.

_____. "The Emergence of the Kamakura Bakufu," in Hall & Mass, MEDIEVAL JAPAN (1974: Yale University Press), 127-156.

_____. "The Origins of Kamakura Justice," *Journal of Japanese Studies* 3.2 (1977), 299-322.

_____. "Jito Land Possession in the Thirteenth Century: The Case of Shitaji Chubun," in Hall and Mass, MEDIEVAL JAPAN (1974: Yale University Press), 157-183.

_____, ed. COURT AND BAKUFU IN JAPAN: ESSAYS IN KAMAKURA HISTORY. 1982: Yale University Press.

_____ & William Hauser, eds. THE BAKUFU IN JAPANESE HISTORY. 1985: Stanford University Press.

John Brownlee. "Crisis as Reinforcement of the Imperial Institution: The Case of the Jokyu Incident, 1221," *Monumenta Nipponica* 30.2 (1975), 193-202.

Kyotsu Hori. "The Economic and Political Effects of the Mongol Wars," in Hall & Mass, MEDIEVAL JAPAN (1974: Yale University Press), 184-198.

Nakaba Yamada. GHENKO: THE MONGOL INVASION OF JAPAN. 1916: Smith, Elder.

Carl Steenstrup. "Pushing the Papers of Kamakura: The Nitty-gritticists versus the Grand Sweeper," *Monumenta Nipponica* 35.3 (1980), 337-346.

FEUDAL JAPAN & THE WARRIOR SOCIETY: The Ashikaga / Muromachi (1333-1568)
& Azuchi / Momoyama (1568-1600) Periods

Martin C. Collcutt. "Muromachi History (1333-1568)," KODANSHA ENCYCLOPEDIA OF JAPAN 3: 172-177.

_____. "Kings of Japan? The Political Authority of the Ashikaga Shoguns," *Monumenta Nipponica* 37.4
(1982), 523-530.

George Elison. "Azuchi-Momoyama History (1568-1600)," KODANSHA ENCYCLOPEDIA OF JAPAN 3: 177-185.

John W. Hall. "Foundations of the Modern Japanese Daimyo," *Journal of Asian Studies* 20.3 (1961). Reprinted
in John W. Hall & Marius Jansen, eds. STUDIES IN THE INSTITUTIONAL HISTORY OF EARLY MODERN
JAPAN (1968: Princeton University Press), 65-77.

George B. Sansom. A HISTORY OF JAPAN, 1334-1615. 1961: Stanford University Press.

H. Paul Varley. IMPERIAL RESTORATION IN MEDIEVAL JAPAN. 1971: Columbia University Press. Covers the
Kemmu Restoration and aftermath, 1333-1392.

_____. THE ONIN WAR: HISTORY OF ITS ORIGINS AND BACKGROUND WITH A SELECTIVE TRANSLATION
OF THE CHRONICLE OF ONIN. 1967: Columbia University Press. Analysis of the great civil war of
1467-1477, which ushered in the period of "high feudalism."

Kenneth Alan Grossberg. JAPAN'S RENAISSANCE: THE POLITICS OF THE MUROMACHI BAKUFU. 1981:
Harvard East Asian Monographs. Reviewed by Peter Arneson in *Journal of Japanese Studies* 9.2 (1983),
385-391.

_____. "From Feudal Chieftain to Secular Monarch," *Monumenta Nipponica* 31.1 (1976), 29-50.

Prescott B. Wintersteen, Jr. "The Early Muromachi Bakufu in Kyoto," in Hall & Mass, MEDIEVAL JAPAN (1974:
Yale University Press), 201-209.

_____. "The Muromachi Shugo and Hanzei," in Hall & Mass, MEDIEVAL JAPAN (1974: Yale University Press),
210-220.

John W. Hall & Takeshi Toyoda, eds. JAPAN IN THE MUROMACHI AGE. 1976: University of California Press.
Contains 18 essays on political, economic, cultural, and religious developments. Reviewed by Mary E.
Berry in *Journal of Japanese Studies* 4.1 (1978), 187-198.

Wendell Cole. KYOTO IN THE MOMOYAMA PERIOD. 1967: University of Oklahoma Press.

George Elison & Bardwell L. Smith, eds. WARLORDS, ARTISTS, AND COMMONERS: JAPAN IN THE
SIXTEENTH CENTURY. 1981: University of Hawaii Press. Reviewed by Barbara Ruch in *Journal of
Japanese Studies* 8.2 (1982), 369-382.

John Hall, Keiji Nagahara & Kozo Yamamura, eds. JAPAN BEFORE TOKUGAWA: POLITICAL CONSOLIDATION
AND ECONOMIC GROWTH, 1500-1650. 1981: Princeton University Press. Contains 11 essays on the
period of daimyo warfare and unification.

Peter Judd Arneson. THE MEDIEVAL JAPANESE DAIMYO: THE OUCHI FAMILY'S RULE OF SUO AND NAGATO
1979: Yale University Press. Covers period from 1333-1573.

David L. Davis. *"Ikki* in Late Medieval Japan," in Hall & Mass, MEDIEVAL JAPAN (1974: Yale University
Press), 221-247. Concerns peasant uprisings.

Osamu Wakita. "The Emergence of the State in Sixteenth-Century Japan: From Oda to Tokugawa," *Journal of
Japanese Studies* 8.2 (1982), 343-367.

_____. "The Kokudaka System: A Device for Unification," *Journal of Japanese Studies* 1.2 (1975), 297-320.

FEUDAL JAPAN & THE WARRIOR SOCIETY: The Ashikaga / Muromachi (1333-1568)
& Azuchi / Momoyama (1568-1600) Periods--II

Neil McMullin. BUDDHISM AND THE STATE IN SIXTEENTH-CENTURY JAPAN. 1984: Princeton University Press. Examines policies of the first great unifier, Oda Nobunaga (1534-1582).

Mary Elizabeth Berry. HIDEYOSHI. 1982: Harvard University Press.

George Elison. "Hideyoshi, the Bountiful Minister," in Elison & Smith, WARLORDS, ARTISTS & COMMONERS (1981: University of Hawaii Press), 223-244.

Walter Dening. THE LIFE OF TOYOTOMI HIDEYOSHI (1536-1598). 1906: Hokuseido.

Adriana Boscaro, transl. 101 LETTERS OF HIDEYOSHI. 1975: Monumenta Nipponica Monographs.

Giuliana Stramigioli. "Hideyoshi's Expansionist Policy on the Asiatic Mainland," *Transactions, Asiatic Society of Japan*, 3rd series, 3 (1954), 74-116.

Arthur L. Sadler. "The Naval Campaign in the Korean War of Hideyoshi (1592-1598)," *Transactions, Asiatic Society of Japan*, 2nd series, 14 (1937), 179-208.

Yoshi S. Kuno. JAPANESE EXPANSION ON THE ASIATIC CONTINENT. 2 volumes. 1937-1940: University of California Press. See volume 1 for Hideyoshi's invasion of Korea.

Homer B. Hulbert. THE HISTORY OF KOREA. 2 volumes. 1905: The Methodist Publishing House. See volume 1 for Hideyoshi's invasion.

Conrad Totman. TOKUGAWA IEYASU: SHOGUN. 1983: Heian International. Based on *Ieyasuden* (The Biography of Ieyasu) by Koya Nakamura.

FEUDAL JAPAN & THE WARRIOR SOCIETY: The "Christian Century" (1549-1650)

Charles R. Boxer. THE CHRISTIAN CENTURY IN JAPAN, 1549-1650. 1951: University of California Press.

_____. THE GREAT SHIP FROM AMACON: ANNALS OF MACAO AND THE OLD JAPAN TRADE, 1555-1640. 1959: Centro de Estudos Historicos Ultramarinos.

_____. A PORTUGUESE EMBASSY TO JAPAN (1644-1647) and THE EMBASSY OF CAPTAIN GONCALO DE SIQUIERIA DE SOUZA TO JAPAN IN 1644-7. 1979: University Publications of America reprint.

_____. PAPERS ON PORTUGUESE, DUTCH, AND JESUIT INFLUENCES IN SIXTEENTH- AND SEVENTEENTH-CENTURY JAPAN. 1979: University Publications of America reprint.

_____ & J.S. Cummins. THE DOMINICAN MISSION IN JAPAN (1602-1622) AND LOPE DE VEGA. 1963: Archivum Fratrum Praedictorum.

Michael Cooper, S.J. "Christianity," KODANSHA ENCYCLOPEDIA OF JAPAN 1: 306-310.

_____, ed. THEY CAME TO JAPAN: AN ANTHOLOGY OF EUROPEAN REPORTS ON JAPAN, 1543-1640. 1965: University of California Press.

_____, transl. & ed. THIS ISLAND OF JAPON: JOAO RODRIGUES' ACCOUNT OF 16TH-CENTURY JAPAN. 1973: Kodansha International.

_____. THE SOUTHERN BARBARIANS: THE FIRST EUROPEANS IN JAPAN. 1971: Kodansha International.

Donald Lach. JAPAN IN THE EYES OF EUROPE: THE SIXTEENTH CENTURY. 1968: University of Chicago Press.

George Elison. "The Cross and the Sword: Patterns of Momoyama History," in George Elison & Bardwell L. Smith, eds. WARLORDS, ARTISTS & COMMONERS (1981: University of Hawaii Press), 55-86.

_____. DEUS DESTROYED: THE IMAGE OF CHRISTIANITY IN EARLY MODERN JAPAN. 1973: Harvard University Press.

George B. Sansom. "Christianity in Japan, 1549-1614," in his THE WESTERN WORLD AND JAPAN (1962: Knopf), 115-133.

Richard H. Drummond. A HISTORY OF CHRISTIANITY IN JAPAN. 1971: William Eerdmans.

Otis Cary. A HISTORY OF CHRISTIANITY IN JAPAN: ROMAN CATHOLIC, GREEK ORTHODOX AND PROTESTANT MISSIONS. 1909: Revell. Reprinted in 1976; covers 1549 to the 20th century.

Frederick Vincent Williams. THE MARTYRS OF NAGASAKI. 1956: Academy Library Guild.

Hubert Cheslik. "The Great Martyrdom in Edo, 1623," *Monumenta Nipponica* 10.1-2 (1955), 1-44.

Montague Paske-Smith, ed. JAPANESE TRADITIONS OF CHRISTIANITY: BEING SOME OLD TRANSLATIONS FROM THE JAPANESE, WITH BRITISH CONSULAR REPORTS OF THE PERSECUTIONS OF 1868-1872. 1930: Kobe.

Henry Smith II, ed. LEARNING FROM "SHOGUN": JAPANESE HISTORY AND WESTERN FANTASY. 1980: Program in Asian Studies, University of California, Santa Barbara. A scholarly response to *Shogun*, the popular novel by James Clavell.

LAND, LABOR & COMMERCE BEFORE 1600

Elizabeth S. Sato. "Shoen," KODANSHA ENCYCLOPEDIA OF JAPAN 7: 155-158.

_____. "The Early Development of the Shoen," in John Hall & Jeffrey Mass, eds. MEDIEVAL JAPAN (1974: Yale University Press), 91-108.

_____. "Oyama Estate and Insei Land Policies," *Monumenta Nipponica* 34.1 (1979) 73-100.

Cornelius J. Kiley. "Estate and Property in the Late Heian Period," in Hall & Mass, MEDIEVAL JAPAN (1974: Yale University Press), 109-124.

Jeffrey P. Mass. "Patterns of Provincial Inheritance in Late Heian Japan," *Journal of Japanese Studies* 9.1 (1983), 67-95.

Peter J. Arneson. "The Struggle for Lordship in Late Heian Japan: The Case of Aki," *Journal of Japanese Studies* 10.1 (1984), 101-141.

Kozo Yamamura. "The Decline of the Ritsuryo System: Hypotheses on Economic & Institutional Change," *Journal of Japanese Studies* 1.1 (1974), 3-37.

_____ et al. "Workshop Papers on the Economic and Institutional History of Medieval Japan," *Journal of Japanese Studies* 1.2 (1975), 255-345.

_____. "Tara in Transition: A Study of a Kamakura Shoen," *Journal of Japanese Studies* 7.2 (1981), 349-391.

Keiji Nagahara. "Landownership Under the Shoen Kokugaryo System," *Journal of Japanese Studies* 1.2 (1975), 269-296.

James Kanda. "Methods of Land Transfer in Medieval Japan," *Monumenta Nipponica* 33.4 (1978), 379-405.

Ryosuke Ishii. "On Japanese Possession of Real Property--A Study of Chigyo in the Middle Ages," *Japan Annual of Law and Politics* 1 (1952), 149-162.

Kanichi Asakawa, ed. THE DOCUMENTS OF IRIKI, ILLUSTRATIVE OF THE DEVELOPMENT OF THE FEUDAL INSTITUTION IN JAPAN. 1955: Japan Society for the Promotion of Science.

_____. LAND & SOCIETY IN MEDIEVAL JAPAN. 1965: Japan Society for the Promotion of Science. Introduction by J.W. Hall and Rizo Takeuchi. Contains 7 essays by the pioneer of English-language studies of Japanese feudal structures.

John H. Wigmore & D.B. Simmons. NOTES ON LAND TENURE AND LOCAL INSTITUTIONS IN OLD JAPAN. 1891; reprinted 1979 by University Publications of America.

Haruko Wakita. "Towards a Wider Perspective on Medieval Commerce," *Journal of Japanese Studies* 1.2 (1975), 321-345.

_____. "Marriage and Property in Premodern Japan from the Perspective of Women's History," *Journal of Japanese Studies* 10.1 (1984), 73-99.

John W. Hall & Takeshi Toyoda, eds. JAPAN IN THE MUROMACHI AGE. 1976: University of California Press.

Mitsuru Miyagawa & Cornelius J. Kiley. "From Shoen to Chigyo: Proprietary Lordship and the Structure of Local Power," in Hall & Toyoda, JAPAN IN THE MUROMACHI AGE (1976: University of California Press), 89-106.

Keiji Nagahara & Kozo Yamamura. "Village Communities and Daimyo Power," in Hall & Toyoda, JAPAN IN THE MUROMACHI AGE (1976: University of California Press), 107-124.

27

LAND, LABOR & COMMERCE BEFORE 1600--II

Takeshi Toyoda, Hiroshi Sugiyama & V. Dixon Morris. "The Growth of Commerce and the Trades," in Hall & Toyoda, JAPAN IN THE MUROMACHI AGE (1976: University of California Press), 129-144.

V. Dixon Morris. "Sakai: From Shoen to Port City," in Hall & Toyoda, JAPAN IN THE MUROMACHI AGE (1976: University of California Press), 145-158.

Takeo Tanaka & Robert Sakai. "Japan's Relations with Overseas Countries," in Hall & Toyoda, JAPAN IN THE MUROMACHI AGE (1976: University of California Press), 159-178.

John W. Hall, Keiji Nagahara & Kozo Yamamura, eds. JAPAN BEFORE TOKUGAWA: POLITICAL CONSOLIDATION & ECONOMIC GROWTH, 1500-1650. 1981: Princeton University Press. Contains essays on land control and commerce under the warring daimyo and late 16th-century unifiers, urbanization, and overall economic growth.

Delmer M. Brown. MONEY ECONOMY IN MEDIEVAL JAPAN: A STUDY IN THE USE OF COINS. 1951: Yale University Press.

Kozo Yamamura. "The Development of Za in Medieval Japan," *Business History Review* 47.4 (1973), 438-465.

Y.T. Wang. OFFICIAL RELATIONS BETWEEN CHINA AND JAPAN, 1368-1549. 1953: Harvard University Press.

Katsumi Mori. "International Relations Between the 10th and 16th Century and the Development of the Japanese International Consciousness," *Acta Asiatica* 2 (1961), 69-93.

_____. "The Beginnings of Overseas Advance of Japanese Merchant Ships," *Acta Asiatica* 23 (1972), 1-24.

Kwan-wei So. JAPANESE PIRACY IN MING CHINA DURING THE MING DYNASTY. 1975: Michigan State University Press.

Benjamin H. Hazard. "The Formative Years of the *Wako*," *Monumenta Nipponica* 22.3-4 (1967), 260-277.

Yosaburo Takekoshi. THE STORY OF THE WAKO: JAPANESE PIONEERS IN THE SOUTHERN REGIONS. Hideo Watanabe, transl. 1940: Kenkyusha.

28

FEUDAL CULTURE BEFORE 1600

Daisetz T. Suzuki. ZEN AND JAPANESE CULTURE. 1959: Pantheon. Includes chapters on swordsmanship, Confucianism, haiku, tea ceremony, and attitudes toward nature.

George B. Sansom. JAPAN: A SHORT CULTURAL HISTORY. Revised edition. 1943: Appleton.

Martin Collcutt. FIVE MOUNTAINS: THE RINZAI ZEN MONASTIC INSTITUTION IN MEDIEVAL JAPAN. 1980: Harvard East Asian Monographs.

William R. LaFleur. THE KARMA OF WORDS: BUDDHISM AND THE LITERARY ARTS IN MEDIEVAL JAPAN. 1983: University of California Press.

Neil McMullin. BUDDHISM & THE STATE IN SIXTEENTH-CENTURY JAPAN. 1985: Princeton University Press.

H. Paul Varley. "Ashikaga Yoshimitsu and the World of Kitayama: Social Change and Shogunal Patronage in Early Muromachi Japan," in John W. Hall & Takeshi Toyoda, eds. JAPAN IN THE MUROMACHI AGE (1976: University of California Press), 183-204.

John Rosenfield. "The Unity of the Three Creeds: A Theme in Japanese Ink Painting of the Fifteenth Century," in Hall & Toyoda, JAPAN IN THE MUROMACHI AGE (1976: University of California Press), 205-226.

Teiji Ito & Paul Novograd. "The Development of Shoin-Style Architecture," in Hall & Toyoda, JAPAN IN THE MUROMACHI AGE (1976: University of California Press), 227-240.

Donald Keene. "The Comic Tradition in Renga," in Hall & Toyoda, JAPAN IN THE MUROMACHI AGE (1976: University of California Press), 241-278.

Barbara Ruch. "Medieval Jongleurs and the Making of a National Literature," in Hall & Toyoda, JAPAN IN THE MUROMACHI AGE (1976: University of California Press), 279-310.

Toshihide Akamatsu & Philip Yampolsky. "Muromachi Zen and the Gozan System," in Hall & Toyoda, JAPAN IN THE MUROMACHI AGE (1976: University of California Press), 313-330.

Stanley Weinstein. "Rennyo and the Shinshu Revival," in Hall & Toyoda, JAPAN IN THE MUROMACHI AGE (1976: University of California Press), 331-350.

George Elison & Bardwell L. Smith, eds. WARLORDS, ARTISTS & COMMONERS: JAPAN IN THE SIXTEENTH CENTURY. 1981: University of Hawaii Press. Includes essays on painting, poetry and song, music, tea.

Margaret H. Childs. *"Chigo Monogatari:* Love Stories or Buddhist Sermons?" *Monumenta Nipponica* 35.2 (1980), 127-152.

Chieko Mulhern. "*Otogi-zoshi:* Short Stories of the Muromachi Period," *Monumenta Nipponica* 29.2 (1974), 181-198.

_____. "Cinderella and the Jesuits: An *Otogi-zoshi* Cycle as Christian Literature," *Monumenta Nipponica* 34.4 (1979), 409-448.

James Araki. *"Otogi-zoshi* and *Nara-ehon:* A Field of Study in Flux," *Monumenta Nipponica* 36.1 (1981), 1-20.

Kakuzo Okakura. THE BOOK OF TEA. 1931: Duffield.

Beatrice Bodar. "Tea and Counsel: The Political Role of Sen Rikyu,"*Monumenta Nipponica* 32.1 (1977), 49-74.

Susan Matisoff. THE LEGEND OF SEMIMARU, BLIND MUSICIAN OF JAPAN. 1978: Columbia University Press.

James Araki. THE BALLAD-DRAMA OF MEDIEVAL JAPAN. 1964: University of California Press.

Donald Keene & Hiroshi Kaneko. *NO:* THE CLASSICAL THEATRE OF JAPAN. 1966: Kodansha International.
Kunio Komparu. THE NOH THEATER: PRINCIPLES & PERSPECTIVES. 1983: Weatherhill.

MEDIEVAL LITERATURE (EXCEPT WAR CHRONICLES) IN TRANSLATION

KENREIMON'IN UKYO NO DAIBU SHU (12th-13th century)

* Philip Tudor Harries, transl. THE POETIC MEMOIRS OF LADY DAIBU. 1980: Stanford University Press.

* James G. Wagner. "The *Kenreimon'in Ukyo no Daibu Shu*," *Monumenta Nipponica* 31.1 (1976), 1-28.

UJI SHUI MONOGATARI (early 13th century)

* D.E. Mills, transl. A COLLECTION OF TALES FROM UJI: A STUDY AND TRANSLATION OF *UJI SHUI MONOGATARI*. 1970: Cambridge University Press.

* John S. Foster, transl. "*Uji Shui Monogatari*" *Monumenta Nipponica* 20.1-2 (1965) 135-208. Translation of 55 tales.

HOJOKI (written in 1212 by Kamo no Chomei, 1153-1216)

* Arthur L. Sadler, transl. THE TEN FOOT SQUARE HUT AND TALES OF THE HEIKE. 1918 and 1921; reprint edition, 1972: Tuttle.

MUMYOSHO (written c. 1200 by Kamo no Chomei)

* Hilda Kato. THE *MUMYOSHO* OF KAMO NO CHOMEI AND ITS SIGNIFICANCE IN JAPANESE LITERATURE. 1968: University of British Columbia.

* Michele Marra. "*Mumyozoshi:* Introduction & Translation," *Monumenta Nipponica* 39.2 (1984), 115-146.

GUKANSHO (written in 1219 by Jien, 1155-1225)

* Delmer Brown and Ichiro Ishida. THE FUTURE AND THE PAST: A TRANSLATION AND STUDY OF THE *GUKANSHO*, AN INTERPRETATIVE HISTORY OF JAPAN WRITTEN IN 1219. 1978: University of California Press.

* J. Rahder. "Miscellany of Personal Views of an Ignorant Fool (Guk/w/ansho)," *Acta Orientalia* 15 (1936), 173-230.

* H. Paul Varley. "The Place of *Gukansho* in Japanese Intellectual History," *Monumenta Nipponica* 34.4 (1979), 479-488.

KINDAI SHUKA (of Fujiwara Teika, 1162-1241)

* Robert H. Brower & Earl Miner, transl. FUJIWARA TEIKA'S "SUPERIOR POEMS OF OUR TIME." 1967: Stanford University Press.

HYAKUNIN ISSHU (famous popular anthology of "100 poems by 100 poets," editorship attributed to Fujiwara Teika in the year 1200)

* Tom Galt, transl. THE LITTLE TREASURY OF ONE HUNDRED PEOPLE, ONE POEM EACH. 1984: Princeton University Press.

* Robert H. Brower. FUJIWARA TEIKA'S HUNDRED-POEM SEQUENCE OF THE SHOJI ERA, 1200. 1978: Monumenta Nipponica Monographs (originally published in 1976 in *Monumenta Nipponica* 31.3 and 31.4).

MEDIEVAL LITERATURE (EXCEPT WAR CHRONICLES) IN TRANSLATION--II

SHASEKISHU (late 13th-century collection of Buddhist *setsuwa*, or "tale literature")

* Robert E. Morrell. SAND AND PEBBLES *(SHASEKISHU):* THE TALES OF MUJU ICHIEN, A VOICE FOR PLURALISM IN KAMAKURA BUDDHISM. 1985: University of New York Press.

IZAYOI NIKKI (recounting journey from Kyoto to Kamakura by the nun Abutsuni, ca. 1277-1280)

* Edwin O. Reischauer & Joseph Yamagiwa. TRANSLATIONS FROM EARLY JAPANESE LITERATURE (1951: Harvard University Press), 1-135.

Herbert Plutschow & Hideichi Fukuda, transl. FOUR JAPANESE TRAVEL DIARIES OF THE MIDDLE AGES. 1981: *Cornell University East Asia Papers.* Translations of "Takakura-in Itsukushima Goko Ki" (25-44); "Shinsho Hoshi Nikki" (45-60); "Miyako no Tsuto" (61-76); "Zenkoji Kiko" (77-86).

ISE DAIJINGU SANKEIKI (14th century)

* Arthur L. Sadler, transl. THE *ISE DAIJINGU SANKEIKI,* OR DIARY OF A PILGRIM TO ISE. 1940: Meiji Japan Society.

TOWAZUGATARI ("autobiography" of former imperial concubine, covering 1271-1306)

* Karen Brazell, transl. THE CONFESSIONS OF LADY NIJO. 1973: Doubleday-Anchor.

* _____. "*Towazugatari:* Autobiography of a Kamakura Court Lady," *Harvard Journal of Asiatic Studies* 31 (1971), 220-233.

TSUREZUREGUSA (of Yoshida Kenko, written ca. 1330-1332)

* Donald Keene, transl. ESSAYS IN IDLENESS: THE *TSUREZUREGUSA* OF KENKO. 1967: Columbia University Press.

* George B. Sansom, transl. "The *Tsurezuregusa* of Yoshida Kaneyoshi," *Transactions, Asiatic Society of Japan,* 1st series, 39 (1911), 1-146.

JINNO SHOTOKI ("Record of the Legitimate Succession of the Divine Emperors" by Kitabatake Chikafusa, 1293-1354)

* H. Paul Varley, transl. A CHRONICLE OF GODS AND KINGS: *JINNO SHOTOKI* OF KITABATAKE CHIKAFUSA. 1980: Columbia University Press.

NO THEATER

* Donald Keene, transl. TWENTY PLAYS OF THE *NO* THEATRE. 1970: Columbia University Press.

* _____ & Hiroshi Kaneko. *NO:* THE CLASSICAL THEATER OF JAPAN. 1966: Kodansha International.

* Arthur Waley, transl. THE *NO* PLAYS OF JAPAN. 1911: Allen & Unwin.

* J. Thomas Rimer & Masakaza Yamazaki, transl. ON THE ART OF THE *NO* DRAMA: THE MAJOR TREATISES OF ZEAMI. 1984: Princeton University Press. The nine major treatises of Zeami Motokiyo (1363-1443), the great master of the *No* theater.

THE "WAY OF THE WARRIOR": General Accounts of Samurai Values and Practices

Martin C. Collcutt. "Bushido," KODANSHA ENCYCLOPEDIA OF JAPAN 1: 221-223.

R. Tsunoda et al., SOURCES OF JAPANESE TRADITION (1958: Columbia University Press), chapters 15-24.

H. Paul Varley. SAMURAI. 1970: Delacorte.

Ivan Morris. THE NOBILITY OF FAILURE: TRAGIC HEROES IN THE HISTORY OF JAPAN. 1975: Holt, Rinehart & Winston.

Louis Frederic. DAILY LIFE IN JAPAN IN THE AGE OF THE SAMURAI, 1185-1603. 1972: Praeger.

William Ritchie Wilson. "The Way of the Bow and Arrow: The Japanese Warrior in *Konjaku Monogatari*," *Monumenta Nipponica* 28.2 (1973), 177-234.

Kenneth Dean Butler. "The *Heike Monogatari* and the Japanese Warrior Ethic," *Harvard Journal of Asiatic Studies* 29 (1969), 93-108.

Tadashi Hasegawa. "The Early Stages of the *Heike Monogatari*," *Monumenta Nipponica* 22.1-2 (1967), 65-81.

Daisetz T. Suzuki. ZEN AND JAPANESE CULTURE. 1959: Pantheon. See especially chapters 4 ("Zen and the Samurai"), and 5-6 ("Zen and Swordmanship").

Joe Hyams. ZEN IN THE MARTIAL ARTS. 1979: Tarcher.

Stephen R. Turnbull. THE SAMURAI: A MILITARY HISTORY. 1977: Macmillan.

_____. THE BOOK OF THE SAMURAI: THE WARRIOR CLASS OF JAPAN. 1982: Arco.

Richard Storry. THE WAY OF THE SAMURAI. 1978: Putnam.

Inazo Nitobe. BUSHIDO, THE SOUL OF JAPAN. 1905: Putnam.

Jack Seward. HARA-KIRI: JAPANESE RITUAL SUICIDE. 1968: Tuttle.

John Allyn. THE FORTY-SEVEN RONIN STORY. 1970: Tuttle.

Kailen Nukariya. THE RELIGION OF THE SAMURAI. 1913: Luzac.

Captain F. Brinkley. SAMURAI: THE INVINCIBLE WARRIORS. 1975: Ohara.

Michael Gibson. THE SAMURAI OF JAPAN. 1969: Wayland.

Toru Sagara. "The Spiritual Strength and Independence in Bushido," *Acta Asiatica* 23 (1973), 91-106.

Robert N. Bellah. "Bushido," in his TOKUGAWA RELIGION (1957: Free Press), 90-106.

Tasuke Kawakami. "Bushido in Its Formative Period," *Annals of the Hitotsubashi Academy* 3 (1952), 65-83.

Noel Perrin. GIVING UP THE GUN: JAPAN'S REVERSION TO THE SWORD, 1543-1879. 1979: Godine.

Caryl Callahan. "Tales of Samurai Honor: Saikaku's *Buke Giri Monogatari*," *Monumenta Nipponica* 34.1 (1979), 1-20. Tales by a famous 17th-century satirist.

_____, transl. IHARA SAIKAKU: TALES OF SAMURAI HONOR *(BUKE GIRI MONOGATARI)*. 1982: Monumenta Nipponica Monographs.

THE "WAY OF THE WARRIOR": General Accounts of Samurai Values and Practices--II

Musashi Miyamoto. A BOOK OF FIVE RINGS: THE CLASSIC GUIDE TO STRATEGY. Victor Harris, transl. 1974: Overlook. A translation of *Go Rin no Sho* by Musashi Miyamoto, Japan's greatest swordsman, written shortly before his death in 1645.

Tsunetomo Yamamoto. *HAGAKURE:* THE BOOK OF THE SAMURAI. William Scott Wilson, transl. 1979: Kodansha International. A translation of a classic statement of the "way of death," written in 1716.

THE "WAY OF THE WARRIOR": War Tales in Translation

KONJAKU MONOGATARI (popular tales collected in early 12th century)

* William Ritchie Wilson. "The Way of the Bow and Arrow: The Japanese Warrior in *Konjaku Monogatari*," *Monumenta Nipponica* 28.2 (1973), 177-234.

SHOMONKI (Japan's earliest war chronicle, concerning events culminating in 940)

* Judith N. Rabinovitch, transl. *SHOMONKI:* THE STORY OF MASAKADO'S REBELLION. 1986: Monumenta Nipponica Monographs.

* Guiliana Stramigioli. "Preliminary Notes on the *Masakado-ki* and the Taira no Masakado Story," *Monumenta Nipponica* 28.3 (1978), 261-293.

MUTSU WAKI (mid 11th-century campaign)

* Helen C. McCullough, transl. "A Tale of Mutsu," *Harvard Journal of Asiatic Studies* 25 (1964-5), 178-211.

HOGEN MONOGATARI (conflict of 1156)

* William R. Wilson, transl. *HOGEN MONOGATARI, TALE OF THE DISORDER IN HOGEN.* 1971: Monumenta Nipponica Monographs.

HEIJI MONOGATARI (conflict of 1159-1160)

* Edwin O. Resichauer & Joseph Yamagiwa, transl. TRANSLATIONS FROM EARLY JAPANESE LITERATURE (1951: Harvard University Press), 377-457.

HEIKE MONOGATARI (the epic clash of the Taira and Minamoto clans, 1180-1185)

* Arthur L. Sadler, transl. THE TEN FOOT SQUARE HUT AND TALES OF THE HEIKE. 1972: Tuttle. Abridged version of translation originally published in *Transactions, Asiatic Society of Japan* volumes of 1918 and 1921.

* Hiroshi Kitagawa & Bruce T. Tsuchida, transl. THE TALE OF THE HEIKE. 2 volumes. 1975: University of Tokyo Press.

AZUMA KAGAMI (about the founding of the Kamakura Shogunate)

* Minoru Shinoda. THE FOUNDING OF THE KAMAKURA SHOGUNATE, 1180-1185--WITH SELECTED TRANSLATIONS FROM THE *AZUMA KAGAMI*. 1960: Columbia University Press.

* William McCullough, transl. "The *Azuma Kagami* Account of the Shokyu War," *Monumenta Nipponica* 23.1-2 (1968), 102-155.

SHOKYUKI (the abortive war against the Bakufu led by Emperor Go-Toba)

* William McCullough, transl. "*Shokyuki:* An Account of the Shokyu War of 1221," *Monumenta Nipponica* 19.1-2 and 19.3-4 (1964), 163-215, 420-455

THE "WAY OF THE WARRIOR":   War Tales in Translation--II

* John S. Brownlee. "The Shokyu War and the Political Rise of the Warriors," *Monumenta Nipponica*
     24.1-2 (1969), 59-77

TAIHEIKI (the great chronicle about the 14th century transition from Kamakura to Ashikaga rule)

* Helen C. McCullough, transl. THE *TAIHEIKI:* A CHRONICLE OF MEDIEVAL JAPAN. 1959:
     Columbia University Press.

SOGA MONOGATARI (c. 1340)

* Thomas J. Cogan. "A Study and Complete Translation of the *Soga Monogatari*," 1982: Ph.D.
     dissertation in Asian Languages and Literature, University of Hawaii.

ONINKI (the civil upheaval of 1467-1477 that ushered in the "Period of Warring States")

* H. Paul Varley. THE ONIN WAR: HISTORY OF ITS ORIGINS AND BACKGROUND, WITH A
     SELECTIVE TRANSLATION OF THE CHRONICLES OF ONIN. 1967: Columbia University Press.

GIKEIKI (15th-century account of Minamoto Yoshitsune, the tragic hero of the 12th century)

* Helen C. McCullough, transl. YOSHITSUNE: A FIFTEENTH-CENTURY JAPANESE CHRONICLE.
     1965: Stanford University Press.

THE "WAY OF THE WARRIOR": Warrior Laws & Codes of Conduct

William Scott Wilson, transl. IDEALS OF THE SAMURAI: WRITINGS OF JAPANESE WARRIORS. 1982: Ohara. Translations of family codes or clan precepts (*kakun*) dating from approximately 1250 to 1600.

Jeffrey Mass. THE DEVELOPMENT OF KAMAKURA RULE, 1180-1250: A HISTORY WITH DOCUMENTS. 1979: Stanford University Press.

J. C. Hall. "Japanese Feudal Laws *(Go Seibai Shikimoku),*" *Transactions, Asiatic Society of Japan*, 1st series, 34 (1906), 1-44.

Carl Steenstrup. HOJO SHIGETOKI (1198-1261) AND HIS ROLE IN THE HISTORY OF POLITICAL AND ETHICAL IDEAS IN JAPAN. 1979: Curzon Press (Scandinavian Institute of Asian Studies Monograph Series 41). Includes translations of "Letter to Nagatoki" (139-157) and "Gokurakuji Letter" (158-198).

John Brownlee. *"Jokkinsho.* A Miscellany of Ten Maxims," *Monumenta Nipponica* 29.2 (1974), 121-162.

Delmer M. Brown. "The Japanese *Tokusei* of 1297," *Harvard Journal of Asiatic Studies* 12 (1949), 188-206.

Kenneth A. Grossberg & Nobuhisa Kanamoto, transl. THE LAWS OF THE MUROMACHI BAKUFU. 1981: Monumenta Nipponica Monographs. Annotated translation of *Kemmu Shikimoku* (1336) and *Muromachi Bakufu Tsuikaho.*

J.C. Hall. "Japanese Feudal Laws, II *(Kemmu Shikimoku),*" *Transactions, Asiatic Society of Japan*, 1st series, 36 (1908), 3-25.

David John Lu. *"Kemmu Shikimoku,"* in his SOURCES OF JAPANESE HISTORY (1974: McGraw-Hill), volume 1, 150-152.

Carl Steenstrup. *"Sata Mirensho:* A Fourteenth-Century Law Primer," *Monumenta Nipponica* 35.4 (1980), 337-346.

_____. "The Imagawa Letter: A Muromachi Warrior's Code of Conduct Which Became a Tokugawa Schoolbook," *Monumenta Nipponica* 28.3 (1973), 295-316.

David John Lu. "Seventeen-Article Injunction of Asakura Toshikage, c. 1480," in his SOURCES OF JAPANESE HISTORY (1974: McGraw-Hill), volume 1, 171-174.

Carl Steenstrup. "Hojo Soun's Twenty-One Articles: The Code of Conduct of the Odawara Hojo," *Monumenta Nipponica* 29.3 (1974), 283-303.

David John Lu. "Hojo Soun's Twenty-One Article Injunction for His Vassals, c. 1495," in his SOURCES OF JAPANESE HISTORY (1974: McGraw-Hill), volume 1, 174-175.

_____. "Takeda Shingen's House Law," in his SOURCES OF JAPANESE HISTORY (1974: McGraw-Hill), volume 1, 175-176. Also a complete translation by W. Rohl in *Oriens Extremus* 6 (1959), 210-235, totaling 99 articles.

_____. "The Hundred Article Code of Chosokabe, 1597," in his SOURCES OF JAPANESE HISTORY (1974: McGraw-Hill), volume 1, 177-181. From John Hall & Marius Jansen, eds. STUDIES IN THE INSTITUTIONAL HISTORY OF EARLY MODERN JAPAN (1968: Princeton University Press), 102-114.

James Murdoch. "Testament of Ieyasu," in his A HISTORY OF JAPAN (1925-1926: Ungar), volume 3, 796-814.

S. Gubbins, transl. "A Samurai Manual," *Transactions and Proceedings of the Japan Society, London* 9 (1910), 140-151.

J.C. Hall, transl. "Teijo's Family Instruction (1763): A Samurai's Ethical Bequest to His Posterity," *Transactions and Proceedings of the Japan Society, London* 14 (1915), 128-156.

Donald Keene, transl. CHUSHINGURA. 1971: Columbia University Press.

Arthur L. Sadler, transl. THE BEGINNER'S BOOK OF BUSHIDO BY DAIDOJI YUZAN *(BUDO SHOSHINSHU)*. 1941: Kokusai Bunka Shinkokai.

Tsunetomo Yamamoto. *HAGAKURE:* THE BOOK OF THE SAMURAI. William Scott Wilson, transl. 1979: Kodansha International. A translation of a classic statement of the "way of death," written in 1716.

Kathryn Sparling, transl. THE WAY OF THE SAMURAI: YUKIO MISHIMA ON *HAGAKURE* IN MODERN LIFE. 1977: Basic Books.

Arai Hakuseki. THE SWORD BOOK IN *HONCHO GUNGIKO* OF ARAI HAKUSEKI & THE BOOK OF *SAME* [Shark Skin]: *KO HI SEI GI* OF INABA TSURIO. Henri L. Joly & Hogitaro Inada, transl. & ed. 1913; reprinted by Tuttle.

Musashi Miyamoto. A BOOK OF FIVE RINGS, A GUIDE TO STRATEGY. Victor Harris, transl. 1974: Overlook.

Walter Dening. JAPAN IN DAYS OF YORE. 1976: East-West Publications.

Ernest W. Clement. "Instructions of a Mito Prince to His Retainers," *Transactions, Asiatic Society of Japan*, 1st series, 26 (1898), 115-153.

37

THE "WAY OF THE WARRIOR": The Martial Arts

Oscar Ratti & Adele Westbrook. SECRETS OF THE SAMURAI: A SURVEY OF THE MARTIAL ARTS OF FEUDAL JAPAN. 1974: Tuttle.

Joe Hyams. ZEN IN THE MARTIAL ARTS. 1979: Tarcher.

Donn F. Draeger & Robert W. Smith. COMPREHENSIVE ASIAN FIGHTING ARTS. 1980: Kodansha International.

Donn F. Draeger. CLASSICAL BUJUTSU. 1973: Weatherhill.

_____. CLASSICAL BUDO. 1974: Weatherhill.

_____ & Gordon Warner. JAPANESE SWORDSMANSHIP: TECHNIQUE AND PRACTICE. 1982: Weatherhill.

Kanzan Sato. THE JAPANESE SWORD. 1983: Kodansha International.

Charles R. Watrall. THE ARTS OF THE JAPANESE SWORD. 1974: Norman Mackenzie Art Gallery.

Basil W. Robinson. THE ARTS OF THE JAPANESE SWORD. 1961: Tuttle.

John M. Yumoto. THE SAMURAI SWORD: A HANDBOOK. 1959: Tuttle.

L.J. Anderson. JAPANESE ARMOUR. 1968: Lionel Leventhal.

Masaaki Hatsumi. NINJUTSU: HISTORY AND TRADITION. 1981: Unique.

Donn F. Draeger. NINJUTSU: THE ART OF INVISIBILITY. 1977: Lotus Press.

Bruce A. Haines. KARATE'S HISTORY AND TRADITIONS. 1968: Tuttle.

P. L. Cuyler. SUMO: FROM RITE TO SPORT. 1979: Weatherhill.

RELIGION: General Works (see items marked ** for more detailed bibliographies)

**Joseph M. Kitagawa. RELIGION IN JAPANESE HISTORY. 1966: Columbia University Press.

** _____. "The Religions of Japan," in Charles J. Adams, ed. A READER'S GUIDE TO THE GREAT RELIGIONS (1965: Free Press), 161-190.

_____. "Religions of Japan," in Wing-tsit Chan et al., THE GREAT ASIAN RELIGIONS (1969: Macmillan), 231-305.

**H. Byron Earhart. JAPANESE RELIGION: UNITY AND DIVERSITY. 3rd edition. 1982: Wadsworth.

_____, ed. RELIGION IN THE JAPANESE EXPERIENCE: SOURCES AND INTERPRETATIONS. 1974: Dickenson.

Ichiro Hori, ed. JAPANESE RELIGION: A SURVEY BY THE AGENCY FOR CULTURAL AFFAIRS. 1972: Kodansha International.

Wm. Theodore DeBary. "Religion," in Arthur Tiedemann, ed. AN INTRODUCTION TO JAPANESE CIVILIZATION (1974: Heath), 309-328.

Masaharu Anesaki. HISTORY OF JAPANESE RELIGION. 1930; reprint edition, 1963: Tuttle.

_____. RELIGIOUS LIFE OF THE JAPANESE PEOPLE. 1961: Kokusai Bunka Shinkokai.

Ryusaku Tsunoda, Wm. Theodore DeBary & Donald Keene, eds. SOURCES OF JAPANESE TRADITION. 1958: Columbia University Press. See especially chapters 2 (early Shinto), 5 (Nara Buddhism), 6-8 (Heian Buddhism), 10-13 (Buddhism and Shinto in the Medieval Period).

Alfred Bloom. "Japan: Religion of a Sacred People in a Sacred Land," in W. Richard Comstock, ed. RELIGION AND MAN (1971: Harper & Row), 336-394.

RELIGION: Shinto

Allan G. Grapard. "Shinto," KODANSHA ENCYCLOPEDIA OF JAPAN 7: 125-132.

Toshio Kuroda. "Shinto in the History of Japanese Religion," *Journal of Japanese Studies* 7.1 (1981), 1-21.

Genchi Kato. A STUDY OF SHINTO: THE RELIGION OF THE JAPANESE NATION. 1926: Barnes & Noble.

Sokyo Ono. SHINTO, THE KAMI WAY. 1962: Bridgeway.

Robert J. Smith. ANCESTOR WORSHIP IN CONTEMPORARY JAPAN. 1974: Stanford University Press. See especially chapters 1 and 2.

D.C. Holtom. "The Meaning of *Kami*," *Monumenta Nipponica* 3.1 and 3.2 (1940), 1-26, 392-413; and *Monumenta Nipponica* 4.2 (1941), 351-394.

_____. THE NATIONAL FAITH OF JAPAN: A STUDY IN MODERN SHINTO. 1938: Dutton.

Jean Herbert. SHINTO: THE FOUNTAINHEAD OF JAPAN. 1967: Allen & Unwin.

Floyd Hiatt Ross. SHINTO, THE WAY OF JAPAN. 1965: Beacon.

Tsunetsugu Muraoka. STUDIES IN SHINTO THOUGHT. 1964: Japanese National Commission for UNESCO.

Joseph W. Mason. THE MEANING OF SHINTO: THE PRIMEVAL FOUNDATIONS OF CREATIVE SPIRIT IN MODERN JAPAN. 1935: Dutton.

Joseph J. Spae. SHINTO MAN. 1972: Oriens Institute for Religious Research.

Haruki Kageyama. THE ARTS OF SHINTO. 1973: Weatherhill.

Kenzo Tange & Teiji Itoh. ISE: PROTOTYPE OF JAPANESE ARCHITECTURE. 1965: Massachusetts Institute of Technology Press.

Donald L. Philippi, transl. *NORITO:* A NEW TRANSLATION OF THE ANCIENT JAPANESE RITUAL PRAYERS. 1959: Kokugakuin.

Genchi Kato & Hikoshiro Hoshino, transl. *KOGOSHUI:* GLEANINGS FROM ANCIENT STORIES. 1926: Barnes & Noble. Memorial presented in 807, revealing Shinto rites and customs.

Felicia Bock, transl. *ENGI-SHIKI:* PROCEDURES OF THE ENGI ERA. 2 volumes. 1970, 1972: Monumenta Nipponica Monographs. A valuable translation of Shinto prayers as recorded in the 9th century.

Karl Florenz. "Ancient Japanese Rituals," *Transactions, Asiatic Society of Japan*, 1st series, 27 (1900), 1-112.

Robert S. Ellwood. THE FEAST OF KINGSHIP: ACCESSION CEREMONIES IN ANCIENT JAPAN. 1973: Monumenta Nipponica Monographs.

D.C. Holtom. THE JAPANESE ENTHRONEMENT CEREMONIES, WITH AN ACCOUNT OF THE IMPERIAL REGALIA. 1928; reprint edition, 1972: Monumenta Nipponica Monographs.

RELIGION: Buddhism

Hajime Nakamura. "Buddhism," KODANSHA ENCYCLOPEDIA OF JAPAN 1: 176-180.

Joseph M. Kitagawa. "The Buddhist Transformation in Japan," *History of Religions* 4 (1965), 319-336.

Daigan & Alicia Matsunaga. FOUNDATION OF JAPANESE BUDDHISM. 2 volumes. 1974, 1976: Buddhist Books International.

Alicia Matsunaga. THE BUDDHIST PHILOSOPHY OF ASSIMILATION: THE HISTORICAL DEVELOPMENT OF THE HONJI-SUIJAKU THEORY. 1969: Monumenta Nipponica Monographs.

Ryusaku Tsunoda et al. SOURCES OF JAPANESE TRADITION. 1958: Columbia University Press. See chapters 5 (Nara), 6 (Tendai), 7 and 8 (Esoteric), 10 (Pure Land), 11 (Nichiren), and 12 (Zen).

Charles Eliot. JAPANESE BUDDHISM. 1935; reprint edition, 1959: Routledge & Kegan Paul.

E. Dale Saunders. BUDDHISM IN JAPAN. 1964: University of Pennsylvania Press.

Kenneth W. Morgan, ed. THE PATH OF THE BUDDHA. 1956: Ronald. See especially 307-363.

Shoko Watanabe. JAPANESE BUDDHISM: A CRITICAL APPRAISAL. 1968: Kokusai Bunka Shinkokai.

Wm. Theodore DeBary, ed. THE BUDDHIST TRADITION IN INDIA, CHINA, AND JAPAN. 1969: Modern Library.

Diana Y. Paul. WOMEN IN BUDDHISM: IMAGES OF THE FEMININE IN THE MAHAYANA TRADITION. 1985: Stanford University Press.

J. H. Kamstra. ENCOUNTER OR SYNCRETISM: THE INITIAL GROWTH OF JAPANESE BUDDHISM. 1967: Brill.

Marinus Willem de Visser. ANCIENT BUDDHISM IN JAPAN: SUTRAS AND CEREMONIES IN THE SEVENTH AND EIGHTH CENTURIES A.D. AND THEIR HISTORY IN LATER TIMES. 2 volumes. 1935: Brill.

Shinsho Hanayama. "Prince Shotoku and Japanese Buddhism," *Philosophical Studies of Japan* 4 (1963), 23-48.

Edwin O. Reischauer, transl. ENNIN'S DIARY: THE RECORD OF A PILGRIMAGE TO CHINA IN SEARCH OF THE LAW. 1955: Ronald.

_____. ENNIN'S TRAVELS IN T'ANG CHINA. 1955: Ronald.

Roy Andrew Miller. THE FOOTPRINTS OF THE BUDDHA: AN EIGHTH-CENTURY OLD JAPANESE POETIC SEQUENCE. 1975: American Oriental Society.

Kyoko Motomochi Nakamura, transl. MIRACULOUS STORIES FROM THE JAPANESE BUDDHIST TRADITION. THE *NIHON RYOIKI* OF THE MONK KYOKAI. 1973: Harvard University Press.

Yoshito S. Hakeda. KUKAI: MAJOR WORKS. 1972: Columbia University Press.

Paul Groner. SAICHO: THE ESTABLISHMENT OF THE JAPANESE TENDAI SCHOOL. 1984: University of California Press.

Allan A. Andrews. THE TEACHINGS ESSENTIAL FOR REBIRTH: A STUDY OF GENSHIN'S *OJOYOSHU*. 1973: Monumenta Nipponica Monographs.

Fernando G. Gutierrez. "Emakimono Depicting the Pains of the Damned," *Monumenta Nipponica* 22.3-4 (1967), 278-289.

Yoshiko K. Dykstra, transl. MIRACULOUS TALES OF THE LOTUS SUTRA FROM ANCIENT JAPAN: THE *DAINIHONKOKU HOKEKYOKENKI* OF PRIEST CHINGEN. 1983: University of Hawaii Press.

41

Robert E. Morrell, transl. SAND AND PEBBLES *(SHASEKISHU):* THE TALES OF MUJU ICHIEN, A VOICE FOR PLURALISM IN KAMAKURA BUDDHISM. 1985: State University of New York Press.

Harper Coates & Ryugaku Ishizuka, transl. and ed. HONEN, THE BUDDHIST SAINT: HIS LIFE AND TEACHING. 5 volumes. 1925: Society for the Publication of Sacred Books of the World.

Alfred Bloom. SHINRAN'S GOSPEL OF PURE GRACE. 1965: University of Arizona Press.

Daisetz T. Suzuki. SHIN BUDDHISM. 1970: Harper & Row.

_____, ed. COLLECTED WRITINGS ON SHIN BUDDHISM. 1974: Harper & Row.

Shinran. THE *KYOGYOSHINSHO.* Daisetz T. Suzuki, transl. 1954: English Publication Bureau.

_____. *TANNISHO:* A TRACT DEPLORING HERESIES OF FAITH. 1962: Higashi Honganji.

Kosho Yamamoto. THE PRIVATE LETTERS OF SHINRAN SHONIN. 1963: Darin Bunko.

_____. THE OTHER POWER. 1965: Darin Bunko.

Luis O. Gomez. "Shinran's Faith and the Sacred Name of Amida," *Monumenta Nipponica* 38.1 (1983), 73-84.

Masaharu Anesaki. NICHIREN, THE BUDDHIST PROPHET. 1949: Harvard University Press.

Laurel Rasplica Rodd. NICHIREN: A BIOGRAPHY. 1978: Center for Asian Studies, Arizona State University.

William R. LaFleur. THE KARMA OF WORDS: BUDDHISM AND THE LITERARY ARTS IN MEDIEVAL JAPAN. 1983: University of California Press.

Neil McMullin. BUDDHISM AND THE STATE IN SIXTEENTH-CENTURY JAPAN. 1985: Princeton University Press.

Margaret H. Childs. "*Chigo Monogatari:* Love Stories or Buddhist Sermons?" *Monumenta Nipponica* 35.2 (1980), 127-151.

James H. Sanford. "Mandalas of the Heart: Two Prose Works by Ikkyu Sojun," *Monumenta Nipponica* 35.3 (1980), 273-298.

*Patricia Armstrong Vessie. ZEN BUDDHISM: A BIBLIOGRAPHY OF BOOKS AND ARTICLES IN ENGLISH, 1892-1975. 1976: University Microfilms International.

*Ruth Fuller Sasaki. "A Bibliography of Translations of Zen (Ch'an) Works," *Philosophy East and West* 10 (1960-1961), 149-166.

Daisetz T. Suzuki. Suzuki (1890-1966) was the pioneer interpreter of Zen to the West. His books in English include ZEN BUDDHISM and ZEN AND JAPANESE CULTURE, and many other titles.

Heinrich Dumoulin. A HISTORY OF ZEN BUDDHISM. 1963: Random House. Translated from the German.

Martin Collcutt. FIVE MOUNTAINS: THE RINZAI ZEN MONASTIC INSTITUTIONS IN MEDIEVAL JAPAN. 1981: Harvard University Press.

Alan W. Watts. THE WAY OF ZEN. 1957: Vintage Books.

Nancy Wilson Ross, ed. THE WORLD OF ZEN. 1960: Random House.

Philip Kapleau, comp. and ed. THE THREE PILLARS OF ZEN: TEACHING, PRACTICE, ENLIGHTENMENT. 1964: Beacon.

Mircea Eliade. FROM PRIMITIVES TO ZEN. 1967: Collins.

Isshu Miura & Ruth Fuller Sasaki. ZEN DUST: THE HISTORY OF THE KOAN AND KOAN STUDY IN RINZAI (LIN-CHI) ZEN. 1967: Harcourt Brace & World.

_____. THE ZEN KOAN: ITS HISTORY AND USE IN RINZAI ZEN. 1965: Harcourt Brace & World.

Philip B. Yampolsky, transl. THE ZEN MASTER HAKUIN: SELECTED WRITINGS. 1985: Columbia University Press.

William R. LaFleur, ed. DOGEN STUDIES. 1985: University of Hawaii Press.

Hee-Jin Kim. DOGEN KIGEN--MYSTICAL REALIST. 1984: University of Arizona Press.

Reiho Masunaga, transl. A PRIMER OF SOTO ZEN: A TRANSLATION OF DOGEN'S *SHOBOGENZO ZUIMONKI*. 1971: University of Hawaii Press.

Eshin Nishimura. UNSUI: A DIARY OF ZEN MONASTIC LIFE. Bardwell L. Smith, ed. 1973: University of Hawaii Press. Charming illustrations.

Jan Fontein & Money L. Hickman. ZEN PAINTING AND CALLIGRAPHY. 1970: Boston Museum of Fine Arts.

RELIGION: Folk Religion

Ichiro Hori. FOLK RELIGION IN JAPAN: CONTINUITY & CHANGE. 1968: University of Chicago Press.

_____. "On the Concept of *Hijiori* (Holy Man)," *Numen* 5 (1958), 128-160, 199-232.

_____. "Rites of Purification and Orgy in Japanese Folk Religion," *Philosophical Studies of Japan* 9 (1969), 61-78.

Hitoshi Miyake. "Folk Religion," in Ichiro Hori, ed. JAPANESE RELIGION (1972: Kodansha International), 121-143.

Joseph Pittau, ed. FOLK CULTURES OF JAPAN AND EAST ASIA. 1966: Monumenta Nipponica Monographs.

Tokihiko Oto. FOLKLORE IN JAPANESE LIFE AND CUSTOMS. 1963: Kokusai Bunka Shinkokai. Useful for illustrations.

Carmen Blacker. "Japan," in Michael Loewe & Carmen Blacker, eds. ORACLES AND DIVINATION (1981: Shambhala), 63-86.

_____. THE CATALPA BOW: A STUDY OF SHAMANISTIC PRACTICES IN JAPAN. 1975: Allen & Unwin.

William P. Fairchild. "Shamanism in Japan," *Folklore Studies* 21 (1962), 1-122.

Hisako Kamata. "'Daughters of the Gods': Shaman Priestesses in Japan and Okinawa," in Pittau, ed. FOLK CULTURES OF JAPAN AND EAST ASIA (1966: Monumenta Nipponica Monographs), 56-73.

Robert J. Smith. ANCESTOR WORSHIP IN CONTEMPORARY JAPAN. 1974: Stanford University Press. See especially chapter 1, "The Historical Perspective" (6-38); and chapter 2, "Spirits, Ghosts, and Gods" (39-68).

C. Ouwehand. NAMAZU-E AND THEIR THEMES: AN INTERPRETIVE APPROACH TO SOME ASPECTS OF JAPANESE FOLK RELIGION. 1964: Brill.

Geoffrey Bownas. JAPANESE RAINMAKING AND OTHER FOLK PRACTICES. 1963: Allen & Unwin.

U. A. Casal. THE FIVE SACRED FESTIVALS OF ANCIENT JAPAN: THEIR SYMBOLISM AND HISTORICAL DEVELOPMENT. 1967: Monumenta Nipponica Monographs.

Fanny Hagin Mayer, transl. JAPANESE FOLK FESTIVALS. 1970: Miura.

Michael Czaja. GODS OF MYTH AND STONE: PHALLICISM IN JAPANESE FOLK RELIGION. 1974: Weatherhill.

Donald Richie & Kenkichi Ito. THE EROTIC GODS: PHALLICISM IN JAPAN. 1967: Zufushinsha.

Genchi Kato. "A Study of the Development of Religious Ideas Among the Japanese People as Illustrated by Japanese Phallicism," *Transactions, Asiatic Society of Japan*, 2nd series, 2, Supplement (1924), 1-70.

Edmund Buckley. "Phallicism in Japan," in Lee Alexander Stone, ed. THE STORY OF PHALLICISM, volume 1 (1927: Pascal Covici), 287-325.

)LKTALES & FOLKLORE

[See also the numerous articles on Japanese folklore and folktales in the journal *Folklore Studies*, later renamed *Asian Folklore Studies*]

nio Yanagita. THE YANAGITA KUNIO GUIDE TO THE JAPANESE FOLK TALE. Fanny Hagin Mayer, ed. and transl. 1986: University of Indiana Press.

roko Ikeda. A TYPE AND MOTIF INDEX OF JAPANESE FOLKLORE. 1971: Tiedeakatemia.

anne P. Algarin. JAPANESE FOLK LITERATURE: A CORE COLLECTION & REFERENCE GUIDE. 1983: Bowker.

igo Seki. "Types of Japanese Folktales," *Asian Folklore Studies* 25 (1966), 1-20.

____, ed. FOLKTALES OF JAPAN. 1963: University of Chicago Press.

nny Hagin Mayer, transl. ANCIENT TALES IN MODERN JAPAN: AN ANTHOLOGY OF JAPANESE FOLK TALES. 1985: University of Indiana Press. 343 folk tales from the *Meii*, the standard Japanese collection.

____. "Available Japanese Folk Tales," *Monumenta Nipponica* 24.3 (1969), 235-247.

chard M. Dorson. STUDIES IN JAPANESE FOLKLORE. 1963: University of Indiana Press. Volume 17 of University of Indiana Folklore Series.

____. FOLK LEGENDS OF JAPAN. 1962: Tuttle.

nio Yanagida. JAPANESE FOLK TALES: A REVISED SELECTION. 1960: Kadokawa.

arrett Bang, transl. MEN FROM THE VILLAGE DEEP IN THE MOUNTAINS AND OTHER JAPANESE FOLK TALES. 1973: Macmillan.

io Sakanishi, transl. JAPANESE FOLK PLAYS: THE INK SMEARED LADY AND OTHER KYOGEN. 1960: Tuttle.

tia R. Isaku. MOUNTAIN STORM, PINE BREEZE: FOLK SONG IN JAPAN. 1984: University of Arizona Press.

onald L. Philippi, transl. SONGS OF GODS, SONGS OF HUMANS: THE EPIC TRADITION OF THE AINU. 1979: Princeton University Press.

arl Etter. AINU FOLKLORE: TRADITIONS AND CULTURE OF THE VANISHING ABORIGINES OF JAPAN. 1949: Wilcox & Follett.

ances Carpenter. PEOPLE FROM THE SKY: AINU TALES FROM NORTHERN JAPAN. 1972: Doubleday.

LITERATURE

**P. E. N. Club. JAPANESE LITERATURE IN EUROPEAN LANGUAGES: A BIBLIOGRAPHY. 2nd edition. 1961 Supplement, 1964: The Japan P. E. N. Club.

Donald Keene. JAPANESE LITERATURE: AN INTRODUCTION FOR WESTERN READERS. 1955: Grove.

_____. "Literature," in Arthur Tiedemann, ed. AN INTRODUCTION TO JAPANESE CIVILIZATION (1974: Heath), 375-421.

Edwin A. Cranston. "Literature," KODANSHA ENCYCLOPEDIA OF JAPAN 5: 28-41.

Shuichi Kato. A HISTORY OF JAPANESE LITERATURE: THE FIRST THOUSAND YEARS. 1979: Kodansha International. First volume of a 3-volume series.

Jin'ichi Konishi. A HISTORY OF JAPANESE LITERATURE: THE ARCHAIC AND ANCIENT AGES (1984: Princeton University Press) and THE EARLY MIDDLE AGES (1986: Princeton University Press). First two volumes of a projected 5-volume survey, translated from the Japanese and edited by Earl Miner.

Edward Putzar. JAPANESE LITERATURE: A HISTORICAL OUTLINE. 1973: University of Arizona Press. An adaptation of Senichi Hisamatsu, ed., *Nihon Bungaku* (1960).

Kokusai Bunka Shinkokai, ed. INTRODUCTION TO CLASSIC JAPANESE LITERATURE. 1948: Kokusai Bunka Shinkokai.

Earl Miner, Hiroko Odagiri & Robert E. Morrell. THE PRINCETON COMPANION TO CLASSICAL JAPANESE LITERATURE. 1985: Princeton University Press.

Earl Miner, ed. PRINCIPLES OF CLASSICAL JAPANESE LITERATURE. 1985: Princeton University Press.

_____. AN INTRODUCTION TO JAPANESE COURT POETRY. 1968: Stanford University Press.

Donald Keene, comp. ANTHOLOGY OF JAPANESE LITERATURE: FROM THE EARLIEST ERA TO THE MID-NINTEENTH CENTURY. 1955: Grove.

Hiroaki Sato & Burton Watson, transl. FROM THE COUNTRY OF EIGHT ISLANDS: AN ANTHOLOGY OF JAPANESE POETRY. 1981: Doubleday.

Yaeko Sato Habein. THE HISTORY OF THE JAPANESE WRITTEN LANGUAGE. 1984: Columbia University Press & University of Tokyo Press.

ENSHOKU: NIHON NO BIJUTSU, 30 volumes. 1970: Kodansha. This lavish collection of "Japanese Art in Full-Color Reproductions," arranged topically rather than chronologically, includes brief English identification of plates at the back of each volume.

obert Treat Paine & Alexander Soper. THE ART AND ARCHITECTURE OF JAPAN. 1955: Penguin. A standard narrative history, but not lavishly illustrated.

ugo Munsterberg. THE ARTS OF JAPAN: AN ILLUSTRATED HISTORY. 1957: Tuttle. See also other works by Munsterberg.

eter Swann. A CONCISE HISTORY OF JAPANESE ART. 1958: Kodansha International.

HE HEIBONSHA SURVEY OF ART. Jointly published by John Weatherhill, Inc. and Heibonsha, this 30-volume adaptation of Heibonsha's popular *Nihon no Bijutsu* series is the best English-language overview of Japanese art history. Authors and titles are as follows:

1. Itsuji Yoshikawa. Major Themes in Japanese Art
2. Namio Egami. The Beginnings of Japanese Art
3. Yasutada Watanabe. Shinto Art: Ise and Izumo Shrines
4. Seiichi Mizuno. Asuka Buddhist Art: Horyu-ji
5. Tsuyoshi Kobayashi. Nara Buddhist Art: Todai-ji
6. Ryoichi Hayashi. The Silk Road and the Shoso-in
7. Minoru O-oka. Temples of Nara and Their Art
8. Takaaki Sawa. Art in Japanese Esoteric Buddhism
9. Toshio Fukuyama. Heian Temples: Byodo-in and Chuson-ji
10. Saburo Ienaga. Painting in the Yamato Style
11. Hisashi Mori. Sculpture of the Kamakura Period
12. Ichimatsu Tanaka. Japanese Ink Painting: Shubun to Sesshu
13. Kiyoshi Hirai. Feudal Architecture of Japan
14. Tsuguyoshi Doi. Momoyama Decorative Painting
15. T. Hayashi, M. Nakamura & S. Hayashiya. Japanese Art and the Tea Ceremony
16. Seiroku Noma. Japanese Costume and Textile Arts
17. Yuzo Yamane. Momoyama Genre Painting
18. Hiroshi Mizuo. Edo Painting: Sotatsu and Korin
19. Yoshitomo Okamoto. The Namban Art of Japan
20. Naomi Okawa. Edo Architecture: Katsura and Nikko
21. Teiji Itoh. Traditional Domestic Architecture of Japan
22. Seiichiro Takahashi. Traditional Woodblock Prints of Japan
23. Yoshiho Yonezawa & Chu Yoshizawa. Japanese Painting in the Literati Style
24. Michiaki Kawakita. Modern Currents in Japanese Art
25. Toru Terada. Japanese Art in World Perspective
26. Kageo Muraoka & Kichiemon Okamura. Folk Arts and Crafts of Japan
27. Yujiro Nakata. The Art of Japanese Calligraphy
28. Masao Hayakawa. Garden Art of Japan
29. Tsugio Mikami. The Art of Japanese Ceramics
30. Saburo Ienaga. Japanese Art: A Cultural Appreciation

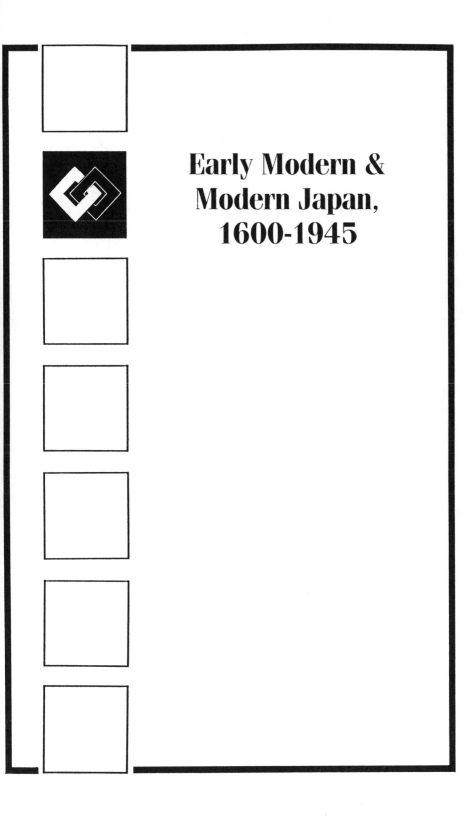

Early Modern & Modern Japan, 1600-1945

EARLY MODERN & MODERN JAPAN,

1600-1945

GENERAL WORKS

Kenneth B. Pyle. THE MAKING OF MODERN JAPAN. 1978: Heath.

Peter Duus. THE RISE OF MODERN JAPAN. 1976: Houghton Mifflin.

Mikiso Hane. JAPAN: A HISTORICAL SURVEY. 1972: Charles Scribner's Sons.

_____. MODERN JAPAN: A HISTORICAL SURVEY. 1986: Westview.

_____. PEASANTS, REBELS AND OUTCASTES: THE UNDERSIDE OF MODERN JAPAN. 1982: Pantheon.

John W. Dower. "E. H. Norman, Japan, and the Uses of History," in Dower, ed. ORIGINS OF THE MODERN JAPANESE STATE: SELECTED WRITINGS OF E. H. NORMAN (1975: Pantheon), 3-101.

Jon Halliday. A POLITICAL HISTORY OF JAPANESE CAPITALISM. 1975: Pantheon.

Edwin O. Reischauer & John K. Fairbank. EAST ASIA: THE GREAT TRADITION. 1960: Houghton Mifflin.

John K. Fairbank, Edwin O. Reischauer & Albert M. Craig. EAST ASIA: THE MODERN TRANSFORMATION. 1965: Houghton Mifflin.

_____. EAST ASIA: TRADITION AND TRANSFORMATION. 1973: Houghton Mifflin. Revised and abridged version of preceding two works.

Edwin O. Reischauer & Albert M. Craig. JAPAN: TRADITION AND TRANSFORMATION. 1977: Houghton Mifflin. Japan sections from preceding survey texts.

Edwin O. Reischauer. JAPAN: THE STORY OF A NATION. 3rd edition. 1980: Knopf.

_____. THE JAPANESE. 1977: Belknap & Harvard University Press.

John W. Hall. JAPAN: FROM PREHISTORY TO MODERN TIMES. 1970: Delacorte. Strongest on premodern.

_____ & Richard Beardsley, eds. TWELVE DOORS TO JAPAN. 1965: McGraw-Hill. A disciplinary approach.

Hugh Borton. JAPAN'S MODERN CENTURY. 2nd edition. 1973: Ronald.

W. G. Beasley. THE MODERN HISTORY OF JAPAN. 3rd edition. 1981: St. Martin's.

Marius B. Jansen. JAPAN AND CHINA: FROM WAR TO PEACE, 1894-1972. 1975: Rand-McNally.

_____. JAPAN AND ITS WORLD: TWO CENTURIES OF CHANGE. 1984: Princeton University Press.

Richard Storry. A HISTORY OF MODERN JAPAN. 1965: Penguin.

Arthur Tiedemann, ed. AN INTRODUCTION TO JAPANESE CIVILIZATION. 1974: Heath. Contains both historical overviews and topical essays by leading scholars.

H. Paul Varley. JAPANESE CULTURE: A SHORT HISTORY. 3rd edition. 1984: University of Hawaii Press.

Barrington Moore, Jr. SOCIAL ORIGINS OF DICTATORSHIP AND DEMOCRACY. 1966: Beacon.

Jean-Pierre Lehmann. THE ROOTS OF MODERN JAPAN. 1982: St. Martin's.

James B. Crowley, ed. MODERN EAST ASIA: ESSAYS IN INTERPRETATION. 1970: Harcourt Brace & World.

Jon Livingston, Joe Moore & Felicia Oldfather, eds. THE JAPAN READER, 1: IMPERIAL JAPAN, 1800-1945. 1973: Pantheon.

GENERAL WORKS--II

_____. THE JAPAN READER, 2: POSTWAR JAPAN. 1973: Pantheon.

The Developing Economies. Special issues on "The Modernization of Japan" in the December publications for 1965, 1966, & 1967, by Japanese scholars.

Seiichi Tohata, ed. THE MODERNIZATION OF JAPAN. 1966: The Institute of Asian Economic Affairs. Articles from the journal *The Developing Economies.*

Robert E. Ward & Dankwart Rustow, eds. POLITICAL MODERNIZATION IN JAPAN & TURKEY. 1964: Princeton University Press.

Princeton University Press Series on "Studies in the Modernization of Japan," 1965-1971:

　　Marius B. Jansen, ed. CHANGING JAPANESE ATTITUDES TOWARD MODERNIZATION. 1965.

　　William E. Lockwood, ed. THE STATE & ECONOMIC ENTERPRISE IN JAPAN. 1965.

　　Ronald P. Dore, ed. ASPECTS OF SOCIAL CHANGE IN MODERN JAPAN. 1967.

　　Robert E. Ward, ed. POLITICAL DEVELOPMENT IN MODERN JAPAN. 1968.

　　Donald Shively, ed. TRADITION AND MODERNIZATION IN JAPANESE CULTURE. 1971.

　　James W. Morley, ed. DILEMMAS OF GROWTH IN PREWAR JAPAN. 1971.

Harry Wray & Hilary Conroy, eds. JAPAN EXAMINED: PERSPECTIVES ON MODERN JAPANESE HISTORY. 1983: University of Hawaii Press. 46 issue-oriented essays by leading scholars.

Sue Henny & Jean-Pierre Lehmann, eds. THEMES AND THEORIES IN MODERN JAPANESE HISTORY. 1985: Athlone.

Albert M. Craig, ed. JAPAN: A COMPARATIVE VIEW. 1979: Princeton University Press.

Tetsuo Najita. JAPAN: THE INTELLECTUAL FOUNDATIONS OF MODERN JAPANESE POLITICS. 1974; 1980: University of Chicago Press.

_____ & J. Victor Koschmann, eds. CONFLICT IN MODERN JAPANESE HISTORY: THE NEGLECTED TRADITION. 1982: Princeton University Press. Eighteen essays focusing on the period from the mid-19th century through the 1920s.

Irwin Scheiner, ed. MODERN JAPAN: AN INTERPRETIVE ANTHOLOGY. 1974: University of California Press.

Ryusaku Tsunoda, Wm. Theodore DeBary & Donald Keene, eds. SOURCES OF JAPANESE TRADITION. 1958: Columbia University Press. Documentary intellectual history; 2 volumes in the paperback edition.

David J. Lu, ed. SOURCES OF JAPANESE HISTORY. 2 volumes. 1974: McGraw-Hill. Wide range of primary materials.

Donald Keene, ed. ANTHOLOGY OF JAPANESE LITERATURE: FROM THE EARLIEST ERA TO THE MID-NINETEENTH CENTURY. 1955: Grove.

_____. MODERN JAPANESE LITERATURE: AN ANTHOLOGY. 1956: Grove.

Janet E. Hunter, ed. CONCISE DICTIONARY OF MODERN JAPANESE HISTORY. 1984: University of California Press.

Michiko Y. Aoki & Margaret B. Dardess, eds. AS THE JAPANESE SEE IT: PAST AND PRESENT. 1981: University of Hawaii Press.

TOKUGAWA: GENERAL

E. H. Norman. "People Under Feudalism," *Bulletin of Concerned Asian Scholars* 9.2 (1977), 56-61.

_____. ORIGINS OF THE MODERN JAPANESE STATE: SELECTED WRITINGS OF E. H. NORMAN. J. W. Dower, ed. 1975: Pantheon. See especially 321-357 on "Late Feudal Society."

John W. Hall. "E. H. Norman on Tokugawa Japan," *Journal of Japanese Studies* 3.2 (1977), 365-374.

_____. "The Nature of Traditional Society: Japan," in Robert E. Ward & Dankwart A. Rustow, eds. POLITICAL MODERNIZATION IN JAPAN AND TURKEY (1964: Princeton University Press), 14-41.

_____. "Tokugawa Japan, 1800-1853," in James B. Crowley, ed. MODERN EAST ASIA: ESSAYS IN INTERPRETATION (1970: Harcourt Brace & World), 62-94.

_____. "Edo History (1600-1868)," KODANSHA ENCYCLOPEDIA OF JAPAN 3: 185-192.

_____. "Rule by Status in Tokugawa Japan," *Journal of Japanese Studies* 1.1 (1974), 39-50.

_____. JAPAN: FROM PREHISTORY TO MODERN TIMES (1970: Delacorte), chapter 10.

_____ & Marius Jansen, eds. STUDIES IN THE INSTITUTIONAL HISTORY OF EARLY MODERN JAPAN. 1968: Princeton University Press. A pioneer collection of 21 essays by leading scholars.

George B. Sansom. A HISTORY OF JAPAN, 1615-1867. 1967: Stanford University Press.

_____. THE WESTERN WORLD AND JAPAN (1950: Knopf), chapters 9-12.

_____. JAPAN: A SHORT CULTURAL HISTORY. Revised edition (1944: Appleton), chapter 7.

Edwin O. Reischauer & John K. Fairbank. EAST ASIA: THE GREAT TRADITION (1958: Houghton Mifflin), chapter 13.

John K. Fairbank, Edwin O. Reischauer & Albert M. Craig. EAST ASIA: TRADITION AND TRANSFORMATION (1973: Houghton Mifflin), chapter 15.

Conrad Totman. POLITICS IN THE TOKUGAWA BAKUFU, 1600-1853. 1967: Harvard University Press.

_____. "Tokugawa Japan," in Arthur Tiedemann, ed. AN INTRODUCTION TO JAPANESE CIVILIZATION (1974: Heath), 97-130

_____. JAPAN BEFORE PERRY: A BRIEF SYNTHESIS. 1982: University of California Press.

_____. TOKUGAWA IEYASU: SHOGUN. 1983: Heian International.

Arthur L. Sadler. THE MAKER OF MODERN JAPAN: THE LIFE OF TOKUGAWA IEYASU. 1937: Allen & Unwin.

Harold Bolitho. TREASURES AMONG MEN: THE FUDAI DAIMYO IN TOKUGAWA JAPAN. 1974: Yale University Press.

Charles J. Dunn. EVERYDAY LIFE IN TRADITIONAL JAPAN. 1969: Putnam.

T. G. Tsukahira. FEUDAL CONTROL IN TOKUGAWA JAPAN: THE *SANKIN KOTAI* SYSTEM. 1966: Harvard East Asian Monographs.

John W. Hall. TANUMA OKITSUGU, 1719-1788: FORERUNNER OF MODERN JAPAN. 1955: Harvard University Press.

TOKUGAWA: GENERAL--II

Herman Ooms. CHARISMATIC BUREAUCRAT: A POLITICAL BIOGRAPHY OF MATSUDAIRA SADANOBU, 1758-1829. 1975: University of Chicago Press.

James L. McClain. KANAZAWA: A SEVENTEENTH-CENTURY JAPANESE CASTLE TOWN. 1982: Yale University Press.

_____. "Castle Towns and Daimyo Authority: Kanazawa in the Years 1583-1630," *Journal of Japanese Studies* 6.2 (1980), 267-299.

Hershel Webb. THE JAPANESE IMPERIAL INSTITUTION IN THE TOKUGAWA PERIOD. 1968: Columbia University Press.

Dan F. Henderson. CONCILIATION AND JAPANESE LAW: TOKUGAWA AND MODERN. 1965: University of Washington Press.

John C. Hall, "Japanese Feudal Laws III--The Tokugawa Legislation, Parts I-III," *Transactions, Asiatic Society of Japan*, 1st series, 38 (1911), 269-331. Translation of laws for nobility, warriors, and commoners.

_____. "Japanese Feudal Laws IV--The Tokugawa Legislation, Part IV," *Transactions, Asiatic Society of Japan* 1st series, 41 (1913), 683-804. Translation of the "Edict in 100 Sections," revised in 1790; accompanied by graphic illustrations of methods of torture and execution.

John Henry Wigmore, ed. MATERIAL FOR THE STUDY OF PRIVATE LAW IN OLD JAPAN. 1964 reprint by University of Tokyo Press of 4 long articles originally published in 1892.

_____. LAW AND JUSTICE IN TOKUGAWA JAPAN: MATERIALS FOR THE HISTORY OF JAPANESE LAW ANT JUSTICE UNDER THE TOKUGAWA SHOGUNATE, 1603-1867. Multi-volume reprint series of basic translations, by University of Tokyo Press.

Torao Haraguchi et al. THE STATUS SYSTEM AND SOCIAL ORGANIZATION OF SATSUMA: A TRANSLATION OF THE *SHUMON TEFUDA ARATAME JOMOKU*. 1975: University of Hawaii Press.

Ronald P. Toby. STATE AND DIPLOMACY IN EARLY MODERN JAPAN: ASIA IN THE DEVELOPMENT OF THE TOKUGAWA BAKUFU. 1983: Princeton University Press.

_____. "Reopening the Question of *Sakoku*: Diplomacy in the Legitimation of the Tokugawa Bakufu," *Journal of Japanese Studies* 3.2 (1977), 323-364.

Keiji Nagahara. "The Historical Premises for the Modernization of Japan: On the Structure of the Tokugawa Shogunate," *Hitosubashi Journal of Economics* 3.1 (October 1962), 61-72.

Anne Walthall. "Peripheries: Rural Culture in Tokugawa Japan," *Monumenta Nipponica* 39.4 (1984), 371-392.

56

TOKUGAWA: ECONOMIC

Sydney Crawcour. "The Premodern Economy," in Arthur E. Tiedemann, ed. AN INTRODUCTION TO JAPANESE CIVILIZATION (1974: Heath), 461-486.

_____. "The Tokugawa Period and Japan's Preparation for Modern Economic Growth," *Journal of Japanese Studies* 1.1 (1974), 113-125.

_____. "The Tokugawa Heritage," in William W. Lockwood, ed. THE STATE AND ECONOMIC ENTERPRISE IN JAPAN (1965: Princeton University Press), 17-44.

_____. "Changes in Japanese Commerce in the Tokugawa Period," in John W. Hall & Marius Jansen, eds. STUDIES IN THE INSTITUTIONAL HISTORY OF EARLY MODERN JAPAN (1968: Princeton University Press), 189-202.

Seymour Broadbridge. "Economic and Social Trends in Tokugawa Japan," *Modern Asian Studies* 8.3 (1974), 347-372.

Daniel L. Spencer. "Japan's Pre-Perry Preparation for Economic Growth," *American Journal of Economics and Sociology* 17 (1958), 195-216.

Junnosuke Sasaki. "Some Remarks on the Economic Foundation of Military Service under the Tokugawa Shogunate System," *Hitotsubashi Journal of Social Studies* 2.1 (1964), 36-53.

Thomas C. Smith. THE AGRARIAN ORIGINS OF MODERN JAPAN. 1959: Stanford University Press.

_____. NAKAHARA: FAMILY FARMING AND POPULATION IN A JAPANESE VILLAGE, 1717-1830. 1977: Stanford University Press.

_____. "Pre-Modern Economic Growth: Japan and the West," *Past and Present* 60 (1973), 127-160.

_____. "Farm Family By-Employments in Pre-Industrial Japan," *Journal of Economic History* 29.4 (1969), 687-715.

_____. "Peasant Families and Population Control in Eighteenth-Century Japan," *Journal of Interdisciplinary History* 6.3 (1976), 417-445.

_____. "The Japanese Village in the Seventeenth Century," *Journal of Economic History* 12.1 (1952), 1-20. Reprinted in Hall & Jansen, STUDIES IN THE INSTITUTIONAL HISTORY OF EARLY MODERN JAPAN (1968: Princeton University Press), 263-282.

_____. "The Land Tax in the Tokugawa Period," *Journal of Asian Studies* 18.1 (1958), 3-20. Reprinted in Hall & Jansen, STUDIES IN THE INSTITUTIONAL HISTORY OF EARLY MODERN JAPAN (1968: Princeton University Press), 283-299.

_____. "The Introduction of Western Industry to Japan During the Last Years of the Tokugawa Period," *Harvard Journal of Asian Studies* 11 (1948), 130-152.

Susan B. Hanley & Kozo Yamamura. ECONOMIC AND DEMOGRAPHIC CHANGE IN PREINDUSTRIAL JAPAN, 1600-1868. 1977: Princeton University Press. See the extended reviews of this work by Dana Morris & Stephen Vlastos in *Journal of Asian Studies* 39.2 (1980), 361-368; and by Harold Bolitho in *Harvard Journal of Asiatic Studies* 39 (1979), 443-448.

_____. "A Quiet Transformation in Tokugawa Economic History," *Journal of Asian Studies* 31.2 (1972), 373-384.

Kozo Yamamura. A STUDY OF SAMURAI INCOME AND ENTREPRENEURSHIP. 1974: Harvard University Press.

_____. "Pre-Industrial Landholding Patterns in Japan and England," in Albert M. Craig, ed. JAPAN: A COMPARATIVE VIEW (1979: Princeton University Press), 276-323.

Isao Soranaka. "The Kansei Reforms--Success or Failure?" *Monumenta Nipponica* 33.1 (1978), 151-164.

William Chambliss. CHIARAIJIMA VILLAGE: LAND TENURE, TAXATION, AND LOCAL TRADE, 1811-1884. 1965: University of Arizona Press.

R. Varner. "The Organized Peasant: The *Wakamonogumi* in the Edo Period," *Monumenta Nipponica* 32.4 (1977), 459-483.

Arne Kalland & Jon Pedersen. "Famine and Population in Fukuoka Domain During the Tokugawa Period," *Journal of Japanese Studies* 10.1 (1984), 31-72.

William B. Hauser. ECONOMIC INSTITUTIONAL CHANGE IN TOKUGAWA JAPAN: OSAKA AND THE KINAI COTTON TRADE. 1974: Cambridge University Press.

Gilbert Rozman. URBAN NETWORKS IN CH'ING CHINA AND TOKUGAWA JAPAN. 1974: Princeton University Press.

_____. "Edo's Importance in the Changing Tokugawa Society," *Journal of Japanese Studies* 1.1 (1974), 113-126.

Takeshi Toyoda. A HISTORY OF PRE-MEIJI COMMERCE IN JAPAN. 1969: Kokusai Bunka Shinkokai.

Charles D. Sheldon. THE RISE OF THE MERCHANT CLASS IN TOKUGAWA JAPAN, 1600-1868. 1958: Augustin.

John G. Roberts. MITSUI: THREE CENTURIES OF JAPANESE BUSINESS. 1973: Weatherhill.

E. S. Crawcour, transl. "Some Observations on Merchants," *Transactions, Asiatic Society of Japan* (1961), 1-139. A translation of Mitsui Takafusa's *Chonin Koken Ron.*

J. Mark Ramseyer. "Thrift and Diligence: House Codes of Tokugawa Merchant Families," *Monumenta Nipponica* 34.2 (1979), 209-230.

"Studies in the History of Foreign Trade in Early Modern Japan." Special issue of *Acta Asiatica* 30 (1976).

Robert J. Smith. "Small Families, Small Households, and Residential Instability: Town and City in 'Pre-Modern' Japan," in Peter Laslett, ed. HOUSEHOLD AND FAMILY IN PAST TIME (1972: Cambridge University Press), 429-471.

_____. "The Domestic Cycle in Selected Commoner Families in Urban Japan, 1757-1858," *Journal of Family History* 3.3 (1978), 219-235.

James Nakamura & Masao Miyamoto. "Social Structure and Population Change: A Comparative Study of Tokugawa Japan and Ch'ing China," *Economic Development and Cultural Change* 30.2 (January 1982), 229-269.

Conrad Totman. THE ORIGINS OF JAPAN'S MODERN FORESTS: THE CASE OF AKITA. 1984: University of Hawaii Press.

_____. "Land-Use Patterns and Afforestation in the Edo Period," *Monumenta Nipponica* 39.1 (1984), 1-10.

William W. Kelly. WATER CONTROL IN TOKUGAWA JAPAN: IRRIGATION ORGANIZATION IN A JAPANESE RIVER BASIN, 1600-1870. 1982: Cornell China-Japan Program.

R. Tsunoda et al. SOURCES OF JAPANESE TRADITION (1958: Columbia University Press), chapters 15-24.

Ronald P. Dore. EDUCATION IN TOKUGAWA JAPAN. 1965: University of California Press.

_____. "The Legacy of Tokugawa Education," in Marius Jansen, ed. CHANGING JAPANESE ATTITUDES
TOWARD MODERNIZATION (1965: Princeton University Press), 99-131.

_____. "Talent and Social Order in Tokugawa Japan," in John Hall & Marius Jansen, eds. STUDIES IN THE
INSTITUTIONAL HISTORY OF EARLY MODERN JAPAN (1968: Princeton University Press), 349-361.

Richard Rubinger. PRIVATE ACADEMIES OF THE TOKUGAWA PERIOD. 1982: Princeton University Press.

Herbert Passin. SOCIETY AND EDUCATION IN JAPAN (1965: Teachers College and East Asian Institute,
Columbia University), chapters 2-3.

Young-chin Kim. "On Political Thought in Tokugawa Japan," *Journal of Politics* 23 (1961), 127-145.

Ichiro Ishida. "Tokugawa Feudal Society and Neo-Confucian Thought," *Pacific Historical Review* 5 (1964), 1-38.

Yoshio Abe. "The Characteristics of Japanese Confucianism," *Acta Asiatica* 33 (1973), 1-21.

_____. "The Development of Neo-Confucianism in Japan, Korea and China," *Acta Asiatica* 17-18 (1969-1970),
16-39.

Tasaburo Ito. "The Book Banning Policy of the Tokugawa Shogunate," *Acta Asiatica* 32 (1972), 36-61.

Masao Maruyama. STUDIES IN THE INTELLECTUAL HISTORY OF TOKUGAWA JAPAN. 1974: Princeton
University Press. Translation by Mikiso Hane of the classic Japanese study.

Tetsuo Najita. "Reconsidering Maruyama Masao's *Studies*," *Japan Interpreter* 11.1 (1976), 97-108.

_____. JAPAN: THE INTELLECTUAL FOUNDATIONS OF MODERN JAPANESE POLITICS. 1974; 1980:
University of Chicago Press.

_____. "Political Economism in the Thought of Dazai Shundai (1680-1747)," *Journal of Asian Studies* 31.4
(1972), 821-839.

_____. "Restorationism in the Political Thought of Yamagata Daini (1725-1767)," *Journal of Asian Studies*
31.1 (1971), 17-30.

_____. "Oshio Heihachiro (1793-1837)," in Albert Craig & Donald Shively, eds. PERSONALITY IN JAPANESE
HISTORY (1970: University of California Press), 155-179.

_____ & Irwin Scheiner, eds. JAPANESE THOUGHT IN THE TOKUGAWA PERIOD, 1600-1868: METHODS
AND METAPHORS. 1978: University of Chicago Press. See the extended reviews by Klaus Kracht in
Journal of Japanese Studies 6.2 (1980), 331-353; Richard Minear in *Harvard Journal of Asiatic Studies*
40 (1980), 285-291; and Harold Bolitho in *Monumenta Nipponica* 35.1 (1980), 89-98. Also the
Bolitho-Harootunian exchange in *Monumenta Nipponica* 35.3 (1980), 368-374.

Peter Nosco, ed. CONFUCIANISM AND TOKUGAWA CULTURE. 1984: Princeton University Press.

Kate Nakai. "The Naturalization of Confucianism in Tokugawa Japan: the Problem of Sinocentrism," *Harvard
Journal of Asiatic Studies* 40.1 (June 1980), 157-199.

Herman Ooms. TOKUGAWA IDEOLOGY: EARLY CONSTRUCTS, 1570-1680. 1985: University of Chicago
Press.

TOKUGAWA: INTELLECTUAL--II

David Nivison & Arthur Wright, eds. CONFUCIANISM IN ACTION. 1959: Stanford University Press. See articles on Japan by DeBary, Hall, and Shively.

W. T. DeBary. NEO-CONFUCIAN ORTHODOXY: THE LEARNING OF THE HEART-AND-MIND. 1981: Columbia University Press.

Thomas C. Smith. "'Merit' As Ideology in the Tokugawa Period," in Ronald Dore, ed. ASPECTS OF SOCIAL CHANGE IN MODERN JAPAN (1967: Princeton University Press), 71-90.

Albert Craig. "Science and Confucianism in Tokugawa Japan," in Marius Jansen, ed. CHANGING JAPANESE ATTITUDES TOWARD MODERNIZATION (1965: Princeton University Press), 133-160.

Hajime Nakamura. "Suzuki Shosan, 1599-1655, and the Spirit of Capitalism in Japanese Buddhism," *Monumenta Nipponica* 22.1-2 (1967), 1-14.

Robert N. Bellah. TOKUGAWA RELIGION: THE VALUES OF PRE-INDUSTRIAL JAPAN. 1957: Free Press.

Ken Ishikawa. "Baigan Ishida's *Shingaku* Doctrine," *Philosophical Studies of Japan* 6 (1965), 1-30.

J. Robertson. "Rooting the Pine: *Shingaku* Methods of Organization," *Monumenta Nipponica* 33.4 (1979), 311-322.

Kojiro Yoshikawa. JINSAI, SORAI, NORINAGA: THREE CLASSICAL PHILOLOGISTS IN MID-TOKUGAWA JAPAN. 1983: University of Tokyo Press.

E. H. Norman. ANDO SHOEKI AND THE ANATOMY OF JAPANESE FEUDALISM. 1949: Special issue of *Transactions, Asiatic Society of Japan.*

Shuichi Kato. THE LIFE AND THOUGHT OF TOMINAGA NAKAMOTO, 1715-1746: A TOKUGAWA ICONOCLAST. 1967: University of British Columbia Press.

J. R. McEwan. THE POLITICAL WRITINGS OF OGYU SORAI. 1962: Cambridge University Press.

Olof G. Lidin. THE LIFE OF OGYU SORAI, A TOKUGAWA CONFUCIAN PHILOSOPHER. 1973: Scandinavian Institute of Asian Studies Monograph Series 19.

_____, transl. OGYU SORAI: DISTINGUISHING THE WAY *(BENDO).* 1970: Monumenta Nipponica Monographs.

Richard Minear, transl. "Ogyu Sorai's *Instructions for Students* : a Translation and Commentary," *Harvard Journal of Asiatic Studies* 36 (1976), 5-81.

Joseph J. Spae. ITO JINSAI: A PHILOSOPHER, EDUCATOR AND SINOLOGIST OF THE TOKUGAWA PERIOD. 1948: Catholic University Press.

Kojiro Yoshikawa. "Ito Jinsai," *Acta Asiatica* 23 (1973), 22-53.

Galen M. Fisher. "The Life and Teaching of Nakae Toju," *Transactions, Asiatic Society of Japan*, 1st series, 36 (1908), 24-94.

_____. "Kumazawa Banzan, His Life and Ideas," *Transactions, Asiatic Society of Japan*, 2nd series, 16 (1938), 223-258.

_____, transl. *Daigaku Wakumon.* A Discussion of Public Questions in the Light of the Great Learning," *Transactions, Asiatic Society of Japan*, 2nd series, 16 (1938), 259-356.

Gino Piovesano. "Miura Baien, 1723-1769, and His Dialectic and Political Ideas," *Monumenta Nipponica* 20.3-4 (1965), 389-421.

Michiko Y. Aoki & Margaret B. Dardess. "The Popularization of Samurai Values: A Sermon by Hosoi Heishu," *Monumenta Nipponica* 31.4 (1976), 400-413; reprinted in Aoki & Dardess, AS THE JAPANESE SEE IT: PAST AND PRESENT (1981: University of Hawaii Press), 59-72.

Ekiken (Ekken) Kaibara. "THE WAY OF CONTENTMENT" AND "GREATER LEARNING FOR WOMEN." 1913; reprint edition, 1979: University Publications of America. Translations of two famous essays by a Neo-Confucion scholar who lived from 1630 to 1714.

Olaf Graf. KAIBARA EKKEN. 1942: Brill.

Joyce Ackroyd, transl. TOLD ROUND A BRUSHWOOD FIRE: THE AUTOBIOGRAPHY OF ARAI HAKUSEKI. 1980: Princeton University Press. Hakuseki lived 1657-1725.

_____, transl. LESSONS FROM HISTORY: ARAI HAKUSEKI'S *TOKUSHI YORON*. 1982: University of Queensland Press.

Kate Wildman-Nakai. "Apologia pro Vita Sua: Arai Hakuseki's Autobiography," *Monumenta Nipponica* 36.2 (1981), 173-186.

Herman Ooms. "Hakuseki's Reading of History," *Monumenta Nipponica* 39.3 (1984), 333-350.

Kokei Tomita. A PEASANT SAGE OF JAPAN: THE LIFE AND WORK OF SONTOKU NINOMIYA. 1912: Harvard University Press.

Hershel Webb. THE JAPANESE IMPERIAL INSTITUTION IN THE TOKUGAWA PERIOD. 1968: Columbia University Press.

David Earl. EMPEROR AND NATION IN JAPAN: POLITICAL THINKERS OF THE TOKUGAWA PERIOD. 1964: University of Washington Press. Focus on Yoshida Shoin.

Shigeru Matsumoto. MOTOORI NORINAGA, 1730-1801. 1970: Harvard University Press.

Tadashi Okubo. "The Thoughts of Mabuchi and Norinaga," *Acta Asiatica* 33 (1973), 68-90.

Richard Devine. "Hirata Atsutane and Christian Sources," *Monumenta Nipponica* 36.1 (1981), 37-54.

Tsuguo Tahara. "The *Kokugaku* Thought," *Acta Asiatica* 33 (1973), 54-67.

Harry D. Harootunian. TOWARD RESTORATION: THE GROWTH OF POLITICAL CONSCIOUSNESS IN TOKUGAWA JAPAN. 1970: University of California Press.

_____. "The Functions of China in Tokugawa Thought," in Akira Iriye, ed. THE CHINESE AND THE JAPANESE (1980: Harvard University Press), 9-36.

J. Victor Koschmann. THE MITO IDEOLOGY: DISCOURSE, REFORM, AND INSURRECTION IN LATE TOKUGAWA JAPAN. 1986: University of California Press.

Bob Tadashi Wakabayashi. ANTI-FOREIGNISM AND WESTERN LEARNING IN EARLY-MODERN JAPAN: THE NEW THESIS OF 1825. 1985: Harvard East Asian Monographs.

Jennifer Robertson. "Sexy Rice: Plant Gender, Farm Manuals, and Grass-Roots Nativism," *Monumenta Nipponica* 39.3 (1984), 233-260.

H. Van Straelen. YOSHIDA SHOIN: FORERUNNER OF THE MEIJI RESTORATION. 1952: Brill.

Donald Keene. THE JAPANESE DISCOVERY OF EUROPE: HONDA TOSHIAKI AND OTHER DISCOVERERS, 1720-1830. 1952. Revised edition, 1969: Stanford University Press.

Carmen Blacker. "Ohashi Totsuan: A Study in Anti-Western Thought," *Transactions, Asiatic Society of Japan* (1959), 147-168.

Richard T. Chang. FROM PREJUDICE TO TOLERANCE: A STUDY OF THE JAPANESE IMAGE OF THE WEST, 1826-1864. 1970: Monumenta Nipponica Monographs.

Winston Davis. "Pilgrimage and World Renewal: A Study of Folk Religion and Social Values in Tokugawa Japan," *History of Religion* 23.2 and 23.3 (1983-84), 97-116, 198-222.

Grant Goodman. THE DUTCH IMPACT ON JAPAN, 1600-1853. 1967: Brill.

George Elison. DEUS DESTROYED: THE IMAGE OF CHRISTIANITY IN EARLY MODERN JAPAN. 1973: Harvard University Press.

Charles R. Boxer. THE CHRISTIAN CENTURY IN JAPAN (1549-1650). 1967: University of California Press.

_____. JAN COMPAIGNE IN JAPAN: AN ESSAY ON THE CULTURAL, ARTISTIC AND SCIENTIFIC INFLUENCE EXERCISED BY THE HOLLANDERS IN JAPAN FROM THE SEVENTEENTH TO THE NINETEENTH CENTURIES. 1950: Martinus Nijhoff.

Masayoshi Sugimoto & David L. Swain. SCIENCE AND CULTURE IN TRADITIONAL JAPAN, 600-1854. 1978: Massachusetts Institute of Technology Press.

Shigeru Nakayama. A HISTORY OF JAPANESE ASTRONOMY. 1969: Harvard University Press.

Hideomi Tuge. HISTORICAL DEVELOPMENT OF SCIENCE AND TECHNOLOGY IN JAPAN. 1961: Kokusai Bunk Sinkokai.

John Z. Bowers. WESTERN MEDICAL PIONEERS IN FEUDAL JAPAN. 1970: Johns Hopkins.

_____. MEDICAL EDUCATION IN JAPAN: FROM CHINESE MEDICINE TO WESTERN MEDICINE. 1965: Harper & Row.

Genpaku Sugita. DAWN OF WESTERN SCIENCE IN JAPAN, OR *RANGAKU KOTOHAJIME*. R. Matsumoto, transl. 1969: Hokuseido. Originally published in 1815.

Calvin French. SHIBA KOKAN: ARTIST, INNOVATOR, AND PIONEER IN THE WESTERNIZATION OF JAPAN. 1974: Weatherhill.

Monumenta Nipponica 19.3-4 (1964), 235-419. Special issue devoted to the early Western influence on Japan in such areas as culture, Dutch language, medicine, geography, astronomy, natural history, the physical sciences, military science, shipbuilding, navigation, and art.

TOKUGAWA: POPULAR CULTURE

Charles J. Dunn. EVERYDAY LIFE IN TRADITIONAL JAPAN. 1969: Putnam.

Oliver Statler. JAPANESE INN. 1961: Secker & Warburg.

Donald Shively. THE LOVE SUICIDE AT AMIJIMA. 1953: Harvard University Press. See introduction on pleasure quarters.

_____. "Bakufu versus Kabuki," *Harvard Journal of Asiatic Studies* 18 (1955), 326-356.

_____. "Sumptuary Regulation and Status in Early Tokugawa Japan," *Harvard Journal of Asiatic Studies* 25 (1964-1965), 123-164.

Lisa Crihfield. "Yoshiwara," KODANSHA ENCYCLOPEDIA OF JAPAN 8: 349-351.

Joseph DeBecker. THE NIGHTLESS CITY, OR THE HISTORY OF THE YOSHIWARA YUKWAKU. 1899; reprint edition, 1971: Tuttle.

Richard Lane. IMAGES FROM THE FLOATING WORLD: THE JAPANESE PRINT. 1978: Putnam.

_____. MASTERS OF THE JAPANESE PRINT: THEIR WORLD AND THEIR WORK. 1962: Doubleday.

James Michener. THE FLOATING WORLD: THE STORY OF JAPANESE PRINTS. 1954: Random House.

Earl Miner, Hiroko Odagiri & Robert E. Morrell. THE PRINCETON COMPANION OF CLASSICAL JAPANESE LITERATURE. 1985: Princeton University Press. Covers literature from earliest times to 1868.

Shuichi Kato. A HISTORY OF JAPANESE LITERATURE: THE YEARS OF ISOLATION. 1979: Kodansha International. Volume 2 of a 3-volume survey.

Donald Keene. WORLD WITHIN WALLS: JAPANESE LITERATURE OF THE PRE-MODERN ERA, 1600-1867. 1976: Holt, Rinehart & Winston.

_____. BUNRAKU: THE ART OF THE JAPANESE PUPPET THEATER. 1965: Kodansha International.

_____, transl. MAJOR PLAYS OF CHIKAMATSU. 1961: Kodansha International.

_____, transl. CHUSHINGURA. 1971: Columbia University Press.

C. Andrew Gerstle. CIRCLES OF FANTASY: CONVENTION IN THE PLAYS OF CHIKAMATSU. 1985: Harvard East Asian Monographs.

Gunji Masakatsu. KABUKI. 1983: Kodansha International.

James R. Brandon, William P. Malm & Donald H. Shively. STUDIES IN KABUKI: ITS ACTING, MUSIC, AND HISTORICAL CONTEXT. 1977: University of Hawaii Press.

James R. Brandon, ed. CHUSHINGURA: STUDIES IN KABUKI AND THE PUPPET THEATER. 1982: University of Hawaii Press.

_____, transl. KABUKI: FIVE CLASSIC PLAYS. 1975: Harvard University Press.

Barbara E. Thornbury. SUKEROKU'S DOUBLE IDENTITY: THE DRAMATIC STRUCTURE OF EDO KABUKI. 1982: Center for Japanese Studies, University of Michigan.

Charles J. Dunn, ed. and transl. THE ACTORS' ANALECTS *(YAKUSHA RONGO)*. 1969: Columbia University Press.

Samuel Leiter. KABUKI ENCYCLOPEDIA: AN ENGLISH-LANGUAGE ADAPTATION OF *KABUKI JITEN*. 1979: Greenwood.

TOKUGAWA: POPULAR CULTURE--II

Faubion Bowers. JAPANESE THEATRE. 1959: Hill & Wang.

Howard Hibbett. THE FLOATING WORLD IN JAPANESE FICTION. 1959: Grove.

Ihara Saikaku (1642-1693). THE JAPANESE FAMILY STOREHOUSE. G. W. Sargent, transl. 1959: Cambridge University Press.

_____. THE LIFE OF AN AMOROUS WOMAN AND OTHER WRITINGS. Ivan Morris, transl. 1963: New Directions.

_____. FIVE WOMEN WHO LOVED LOVE. W. T. DeBary, transl. 1956: Tuttle.

_____. TALES OF JAPANESE JUSTICE. T. Kondo & A. Marks, transl. 1980: University of Hawaii Press.

_____. THIS SCHEMING WORLD. M. Takatsuka & D. C. Stubbs, transl. 1965: Tuttle.

_____. WORLDLY MENTAL CALCULATIONS. B. Befu, transl. 1976: University of California Press.

_____. THE LIFE OF AN AMOROUS MAN. K. Hamada, transl. 1964: Tuttle.

_____. COMRADE LOVES OF THE SAMURAI. E. Powys Mathers, transl. 1981: Tuttle.

_____. TALES OF SAMURAI HONOR. C. A. Callahan, transl. 1982: Monumenta Nipponica Monographs.

Robert W. Leutner. SHIKITEI SANBA AND THE COMIC TRADITION IN EDO FICTION. 1985: Harvard-Yenching Institute Monograph Series.

Ikku Jippensha. *HIZAKURIGE,* OR SHANKS' MARE. Thomas Satchell, transl. The most famous comic novel of feudal Japan, written in 1802; reprinted 1960: Tuttle.

Jack Rucinski. "A Japanese Burlesque: *Nise Monogatari,*" *Monumenta Nipponica* 30.1 (1975), 1-18.

Carolyn Haynes. "Parody in Kyogen: Makura Monogurui and Tako," *Monumenta Nipponica* 39.3 (1984), 261-280.

Haruko Iwasaki. "Portrait of a Daimyo: Comical Fiction by Matsudaira Sadanobu," *Monumenta Nipponica* 38.1 (1983), 1-48.

R. H. Blyth. EDO SATIRICAL VERSE ANTHOLOGIES. 1961: Hokuseido.

_____. JAPANESE LIFE AND CHARACTER IN SENRYU. 1960: Hokuseido.

_____. ORIENTAL HUMOR. 1959: Hokuseido.

_____. HAIKU. 4 volumes. 1950-1952: Hokuseido.

Basho. THE NARROW ROAD TO THE DEEP NORTH, AND OTHER TRAVEL SKETCHES. Nobuyuki Yuasa, transl. 1966: Penguin. Five travel sketches by the greatest haiku poet, Matsuo Basho (1644-1694).

Akinari Ueda. *UGETSU MONOGATARI:* TALES OF MOONLIGHT AND RAIN. 1980: Hokuseido. "Gothic" tales first published in 1776.

David Chibbett. THE HISTORY OF JAPANESE PRINTING AND BOOK ILLUSTRATION. 1977: Kodansha International.

Kogoro Yoshida. TANROKUBON: RARE BOOKS OF SEVENTEENTH-CENTURY JAPAN. 1984: Kodansha International & Harper & Row.

Martin C. Collcutt. "Bushido," KODANSHA ENCYCLOPEDIA OF JAPAN 1: 221-223.

William Scott Wilson, ed. IDEALS OF THE SAMURAI: WRITINGS OF JAPANESE WARRIORS. 1982: Ohara.

Daisetz T. Suzuki. ZEN AND JAPANESE CULTURE. 1959: Pantheon. See especially chapters 4 ("Zen and the Samurai"), and 5-6 ("Zen and Swordsmanship").

Inazo Nitobe. BUSHIDO: THE SOUL OF JAPAN. 1899: Putnam.

Donn F. Draeger & Gordon Warner. JAPANESE SWORDMANSHIP: TECHNIQUE AND PRACTICE. 1982: Weatherhill.

Donn F. Draeger & Robert W. Smith. COMPREHENSIVE ASIAN FIGHTING ARTS. 1980: Kodansha International.

Donn F. Draeger. CLASSICAL BUJUTSU. 1973: Weatherhill.

_____. CLASSICAL BUDO. 1974: Weatherhill.

_____. NINJUTSU: THE ART OF INVISIBILITY. 1977: Lotus Press.

Oscar Ratti & Adele Westbrook. SECRETS OF THE SAMURAI: A SURVEY OF THE MARTIAL ARTS OF FEUDAL JAPAN. 1973: Tuttle.

Joe Hyams. ZEN IN THE MARTIAL ARTS. 1979: Tarcher.

Bruce A. Haines. KARATE'S HISTORY AND TRADITIONS. 1968: Tuttle.

John Allyn. THE FORTY-SEVEN RONIN STORY. 1970: Tuttle.

Jack Seward. HARA-KIRI: JAPANESE RITUAL SUICIDE. 1968: Tuttle.

Musashi Miyamoto. A BOOK OF FIVE RINGS: THE CLASSIC GUIDE TO STRATEGY. Victor Harris, transl. 1974: Overlook. Written in 1645 by the most renowned swordsman of feudal Japan.

Tsunetomo Yamamoto. HAGAKURE: THE BOOK OF THE SAMURAI. William Scott Wilson, transl. 1979: Kodansha International. A classic text written in 1716.

Noel Perrin. GIVING UP THE GUN: JAPAN'S REVERSION TO THE SWORD, 1543-1879. 1979: Godine.

Ihara Saikaku. COMRADE LOVES OF THE SAMURAI. E. Powys Mathers, transl. 1981: Tuttle.

_____. TALES OF SAMURAI HONOR. C. A. Callahan, transl. 1982: Monumenta Nipponica Monographs.

BAKUMATSU / RESTORATION

John W. Dower, ed. ORIGINS OF THE MODERN JAPANESE STATE: SELECTED WRITINGS OF E. H. NORMAN. 1975: Pantheon. Includes Norman's classic *Japan's Emergence As a Modern State* (1940) and *Feudal Background of Japanese Politics* (1944).

E. H. Norman. SOLDIER AND PEASANT IN JAPAN: THE ORIGINS OF CONSCRIPTION. 1965: Institute of Pacific Relations; reprint of articles originally published in *Pacific Affairs*, March and June 1943.

Albert Craig. CHOSHU IN THE MEIJI RESTORATION, 1853-1868. 1961: Harvard University Press.

_____. "The Restoration Movement in Choshu," *Journal of Asian Studies* 18.2 (1959), 187-198.

Marius Jansen. SAKAMOTO RYOMA AND THE MEIJI RESTORATION. 1961: Princeton University Press.

_____ & Gilbert Rozman, eds. JAPAN IN TRANSITION: FROM TOKUGAWA TO MEIJI. 1986: Princeton University Press.

Thomas C. Smith. "The Discontented," *Journal of Asian Studies* 21.2 (1962), 215-219. Review of above monographs by Craig and Jansen.

_____. "Old Values and New Techniques in the Modernization of Japan," *Far Eastern Quarterly* 14.3 (1955); reprinted in John A. Harrison, ed. JAPAN (1972: University of Arizona Press), 1-9.

_____. "Japan's Aristocratic Revolution," *Yale Review* (1961), 370-383; reprinted in Jon Livingston et al., IMPERIAL JAPAN, 1800-1945 (1973: Pantheon), 91-101.

George B. Sansom. "Forerunners of the Restoration Movement," in his THE WESTERN WORLD AND JAPAN (1965: Knopf), 248-274.

Masakazu Iwata. "Forces Behind the Restoration Movement," in his OKUBO TOSHIMICHI: THE BISMARK OF JAPAN (1964: University of California Press), 103-111.

Marlene Mayo. "Late Tokugawa and Early Meiji," in Arthur Tiedemann, ed. AN INTRODUCTION TO JAPANESE CIVILIZATION (1974: Heath), 131-180.

Tetsuo Najita. "Restorationism in Late Tokugawa," in his JAPAN (1974: University of Chicago Press), 43-68.

W. G. Beasley, ed. SELECT DOCUMENTS ON JAPANESE FOREIGN POLICY, 1853-1868. 1955: Oxford University Press.

_____. THE MEIJI RESTORATION. 1972: Stanford University Press.

_____. "Self-Strengthening and Restoration: Chinese and Japanese Responses to the West in the mid-Nineteenth Century," *Acta Asiatica* 34 (1974), 91-107.

H. D. Harootunian. Review of Beasley's MEIJI RESTORATION in *Journal of Asian Studies* 33.4 (1974), 661-672.

_____. TOWARD RESTORATION: THE GROWTH OF POLITICAL CONSCIOUSNESS IN TOKUGAWA JAPAN. 1970: University of California Press. See especially 403-410 ("The Restoration Reconsidered").

Thomas M. Huber. THE REVOLUTIONARY ORIGINS OF MODERN JAPAN. 1981: Stanford University Press.

Conrad Totman. THE COLLAPSE OF THE TOKUGAWA BAKUFU, 1862-1868. 1980: University of California Press.

_____. "From *Sakoku* to *Kaikoku:* The Transformation of Foreign-Policy Attitudes, 1853-1868," *Monumenta Nipponica* 35.1 (1980), 1-19.

BAKUMATSU / RESTORATION--II

_____. "Ethnicity in the Meiji Restoration: An Interpretive Essay," *Monumenta Nipponica* 37.3 (1982), 269-288.

Paul Akamatsu. MEIJI 1868: REVOLUTION AND COUNTERREVOLUTION IN JAPAN. 1972: Harper & Row.

Yoshio Sakata & John W. Hall. "The Motivation of Political Leadership in the Meiji Restoration," *Journal of Asian Studies* 16.1 (1956); reprinted in Harrison, JAPAN (1972: University of Arizona Press), 179-198.

John W. Hall. "The Meiji Restoration and its Meaning," in his JAPAN: FROM PREHISTORY TO MODERN TIMES (1970: Delacorte), 265-272.

Jean-Pierre Lehmann. THE ROOTS OF MODERN JAPAN. 1982: St. Martin's.

Neil Waters. JAPAN'S LOCAL PRAGMATISTS: THE TRANSITION FROM BAKUMATSU TO MEIJI IN THE KAWASAKI REGION. 1983: Harvard East Asian Monographs.

Peter Frost. THE BAKUMATSU CURRENCY CRISIS. 1970: Harvard East Asian Monographs.

Masao Miyoshi. AS WE SAW THEM: THE FIRST JAPANESE EMBASSY TO THE UNITED STATES (1860). 1979: University of California Press.

Lewis Bush. 77 SAMURAI: JAPAN'S FIRST EMBASSY TO AMERICA. 1968: Kodansha International. Based on the book by Itsuro Hattori.

John McMaster. "Alcock and Harris: Foreign Diplomacy in Bakumatsu Japan," *Monumenta Nipponica* 22.4 (1967), 305-367.

Shozo Fujita. "Spirit of the Meiji Restoration," *Japan Interpreter* 6.1 (1970), 70-97.

Pat Barr. THE COMING OF THE BARBARIANS: THE OPENING OF JAPAN TO THE WEST. 1967: Macmillan.

S. E. Morison. "OLD BRUIN": COMMODORE MATTHEW C. PERRY, 1794-1858. 1967: Little, Brown.

Arthur Walworth. BLACK SHIPS OFF JAPAN. 1946: Knopf.

Oliver Statler. SHIMODA STORY. 1969: Random House.

Hazel J. Jones. LIVE MACHINES: HIRED FOREIGNERS AND MEIJI JAPAN. 1980: University of British Columbia Press.

_____. "Bakumatsu Foreign Employees," *Monumenta Nipponica* 29.3 (1974), 305-328.

Ardath W. Burks, ed. THE MODERNIZERS: OVERSEAS STUDENTS, FOREIGN EMPLOYEES, AND MEIJI JAPAN. 1984: Westview.

CONFLICT & REBELLION IN TOKUGAWA & EARLY MEIJI

Tetsuo Najita & J. Victor Koschmann, eds. CONFLICT IN MODERN JAPANESE HISTORY: THE NEGLECTED TRADITION. 1982: Princeton University Press. See especially essays by Koschmann, Huber, Steele, Hashimoto, and Vlastos.

Hugh Borton. PEASANT UPRISINGS IN JAPAN OF THE TOKUGAWA PERIOD. 1968: Paragon reprint; originally published in *Transactions, Asiatic Society of Japan*, 1938.

Herbert P. Bix. PEASANT PROTEST IN FEUDAL JAPAN, 1590-1884. 1986: Yale University Press.

_____. "Miura Meisuke, or Peasant Rebellion Under the Banner of 'Distress'," *Bulletin of Concerned Asian Scholars* 10.2 (1978), 18-26.

Stephen Vlastos. PEASANT PROTESTS AND UPRISINGS IN TOKUGAWA JAPAN. 1986: University of California.

Anne Walthall. SOCIAL CONFLICT AND POPULAR CULTURE IN EIGHTEENTH-CENTURY JAPAN. 1986: University of Arizona Press.

_____. "Narratives of Peasant Uprisings in Japan," *Journal of Asian Studies* 42.3 (May 1983), 571-588.

William Kelly. DEFERENCE & DEFIANCE IN NINETEENTH-CENTURY JAPAN. 1985: Princeton University Press.

W. Donald Burton. "Peasant Struggle in Japan, 1590-1760," *Journal of Peasant Studies* 5.2 (1978), 135-171.

Tetsuo Najita. "Oshio Heihachiro (1793-1837)," in Albert Craig & Donald Shively, eds. PERSONALITY IN JAPANESE HISTORY (1970: University of California Press), 155-179.

J. Rahder. "Record of the Kurume Uprising," *Acta Orientalia* 14 (1936), 81-108.

Yoshio Sugimoto. "Structural Sources of Popular Revolts and the Tobaku Movement at the Time of the Meiji Restoration," *Journal of Asian Studies* 34.4 (1975), 875-889.

Patricia Sippel. "Popular Protest in Early Modern Japan: The Bushu Outburst," *Harvard Journal of Asiatic Studies* 37 (1977), 273-322.

Irwin Scheiner. "Benevolent Lords and Honorable Peasants: Rebellion and Peasant Consciousness in Tokugawa Japan," in T. Najita & I. Scheiner, eds. JAPANESE THOUGHT IN THE TOKUGAWA PERIOD, 1600-1868 (1978: University of Chicago Press), 39-62.

_____."The Mindful Peasant: Sketches for a Study of Rebellion,"*Journal of Asian Studies* 32.4 (1973), 579-591.

E. H. Norman. SOLDIER AND PEASANT IN JAPAN: THE ORIGINS OF CONSCRIPTION. Originally published in *Pacific Affairs* 16.1 and 16.2 (1943). Published separately in 1943, with reprint edition in 1965 by the Institute of Pacific Relations.

Thomas Huber. THE REVOLUTIONARY ORIGINS OF MODERN JAPAN. 1981: Stanford University Press.

Nobutake Ike. THE BEGINNINGS OF POLITICAL DEMOCRACY IN JAPAN. 1950: Johns Hopkins.

Roger Bowen. REBELLION AND DEMOCRACY IN MEIJI JAPAN: A STUDY OF COMMONERS IN THE POPULAR RIGHTS MOVEMENT. 1980: University of California Press.

_____. "Rice Roots Democracy and Popular Rebellion in Meiji Japan," *Journal of Peasant Studies* 6.1 (1978), 3-39.

James H. Buck. "The Satsuma Rebellion of 1877--From Kagoshima Through the Seige of Kumamoto Castle," *Monumenta Nipponica* 28.4 (1973), 427-446

Augustus H. Mounsey. THE SATSUMA REBELLION: AN EPISODE OF MODERN JAPANESE HISTORY. 1979 reprint of 1879 account of the great rebellion of 1877: University Publications of America.

MEIJI: STATE & POLITICS

E. H. Norman. JAPAN'S EMERGENCE AS A MODERN STATE (1940) and FEUDAL BACKGROUND OF JAPANESE POLITICS (1944); reprinted in J. W. Dower, ed. ORIGINS OF THE MODERN JAPANESE STATE (1975: Pantheon).

_____. SOLDIER AND PEASANT IN JAPAN: THE ORIGINS OF CONSCRIPTION. Originally published in *Pacific Affairs* 16.1 and 16.2 (1943). Published separately in 1943, with reprint edition in 1965 by the Institute of Pacific Relations.

John W. Dower. "E. H. Norman, Japan, and the Uses of History." Introduction to ORIGINS (cited above), 3-101. A critique of "modernization theory" and the values of "value-free" scholarship.

Shigeki Toyama. "The Appreciation of Norman's Historiography," *Japan Interpreter* 13.1 (1980), 1-14.

_____. "The Meiji Restoration and the Present Day," *Bulletin of Concerned Asian Scholars* 2.1 (1969), 10-14.

Marius Jansen. "The Meiji State: 1868-1912," in James B. Crowley, ed. MODERN EAST ASIA: ESSAYS IN INTERPRETATION (1970: Harcourt Brace & World), 95-121.

_____. "Meiji History (1868-1912)," KODANSHA ENCYCLOPEDIA OF JAPAN 3: 192-197.

Marlene J. Mayo. "Late Tokugawa and Early Meiji Japan," in Arthur E. Tiedemann, ed. AN INTRODUCTION TO JAPANESE CIVILIZATION (1974: Heath), 131-180.

Roger F. Hackett. "The Era of Fulfillment, 1877-1911," in Tiedemann, AN INTRODUCTION TO JAPANESE CIVILIZATION (1974: Heath), 181-215.

Osamu Kuno. "The Meiji State, Minponshugi, and Ultranationalism," in J. Victor Koschmann, ed. AUTHORITY AND THE INDIVIDUAL IN JAPAN (1978: University of Tokyo Press), 60-80.

Joseph Pittau. "The Meiji Political System: Different Interpretations," in Joseph Roggendorf, ed. STUDIES IN JAPANESE CULTURE: TRADITION AND EXPERIMENT (1965: Monumenta Nipponica Monographs), 99-122.

Barrington Moore, Jr. SOCIAL ORIGINS OF DICTATORSHIP AND DEMOCRACY (1966: Beacon), chapter 5.

Ellen Kay Trimberger. REVOLUTION FROM ABOVE: MILITARY BUREAUCRATS AND DEVELOPMENT IN JAPAN, TURKEY, EGYPT, AND PERU. 1978: Transactions.

Robert A. Scalapino. DEMOCRACY AND THE PARTY MOVEMENT IN PREWAR JAPAN. 1953: University of California Press.

Nobutake Ike. THE BEGINNINGS OF POLITICAL DEMOCRACY IN JAPAN. 1950: Johns Hopkins.

Roger W. Bowen. REBELLION AND DEMOCRACY IN MEIJI JAPAN: A STUDY OF COMMONERS IN THE POPULAR RIGHTS MOVEMENT. 1980: University of California Press.

George M. Beckmann. THE MAKING OF THE MEIJI CONSTITUTION: THE OLIGARCHS AND THE CONSTITUTIONAL DEVELOPMENT OF JAPAN, 1868-1891. 1957: University of Kansas Press.

George Akita. FOUNDATIONS OF CONSTITUTIONAL GOVERNMENT IN MODERN JAPAN, 1868-1900. 1967: Harvard University Press.

Hirobumi Ito. COMMENTARIES ON THE CONSTITUTION OF THE EMPIRE OF JAPAN. Miyoji Ito, transl. 1931: Igirisu-horitsu gakko.

Joseph Pittau. POLITICAL THOUGHT IN EARLY MEIJI JAPAN, 1868-1889. 1967: Harvard University Press.

Johannes Siemes. HERMAN ROESLER AND THE MAKING OF THE MEIJI STATE. 1968: Monumenta Nipponica Monographs & Tuttle.

Ryosuke Ishii, ed. JAPANESE LEGISLATION IN THE MEIJI ERA. 1958: Obunsha.

R. H. P. Mason. JAPAN'S FIRST GENERAL ELECTION: 1890. 1969: Cambridge University Press.

Robert M. Spaulding. IMPERIAL JAPAN'S HIGHER CIVIL SERVICE EXAMINATIONS. 1967: Princeton University Press.

Masakazu Iwata. OKUBO TOSHIMICHI, THE BISMARK OF JAPAN. 1964: University of California Press.

Roger F. Hackett. YAMAGATA ARITOMO IN THE RISE OF MODERN JAPAN, 1838-1922. 1971: Harvard University Press.

Yoshitaka Oka. FIVE POLITICAL LEADERS OF MODERN JAPAN. 1985: University of Tokyo Press. Includes essays on Ito Hirobumi and Okuma Shigenobu.

Joyce C. Lebra. OKUMA SHIGENOBU: STATESMAN OF MEIJI JAPAN. 1973: Australian National University Press.

_____. "Okuma Shigenobu and the 1881 Political Crisis," *Journal of Asian Studies* 16.4 (1959), 475-487.

Andrew Fraser. "The Expulsion of Okuma from the Government in 1881," *Journal of Asian Studies* 26.2 (1967), 213-236.

George E. Uyehara. THE POLITICAL DEVELOPMENT OF JAPAN, 1867-1909. 1910: Dutton.

Walter McLaren. POLITICAL HISTORY OF JAPAN DURING THE MEIJI ERA, 1867-1912. 1916: Russell.

Roger Hackett. "Political Modernization and the Meiji Genro," in Robert E. Ward, ed. POLITICAL DEVELOPMENT IN MODERN JAPAN (1973: Princeton University Press), 65-97.

_____. "The Meiji Leaders and Modernization: The Case of Yamagata Aritomo," in Marius Jansen, ed. CHANGING JAPANESE ATTITUDES TOWARD MODERNIZATION (1965: Princeton University Press), 243-273.

John W. Hall. "A Monarch for Modern Japan," in Ward, POLITICAL DEVELOPMENT IN MODERN JAPAN (1973: Princeton University Press), 11-64.

Bernard Silberman. MINISTERS OF MODERNIZATION: ELITE MOBILITY IN THE MEIJI RESTORATION, 1868-1873. 1964: University of Arizona Press.

_____. "Bureaucratic Development and the Structure of Decision-Making in the Meiji Period," in John A. Harrison, ed. JAPAN (1973: University of Arizona Press), 69-82. Originally published in *Journal of Asian Studies*, 27.1 (1967).

David Wurfel, ed. MEIJI JAPAN'S CENTENNIAL: ASPECTS OF POLITICAL THOUGHT AND ACTION. 1968: University of Kansas Press.

Harry D. Harootunian. "The Progress of Japan and the Samurai Class, 1868-1882," *Pacific Historical Review* 28 (1959), 255-266

_____. "The Economic Rehabilitation of the Samurai in the Early Meiji Period," *Journal of Asian Studies* 19.4 (1960), 434-444

George B. Sansom. "Early Meiji: Western Influences," in his THE WESTERN WORLD AND JAPAN (1965: Knopf), 378-442.

Shigeki Toyama. "Reforms of the Meiji Restoration and the Birth of Modern Intellectuals," *Acta Asiatica* 13 (1967), 55-99.

Osamu Kuno. "The Meiji State, Minponshugi, and Ultranationalism," in J. Victor Koschmann, ed. AUTHORITY AND THE INDIVIDUAL IN JAPAN (1978: University of Tokyo Press), 60-80.

Daikichi Irokawa. THE CULTURE OF THE MEIJI PERIOD. Marius Jansen, transl. & ed. 1985: Princeton University Press.

_____. "Freedom and the Concept of People's Rights," *Japan Quarterly* 14.2 (1967), 175-183.

Carol Gluck. JAPAN'S MODERN MYTHS: IDEOLOGY IN THE LATE MEIJI PERIOD. 1985: Princeton University Press.

Masaaki Kosaka. JAPANESE THOUGHT IN THE MEIJI ERA. 1958. See series citation on page 73.

Marius Jansen, ed. CHANGING JAPANESE ATTITUDES TOWARD MODERNIZATION. 1965: Princeton University Press.

Herbert Passin. SOCIETY AND EDUCATION IN JAPAN. 1965: Teachers College and East Asian Institute, Columbia University.

Carmen Blacker. THE JAPANESE ENLIGHTENMENT: A STUDY OF THE WRITINGS OF FUKUZAWA YUKICHI. 1964: Cambridge University Press.

Yukichi Fukuzawa. THE AUTOBIOGRAPHY OF YUKICHI FUKUZAWA. Eiichi Kiyooka, transl. 1966: Columbia University Press.

_____. AN ENCOURAGEMENT OF LEARNING. David A. Dilworth & Umeyo Hirano, transl. 1969: Monumenta Nipponica Monographs.

_____. AN OUTLINE OF A THEORY OF CIVILIZATION. 1973: David A. Dilworth & G. Cameron Hurst, transl. 1973: Monumenta Nipponica Monographs.

_____. THE SPEECHES OF FUKUZAWA: A TRANSLATION AND CRITICAL STUDY. Wayne H. Oxford, transl. 1973: Hokuseido.

_____. FUKUZAWA YUKICHI ON EDUCATION. Eiichi Kiyooka and Kazuyoshi Nakayama, transl. 1985: University of Tokyo Press.

William R. Braisted, transl. and ed. *MEIROKU ZASSHI*, JOURNAL OF THE JAPANESE ENLIGHTENMENT 1976: Harvard University Press.

Albert Craig. "Fukuzawa Yukichi: The Political Foundations of Meiji Nationalism," in Robert E. Ward, ed. POLITICAL DEVELOPMENT IN MODERN JAPAN (1973: Princeton University Press), 99-148.

Earl Kinmonth. "Fukuzawa Reconsidered: *Gakumon no Susume* and Its Audience," *Journal of Asian Studies* 37.4 (1978), 677-696.

_____. "Nakamura Keiu and Samuel Smiles: a Victorian Confucian and a Confucian Victorian," *American Historical Review* 85.3 (1980), 535-556.

_____. THE SELF-MADE MAN IN MEIJI JAPANESE THOUGHT: FROM SAMURAI TO SALARY MAN. 1981: University of California Press.

71

Thomas Havens. NISHI AMANE AND MODERN JAPANESE THOUGHT. 1970: Princeton University Press.

Ivan Hall. MORI ARINORI. 1973: Harvard University Press.

Alan Grapard. "Japan's Ignored Cultural Revolution," *History of Religions* 23 (1984), 240-265.

Irwin Scheiner. CHRISTIAN CONVERTS AND SOCIAL PROTEST IN MEIJI JAPAN. 1970: University of California Press.

F. G. Notehelfer. AMERICAN SAMURAI: CAPTAIN L. L. JANES AND JAPAN. 1984: Princeton University Press.

Donald Shively, ed. TRADITION AND MODERNIZATION IN JAPANESE CULTURE. 1971: Princeton University Press. See especially Shively's essay "The Japanization of the Middle Meiji," 77-119.

_____. "Motoda Eifu: Confucian Lecturer to the Meiji Emperor," in David Nivison & Arthur Wright, eds. CONFUCIANISM IN ACTION (1959: Stanford University Press), 302-333.

Hilary Conroy, Sandra Davis & Wayne Patterson, eds. JAPAN IN TRANSITION: THOUGHT AND ACTION IN THE MEIJI ERA, 1868-1912. 1985: Farleigh Dickinson University Press.

Warren W. Smith. CONFUCIANISM IN MODERN JAPAN: A STUDY OF CONSERVATISM IN JAPANESE INTELLECTUAL HISTORY. 1959: Hokuseido.

Kenneth B. Pyle. THE NEW GENERATION IN MEIJI JAPAN: PROBLEMS IN CULTURAL IDENTITY, 1885-1895. 1969: Stanford University Press.

_____. "Advantages of Followership: German Economics and Japanese Bureaucrats, 1890-1925," *Journal of Japanese Studies* 1.1 (1974), 127-164.

Peter Duus. "Whig History, Japanese Style: the Min'yusha Historians and the Meiji Restoration," *Journal of Asian Studies* 33.3 (1974), 415-436.

Masao Maruyama. "Fukuzawa, Uchimura, and Okakura," *Developing Economies* 4.4 (1966), 594-611.

Ray A. Moore, ed. CULTURE AND RELIGION IN JAPANESE-AMERICAN RELATIONS: ESSAYS ON UCHIMURA KANZO, 1861-1930. 1981: Center for Japanese Studies, University of Michigan.

Takeo Doi. "Uchimura Kanzo: Japanese Christianity in Comparative Perspective," in Albert Craig, ed. JAPAN: A COMPARATIVE VIEW (1979: Princeton University Press), 182-213.

Katsuichiro Kamei. "Uchimura Kanzo, Intolerant Believer," *Japan Interpreter* 10.1 (1975), 16-43.

Kanzo Uchimura. HOW I BECAME A CHRISTIAN: OUT OF MY DIARY, BY A "HEATHEN CONVERT." 1895: Keiseisha; reprinted 1968: Modern Literature House.

John Caiger. "The Aims and Content of School Courses in Japanese History, 1872-1945," in Edmund R. Skryzpczak, ed. JAPAN'S MODERN CENTURY (1968: Tuttle), 51-82.

Donald J. Roden. SCHOOLDAYS IN IMPERIAL JAPAN: A STUDY IN THE CULTURE OF A STUDENT ELITE. 1980: University of California Press.

_____. "'Monasticism' and the Paradox of the Meiji Higher Schools," *Journal of Asian Studies* 37.3 (1978), 413-425.

John D. Pierson. TOKUTOMI SOHO, 1863-1957: A JOURNALIST FOR MODERN JAPAN. 1980: Princeton University Press.

James L. Huffman. POLITICS OF THE MEIJI PRESS: THE LIFE OF FUKUCHI GEN'ICHIRO. 1980: University of Hawaii Press.

Janet A. Walker. THE JAPANESE NOVEL OF THE MEIJI PERIOD AND THE IDEAL OF INDIVIDUALISM. 1979: Princeton University Press.

Richard J. Bowring. MORI OGAI AND THE MODERNIZATION OF JAPANESE CULTURE. 1979: Cambridge University Press.

Byron K. Marshall. "Professors and Politics: The Meiji Academic Elite," Journal of Japanese Studies 3.1 (1977), 71-97.

James R. Bartholomew. "Japanese Modernization and the Imperial Universities, 1876-1920," Journal of Asian Studies 37.2 (1978), 251-271.

_____. "Science, Bureaucracy, and Freedom in Meiji and Taisho Japan," in Tetsuo Najita & J. Victor Koschmann, eds. CONFLICT IN MODERN JAPANESE HISTORY (1982: Princeton University Press), 226-257.

Jay Rubin. INJURIOUS TO PUBLIC MORALS: WRITERS AND THE MEIJI STATE. 1984: University of Washington Press.

Donald Keene. "The Sino-Japanese War of 1894-95 and Japanese Culture," in his LANDSCAPES AND PORTRAITS: APPRECIATIONS OF JAPANESE CULTURE (1971: Kodansha International), 259-299.

Edward Seidensticker. LOW CITY, HIGH CITY: TOKYO FROM EDO TO THE EARTHQUAKE: HOW THE SHOGUN'S ANCIENT CAPITAL BECAME A GREAT MODERN CITY, 1867-1923. 1983: Knopf.

Robert Lyons Danly. IN THE SHADE OF SPRING LEAVES: THE LIFE AND WRITINGS OF HIGUCHI ICHIYO, A WOMAN OF LETTERS IN MEIJI JAPAN. 1981: Yale University Press.

Lawrence R. Kominz. "Pilgrimage to Tolstoy: Tokutomi Roka's Junrei Kiko," Monumenta Nipponica 41.1 (1986), 51-101.

Centenary Cultural Council Series on JAPANESE CULTURE IN THE MEIJI ERA. Edited by Kaikoku Hyakunen Kinen Bunka Jigyokai, 1955-1958. All volumes translated from the Japanese.

1. Yoshie Okazaki. JAPANESE LITERATURE IN THE MEIJI ERA.
2. Hideo Kishimoto. JAPANESE RELIGION IN THE MEIJI ERA.
3. Toyotaka Komiya. JAPANESE MUSIC AND DRAMA IN THE MEIJI ERA.
4. Kunio Yanagita. JAPANESE MANNERS AND CUSTOMS IN THE MEIJI ERA.
5. Keizo Shibusawa. JAPANESE LIFE AND CULTURE IN THE MEIJI ERA.
6. _____. JAPANESE SOCIETY IN THE MEIJI ERA.
7. Jintaro Fujii. OUTLINE OF JAPANESE HISTORY IN THE MEIJI ERA.
8. Naoteru Uyeno. JAPANESE ARTS AND CRAFTS IN THE MEIJI ERA.
9. Masaaki Kosaka. JAPANESE THOUGHT IN THE MEIJI ERA.
10. Ryosuke Ishii. JAPANESE LEGISLATION IN THE MEIJI ERA.

Centenary Cultural Council Series on A HISTORY OF JAPANESE-AMERICAN CULTURAL RELATIONS, 1853-1926.

1. Keishi Ohara. JAPANESE TRADE AND INDUSTRY IN THE MEIJI-TAISHO ERA.
2. Ki Kimura. JAPANESE LITERATURE: MANNERS AND CUSTOMS IN THE MEIJI-TAISHO ERA
3. Hikomatsu Kamikawa. JAPANESE-AMERICAN DIPLOMATIC RELATIONS IN THE MEIJI-TAISHO ERA.

73

TOKUGAWA-MEIJI: FIRST-HAND MATERIALS

Michael Cooper, ed. THEY CAME TO JAPAN: AN ANTHOLOGY OF EUROPEAN REPORTS ON JAPAN, 1543-1640. 1965: University of California Press.

Richard Blaker. THE NEEDLE WATCHER: THE WILL ADAMS STORY, BRITISH SAMURAI. 1973: Tuttle.

Richard Cocks. DIARY OF RICHARD COCKS, CAPE-MERCHANT IN THE ENGLISH FACTORY IN JAPAN, 1615-1622. 2 volumes. N. Murakami, ed. 1899: Sankosha.

Englebert Kaempfer. HISTORY OF JAPAN... 1690-1692. 3 volumes. J. G. S. Schenchzer, transl. 1906: MacLehose.

C. P. Thunberg. TRAVELS IN EUROPE, AFRICA, AND ASIA. 4 volumes. 1795: Dandre.

V. M. Golovnin. MEMOIRS OF A CAPTIVITY IN JAPAN. 3 volumes. 1824; reprinted in 1973: Henry Colburn.

Philipp Franz von Siebold. MANNERS AND CUSTOMS OF THE JAPANESE. 1930: Japan-Institut.

Illustrated London News. 1842-1975.

E. O. Reischauer, ed. JAPAN. 1974. Facsimile articles from *The New York Times* beginning in the 1850s.

Jean-Pierre Lehmann. THE IMAGE OF JAPAN FROM FEUDAL ISOLATION TO WORLD POWER, 1850-1905. 1978: Allen & Unwin.

Colin Holmes & A. H. Ion. "Bushido and the Samurai: Images in British Public Opinion, 1894-1914," *Modern Asian Studies* 14.2 (1980), 309-329.

Roger Pineau, ed. THE JAPANESE EXPEDITION 1852-1854. THE PERSONAL JOURNAL OF COMMODORE MATTHEW C. PERRY. 1969: Smithsonian Institution.

Francis L. Hawks, ed. NARRATIVE OF THE EXPEDITION OF AN AMERICAN SQUADRON... UNDER COMMODORE M. C. PERRY. 3 volumes. 1856: Nicholson.

James Morrow. A SCIENTIST WITH PERRY IN JAPAN: THE JOURNAL OF DR. JAMES MORROW. Allan B. Cole, ed. 1947: University of North Carolina Press.

George Henry Preble. THE OPENING OF JAPAN: A DIARY OF DISCOVERY IN THE FAR EAST, 1853-1856. 1962: Tuttle.

Townsend Harris. THE COMPLETE JOURNAL OF TOWNSEND HARRIS. Revised edition. M. E. Cosenza, ed. 1959: Tuttle.

Henry C. J. Heusken. JAPAN JOURNAL, 1855-1861. Jeannette C. Van der Corput & Robert C. Wilson, eds. 1964: Rutgers University Press.

L. Oliphant. NARRATIVE OF THE EARL OF ELGIN'S MISSION TO CHINA AND JAPAN IN THE YEARS 1857, 1858, 1859. 2 volumes. 1860: Blackwood.

Sir Rutherford Alcock. THE CAPITAL OF THE TYCOON: A NARRATIVE OF THREE YEARS' RESIDENCE IN JAPAN. 2 volumes. 1863: Harper.

Sir Ernest M. Satow. A DIPLOMAT IN JAPAN. 1921: Seeley Service.

William E. Griffis. THE MIKADO'S EMPIRE. 1876: Harper. 2 volumes; see especially volume 2, "Personal Experiences, Observations, and Studies in Japan."

_____. AN AMERICAN TEACHER IN EARLY MEIJI JAPAN. 1976: University of Hawaii Press. Excerpts from the Griffis diary compiled by Edward Beauchamp.

John R. Black. YOUNG JAPAN: YOKOHAMA AND YEDO. A NARRATIVE OF THE SETTLEMENT AND THE CITY FROM THE SIGNING OF THE TREATIES IN 1858 TO THE CLOSE OF THE YEAR 1879. 2 volumes. 1969: Oxford University Press.

Edward S. Morse. JAPAN DAY BY DAY. 2 volumes. 1936: The Morse Society. Covers 1877-1883.

Erwin O. E. Von Baelz. AWAKENING JAPAN: THE DIARY OF A GERMAN DOCTOR. 1932: Viking.

Clara A. N. Whitney. CLARA'S DIARY: AN AMERICAN GIRL IN MEIJI JAPAN. M. William Steele & Tamiko Ichimata, eds. 1983: Kodansha International.

Isabella L. Bird. UNBEATEN TRACKS IN JAPAN: AN ACCOUNT OF TRAVELS ON HORSEBACK IN THE INTERIOR INCLUDING VISITS TO THE ABORIGINES OF YEZO AND THE SHRINES OF NIKKO AND ISE. 2 volumes. 1881: Putnam.

Mary Crawford Fraser. A DIPLOMAT'S WIFE IN JAPAN: SKETCHES AT THE TURN OF THE CENTURY. Hugh Cortazzi, ed. 1984: Weatherhill.

P. Pratt. HISTORY OF JAPAN: COMPILED FROM THE RECORDS OF THE ENGLISH EAST INDIA COMPANY. M. Paske-Smith, ed. 1931: J. L. Thompson.

Sir Thomas S. Raffles. REPORT ON JAPAN TO THE SECRET COMMITTEE OF THE ENGLISH EAST INDIA COMPANY. 1929: J. L. Thompson.

Basil Hall Chamberlain. THINGS JAPANESE. BEING NOTES ON VARIOUS SUBJECTS CONNECTED WITH JAPAN FOR THE USE OF TRAVELLERS AND OTHERS. 6th edition. 1939: Kegan Paul.

Douglas Sladen. QUEER THINGS ABOUT JAPAN. 1904: Treherne.

Walter W. McLaren. A POLITICAL HISTORY OF JAPAN DURING THE MEIJI ERA, 1867-1912. 1916; reprinted 1965: Russell.

Lafcadio Hearn (1850-1904). See the numerous works by this most famous of the early interpreters of Japan to the West.

Pat Barr. THE DEER CRY PAVILION: A STORY OF WESTERNERS IN JAPAN, 1868-1905. 1968: Macmillan.

Harold S. Williams. FOREIGNERS IN MIKADOLAND. 1963: Tuttle.

_____. TALES OF FOREIGN SETTLEMENTS IN JAPAN. 1958: Tuttle.

_____. SHADES OF THE PAST; OR INDISCREET TALES OF JAPAN. 1959: Tuttle.

R. Tsunoda et al. SOURCES OF JAPANESE TRADITION. 1958: Columbia University Press.

David J. Lu. SOURCES OF JAPANESE HISTORY. 2 volumes. 1974: McGraw-Hill.

Shunsuke Kamei. "Japanese See America: A Century of Firsthand Impressions," *Japan Interpreter* 9.1 (1976), 6-35. Selections from seventeen individuals.

"Diary of an Official of the Bakufu," *Transactions, Asiatic Society of Japan*, 2nd series, 8 (1930), 98-119.

Ernest M. Satow, transl. *KINSE SHIRIAKU*: A HISTORY OF JAPAN [1853-1869]. 1873: Japan Mail.

W. G. Beasley, ed. SELECT DOCUMENTS ON JAPANESE FOREIGN POLICY, 1853-1868. 1955: Oxford University Press.

W. W. McLaren, ed. JAPANESE GOVERNMENT DOCUMENTS, *Transactions, Asiatic Society of Japan*, 1st series, 42 (1914).

Centre for East Asian Cultural Studies. MEIJI JAPAN THROUGH CONTEMPORARY SOURCES. 3 volumes. 1970: Center for East Asian Cultural Studies.

The Far East, volumes 1-7 (1870-1875).

Takayoshi Kido. THE DIARY OF KIDO TAKAYOSHI. Sidney DeVere Brown & Akiko Hirota, transl. 1984-1986: University of Tokyo Press. Volume 1 covers 1868-1871; volume 2, 1871-1874; and volume 3, 1874-1877.

William Braisted, transl. and ed. *MEIROKU ZASSHI*:, JOURNAL OF THE JAPANESE ENLIGHTENMENT. 1976: Harvard University Press. The major journal of the early reformers, 1874-1875.

Yukichi Fukuzawa (1835-1901). THE AUTOBIOGRAPHY OF FUKUZAWA YUKICHI. 1966: Hokuseido.

_____. AN ENCOURAGEMENT OF LEARNING. 1969: Monumenta Nipponica Monographs.

_____. AN OUTLINE OF A THEORY OF CIVILIZATION. 1973: Monumenta Nipponica Monographs.

_____. THE SPEECHES OF FUKUZAWA: A TRANSLATION AND CRITICAL STUDY. 1973: Hokuseido.

_____. FUKUZAWA YUKICHI ON EDUCATION. 1985: University of Tokyo Press.

Chomin Nakae. A DISCOURSE ON GOVERNMENT: NAKAE CHOMIN AND HIS *SANSUIJIN KEIRIN MONDO*. Margaret Dardess, transl. 1977: Program in East Asian Studies, Western Washington State College.

_____. A DISCOURSE BY THREE DRUNKARDS ON GOVERNMENT. Nobuko Tsukui, transl. 1984: Weatherhill.

Kakuzo Okakura. THE IDEALS OF THE EAST. 1903: Dutton.

_____. THE AWAKENING OF JAPAN. 1905: Century.

_____. THE BOOK OF TEA: A JAPANESE HARMONY OF ART, CULTURE AND THE SIMPLE LIFE. 2nd edition. 1935: Angus & Robertson.

Department of Education, Japan. OUTLINES OF THE MODERN EDUCATION IN JAPAN. 1893: Department of Education, Japan.

Alfred Stead, ed. JAPAN BY THE JAPANESE: SURVEY BY HIGHEST AUTHORITIES. 2 volumes. 1904: Heinemann.

F. Brinkley, ed. JAPAN: DESCRIBED AND ILLUSTRATED BY THE JAPANESE. 1897: Millet.

Shigenobu Okuma, comp. FIFTY YEARS OF NEW JAPAN. 2 volumes. 1909: Dutton. Articles by prominent
     Japanese leaders.

Inazo Nitobe. BUSHIDO: THE SOUL OF JAPAN. 10th edition. 1905: Putnam.

_____. THE JAPANESE NATION. ITS LAND, ITS PEOPLE, ITS LIFE. 1912: Putnam.

_____ et al. WESTERN INFLUENCES IN MODERN JAPAN. 1931: University of Chicago Press.

_____. THE WORKS OF INAZO NITOBE. 5 volumes. 1972: University of Tokyo Press.

Toten Miyazaki. MY THIRTY-THREE YEARS' DREAM: THE AUTOBIOGRAPHY OF MIYAZAKI TOTEN.
     Shinkichi Eto & Marius B. Jansen, transl. 1984: Princeton University Press.

ECONOMIC DEVELOPMENT

"Economic History," THE KODANSHA ENCYCLOPEDIA OF JAPAN 2:146-165. Essays by William Hauser on the economy to 1867 (146-151), Kazuo Yamaguchi on the early modern economy to 1945 (151-154), Martin Bronfenbrenner on the 1945-1952 occupation period (154-158), and Hugh Patrick on the postwar and contemporary economy (158-165).

Takafusa Nakamura. ECONOMIC GROWTH IN PREWAR JAPAN. 1982: University of Tokyo Press.

_____. THE POSTWAR JAPANESE ECONOMY: ITS DEVELOPMENT AND STRUCTURE. 1981: University of Tokyo Press.

Kazushi Ohkawa & Henry Rosovsky. "A Century of Japanese Economic Growth," in William Lockwood, ed. THE STATE AND ECONOMIC ENTERPRISE IN JAPAN (1965: Princeton University Press), 47-92.

George Allen. A SHORT ECONOMIC HISTORY OF MODERN JAPAN. Revised edition. 1962: Macmillan.

William Lockwood. THE ECONOMIC DEVELOPMENT OF JAPAN: GROWTH AND STRUCTURAL CHANGE, 1868-1938. 1954. Expanded edition, 1968: Princeton University Press.

_____, ed. THE STATE AND ECONOMIC ENTERPRISE IN JAPAN. 1965: Princeton University Press.

Kunio Yoshihara. JAPANESE ECONOMIC DEVELOPMENT: A SHORT INTRODUCTION. 1979: Oxford University Press.

Bank of Japan. HUNDRED YEAR STATISTICS OF THE JAPANESE ECONOMY. 1966: Nihon Ginko.

Kazushi Ohkawa, Miyohei Shinohara & Mataji Umemura, eds. LONG-TERM ECONOMIC STATISTICS OF JAPAN. 1965: Toyo Keizaishi Shimposha. 14 volumes; the standard set of statistics.

_____, Miyohei Shinohara, with Larry Meissner. PATTERNS OF JAPANESE ECONOMIC DEVELOPMENT: A QUANTITATIVE APPRAISAL. 1979: Yale University Press. Synthesis of the preceding 14-volume series.

_____ & Lawrence Klein, eds. ECONOMIC GROWTH: THE JAPANESE EXPERIENCE SINCE THE MEIJI ERA (Proceedings of the 1st Conference). 1968: R. D. Irwin.

_____ & Yujiro Hayami, eds. ECONOMIC GROWTH: THE JAPANESE EXPERIENCE SINCE THE MEIJI ERA (Proceedings of the 2nd Conference). 1973: Japan Economic Research Center (Tokyo).

_____ & Henry Rosovsky. JAPANESE ECONOMIC GROWTH: TREND ACCELERATION IN THE TWENTIETH CENTURY. 1973: Stanford University Press.

_____ & Henry Rosovsky. "Capital Formation in Japan," in THE INDUSTRIAL ECONOMIES--CAPITAL, LABOR & ENTERPRISE: THE UNITED STATES, JAPAN & RUSSIA, volume 7, part 2 of THE CAMBRIDGE ECONOMIC HISTORY OF EUROPE (1978: Cambridge University Press), 134-165.

_____. DIFFERENTIAL STRUCTURE AND AGRICULTURE: ESSAYS ON DUALISTIC GROWTH. 1972: Kinokuniya.

_____, Bruce Johnson & Hiromatsu Kaneda. AGRICULTURE AND ECONOMIC GROWTH: JAPAN'S EXPERIENCE. 1969: University of Tokyo Press.

Penelope Francks. TECHNOLOGY AND AGRICULTURAL DEVELOPMENT IN PRE-WAR JAPAN. 1982: Yale University Press.

Yujiro Hayami. A CENTURY OF AGRICULTURAL GROWTH IN JAPAN: ITS RELEVANCE TO ASIAN DEVELOPMENT. 1975: University of Minnesota Press.

Takekazu Ogura. AGRICULTURAL DEVELOPMENT IN MODERN JAPAN. Revised edition. 1968: Fuji.

James Nakamura. AGRICULTURAL PRODUCTION AND THE ECONOMIC DEVELOPMENT OF JAPAN, 1873-1922. 1966: Princeton University Press. See also Henry Rosovsky's review of this work under the title "Rumbles in the Ricefields: Professor Nakamura vs. the Official Statistics" in *Journal of Asian Studies* 27.2 (1968), 347-360.

_____. "Growth of Japanese Agriculture, 1875-1920," in William Lockwood, ed. THE STATE AND ECONOMIC ENTERPRISE IN JAPAN (1965: Princeton University Press), 249-324.

Miyohei Shinohara. STRUCTURAL CHANGES IN JAPAN'S ECONOMIC DEVELOPMENT. 1970: Kinokuniya.

Allen Kelley & Jeffrey Williamson. LESSONS FROM JAPANESE DEVELOPMENT: AN ANALYTIC ECONOMIC HISTORY. 1974: University of Chicago Press.

Henry Rosovsky. CAPITAL FORMATION IN JAPAN, 1868-1940. 1961: Free Press.

Koichi Emi. GOVERNMENTAL FISCAL ACTIVITY AND ECONOMIC GROWTH IN JAPAN, 1868-1960. 1963: Kinokuniya.

T. F. M. Adams & Iwao Hoshii. A FINANCIAL HISTORY OF MODERN JAPAN. 1964: Research (Tokyo).

Raymond W. Goldsmith. FINANCIAL DEVELOPMENT OF JAPAN, 1868-1977. 1983: Yale University Press.

_____. THE FINANCIAL DEVELOPMENT OF INDIA, JAPAN, AND THE UNITED STATES. 1983: Yale University Press.

Fuji Bank, ed. BANKING IN MODERN JAPAN. 1961. A 245-page Special Issue of *Fuji Bank Bulletin* 11.4.

S. Broadbridge. INDUSTRIAL DUALISM IN JAPAN. 1967: Aldine.

Martin Bronfenbrenner. "Some Lessons of Japan's Economic Development, 1853-1938," *Pacific Affairs* 34.1 (1961), 7-27.

Thomas C. Smith. POLITICAL CHANGE AND INDUSTRIAL DEVELOPMENT IN JAPAN: GOVERNMENTAL ENTERPRISE, 1868-1880. 1955: Stanford University Press.

Henry Rosovsky. "Japan's Transition to Modern Economic Growth, 1869-1885," in his INDUSTRIALIZATION IN TWO SYSTEMS. 1966: Wiley.

Shigeto Tsuru. "The Take-Off of Japan, 1868-1900," in his ESSAYS ON ECONOMIC DEVELOPMENT (1968: Kinokuniya), 105-122.

Yoshio Ando. "The Formation of Heavy Industry--One of the Processes of Industrialization in the Meiji Period," *Developing Economies* 3.4 (1965), 450-470.

Allen Kelley & Jeffrey Williamson. "Writing History Backwards: Meiji Japan Revisited," *Journal of Economic History* 31.4 (1971), 729-776.

Johannes Hirschmeier. THE ORIGINS OF ENTREPRENEURSHIP IN MEIJI JAPAN. 1964: Harvard University Press.

_____ & Tsunehiko Yui. THE DEVELOPMENT OF JAPANESE BUSINESS, 1600-1980. 1981: Allen & Unwin.

Harvard Graduate School of Business Administration. *Business History Review* 46.1 (1970): "Special Issue: Japanese Entrepreneurship."

Byron Marshall. CAPITALISM AND NATIONALISM IN PREWAR JAPAN: THE IDEOLOGY OF THE BUSINESS ELITE, 1868-1941. 1967: Stanford University Press.

Kozo Yamamura. "A Re-examination of Entrepreneurship in Meiji Japan (1868-1912)," *Economic History Review* 21.1 (1968), 144-158.

_____. "Entrepreneurship, Ownership, and Management in Japan," in THE INDUSTRIAL ECONOMIES-- CAPITAL, LABOR & ENTERPRISE: THE UNITED STATES, JAPAN & RUSSIA, volume 7, part 2 of THE CAMBRIDGE ECONOMIC HISTORY OF EUROPE (1978: Cambridge University Press), 134-165.

_____. "Success Illgotten? The Role of Meiji Militarism in Japan's Technical Progress," *Journal of Economic History* 37.1 (1977), 113-135.

_____. "The Japanese Economy, 1911-1930: Concentration, Conflicts, and Crises," in B. Silberman & H. Harootunian, eds. JAPAN IN CRISIS (1974: Princeton University Press), 299-328.

_____. "Then Came the Great Depression: Japan's Interwar Years," in Herman van der Wee, ed. THE GREAT DEPRESSION REVISITED (1972: Martinus Nijhoff), 182-211.

_____. "Zaibatsu, Prewar and Zaibatsu, Postwar," *Journal of Asian Studies* 23.4 (1964), 539-554.

Kazuo Shibagaki. "The Early History of the Zaibatsu," *Developing Economies* 4.4 (1966), 535-566.

John Roberts. MITSUI: THREE CENTURIES OF JAPANESE BUSINESS. 1973: Weatherhill.

Oland B. Russell. THE HOUSE OF MITSUI. 1939: Little, Brown.

Mark Fruin. KIKKOMAN: COMPANY, CLAN, AND COMMUNITY. 1983: Harvard University Press.

William D. Wray. MITSUBISHI AND THE N.Y.K., 1870-1914: BUSINESS STRATEGY IN THE JAPANESE SHIPPING INDUSTRY. 1984: Harvard East Asian Monographs.

Hugh T. Patrick. "The Economic Muddle of the 1920's," in James W. Morley, ed. DILEMMAS OF GROWTH IN PREWAR JAPAN (1971: Princeton University Press), 211-266.

Arthur E. Tiedemann. "Big Business and Politics in Prewar Japan," in Morley, DILEMMAS OF GROWTH IN PREWAR JAPAN (1971: Princeton University Press), 267-316.

Yukio Cho. "Exposing the Incompetence of the Bourgeoisie: The Financial Panic of 1927," *Japan Interpreter* 8.4 (1974), 492-501.

_____. "Keeping Step with the Military: The Beginning of the Automobile Age," *Japan Interpreter* 7.2 (1972), 168-178.

_____. "From the Showa Economic Crisis to Military Economy--with Special Reference to the Inoue and Takahashi Financial Policies," *Developing Economies* 5.4 (1967), 568-596.

Mitsuharu Ito. "Munitions Unlimited: The Controlled Economy," *Japan Interpreter* 7.3-4 (1972), 353-363.

Makoto Takahashi. "The Development of Wartime Economic Controls," *Developing Economies* 5.4 (1967), 648-665.

Myra Wilkins. "American-Japanese Direct Foreign Investment Relationships, 1930-1952," *Business History Review* (1982), 497-518.

)orothy Borg & Shumpei Okamoto, eds. PEARL HARBOR AS HISTORY: JAPANESE-AMERICAN RELATIONS, 1931-1941. 1973: Columbia University Press. See especially articles by Katsuro Yamamura (on Finance Ministry) and Hideichiro Nakamura (on Japan Economic Federation).

'halmers Johnson. MITI AND THE JAPANESE MIRACLE: THE GROWTH OF INDUSTRIAL POLICY, 1925-1975. 1982: Stanford University Press. Especially chapters 3-5.

. G. Shumpeter, ed. THE INDUSTRIALIZATION OF JAPAN AND MANCHUKUO, 1930-1940. 1940: Macmillan.

.ate L. Mitchell. INDUSTRIALIZATION OF THE WESTERN PACIFIC. 1942: Institute of Pacific Relations.

dwin W. Pauley. REPORT ON JAPANESE REPARATIONS TO THE PRESIDENT OF THE UNITED STATES, NOVEMBER 1945 TO APRIL 1946. Department of State Publication 3174, Far Eastern Series 25. The Pauley Report.

I. S. Department of State. REPORT OF THE MISSION ON JAPANESE COMBINES, PART I, ANALYTICAL AND TECHNICAL DATA. Department of State Publication 2628, Far Eastern Series 14. 1946. The Edwards Report.

erome B. Cohen. THE JAPANESE ECONOMY IN WAR AND RECONSTRUCTION. 1949: University of Minnesota Press.

'. A. Bisson. JAPAN'S WAR ECONOMY. 1945: Macmillan.

_____. ZAIBATSU DISSOLUTION IN JAPAN. 1954: University of California Press.

:leanor M. Hadley. ANTI-TRUST IN JAPAN. 1970: Princeton University Press.

_____. "Zaibatsu" and "Zaibatsu Dissolution," KODANSHA ENCYCLOPEDIA OF JAPAN 8: 361-366.

Mitsubishi Economic Research Institute, ed. MITSUI-MITSUBISHI-SUMITOMO: PRESENT STATUS OF THE FORMER ZAIBATSU ENTERPRISES. 1955: Mitsubishi Economic Research Institute.

{ichard Rice. "Economic Mobilization in Wartime Japan: Business, Bureaucracy, and Military in Conflict," Journal of Asian Studies 38.4 (1979), 689-706.

Mikio Sumiya & Koji Taira, eds. AN OUTLINE OF JAPANESE ECONOMIC HISTORY, 1603-1940. 1979: University of Tokyo Press.

{eiichiro Nakagawa, ed. STRATEGY AND STRUCTURE OF BIG BUSINESS. 1976: University of Tokyo Press.

_____, ed. SOCIAL ORDER AND ENTREPRENEURSHIP. 1977: University of Tokyo Press.

_____, ed. MARKETING AND FINANCE IN THE COURSE OF INDUSTRIALIZATION. 1978: University of Tokyo Press.

_____, ed. GOVERNMENT AND BUSINESS. 1980: University of Tokyo Press.

_____ & Tsunehiko Yui. SHIPPING BUSINESS IN THE 19TH AND 20TH CENTURIES. 1984: University of Tokyo Press.

LABOR & INDUSTRIAL RELATIONS

"Labor," THE KODANSHA ENCYCLOPEDIA OF JAPAN 4: 343-360. Essays on labor history by Solomon Levine, Robert Evans, Jr., and Ken Kurita.

Joe B. Moore. "The Japanese Worker," *Bulletin of Concerned Asian Scholars* 6.3 (1974), 35-47. A critical evaluation of basic works in this field.

"Essays on 'The Japanese Employment System'," *Journal of Japanese Studies* 4.2 (1978), 225-300. Includes Sydney Crawcour, "The Japanese Employment System" (225-245); Robert E. Cole, "The Late-Developer Hypothesis: An Evaluation of its Relevance for Japanese Employment Practices" (247-265); and W. Mark Fruin, "The Japanese Company Controversy: Ideology and Organization in a Historical Perspective" (267-300). See also Ronald Dore, "More About Late Development," *Journal of Japanese Studies* 5.1 (1979), 137-151.

Kazuo Okochi, Bernard Karsh & Solomon B. Levine, eds. WORKERS AND EMPLOYERS IN JAPAN: THE JAPANESE EMPLOYMENT RELATIONS SYSTEM. 1974: Princeton University Press.

Mikio Sumiya. "The Emergence of Modern Japan" and "Contemporary Arrangements: An Overview," in Okochi, Karsh & Levine, WORKERS AND EMPLOYERS IN JAPAN (1974: Princeton University Press), 15-48, 49-87.

_____. "The Japanese System of Industrial Relations," in Peter Doeringer, ed. INDUSTRIAL RELATIONS IN INTERNATIONAL PERSPECTIVE: ESSAYS ON RESEARCH AND POLICY (1981: Holmes & Meier), 287-323.

_____. "The Development of Japanese Labor Relations," *Developing Economies* 4.4 (1966), 499-515.

_____. SOCIAL IMPACT OF INDUSTRIALIZATION IN JAPAN. 1963: University of Tokyo Press.

Hugh Patrick, ed. JAPANESE INDUSTRIALIZATION AND ITS SOCIAL CONSEQUENCES. 1976: University of California Press. See especially the historically oriented articles by Hazama on life styles of industrial workers; Cole & Tominaga on changing occupational structure; Saxonhouse on women in cotton spinning; Chubachi & Taira on poverty.

Solomon Levine & Hisashi Kawada. HUMAN RESOURCES IN JAPANESE INDUSTRIAL DEVELOPMENT. 1980: Princeton University Press.

Koji Taira. ECONOMIC DEVELOPMENT AND THE LABOR MARKET IN JAPAN. 1970: Columbia University Press.

_____. "Factory Labor and the Industrial Revolution in Japan," in THE INDUSTRIAL ECONOMIES--CAPITAL, LABOR & ENTERPRISE: THE UNITED STATES, JAPAN & RUSSIA, volume 7, part 2 of THE CAMBRIDGE ECONOMIC HISTORY OF EUROPE (1978: Cambridge University Press), 166-214.

Ron Napier. "The Transformation of the Japanese Labor Market, 1894-1937," in T. Najita & J. V. Koschmann, eds. CONFLICT IN MODERN JAPANESE HISTORY (1982: Princeton University Press), 342-365.

Ernest J. Notar. "Japan's Wartime Labor Policy: A Search for Method," *Journal of Asian Studies* 44.2 (1985), 311-328.

Andrew Gordon. THE EVOLUTION OF LABOR RELATIONS IN JAPAN: HEAVY INDUSTRY, 1853-1955. 1985: Harvard East Asian Monographs.

Thomas O. Wilkenson. THE URBANIZATION OF JAPANESE LABOR, 1868-1955. 1966: University of Massachusetts Press.

Gary D. Allinson. JAPANESE URBANISM: INDUSTRY AND POLITICS IN KARIYA, 1872-1972. 1975: University of California Press.

azuo Okochi. LABOR IN MODERN JAPAN. 1958: Science Council of Japan.

F. Ayusawa. A HISTORY OF LABOR IN MODERN JAPAN. 1966: University of Hawaii Press.

aishiro Shirai & Haruo Shimada. "Japan," in John T. Dunlop & Walter Galenson, eds. LABOR IN THE TWENTIETH CENTURY (1978: Academic Press), 241-322.

obert Scalapino. "Japan," in Walter Galenson, ed. LABOR AND ECONOMIC DEVELOPMENT (1959: Wiley), 75-145.

____. THE EARLY JAPANESE LABOR MOVEMENT: LABOR AND POLITICS IN A DEVELOPING SOCIETY. 1984: University of California Press.

asue Aoki Kidd. "Women Workers in the Japanese Cotton Mills: 1880-1920," *Cornell University East Asian Papers* 20 (1978).

. Patricia Tsurumi. "Female Textile Workers and the Failure of Early Trade Unionism in Japan," *History Workshop* 18 (1984), 3-27.

homas C. Smith. "The Right to Benevolence: Dignity and Japanese Workers, 1890-1920," *Comparative Studies in Society and History* 26.4 (1984), 587-613.

tephen S. Large. THE YUAIKAI, 1912-1919: THE RISE OF LABOR IN JAPAN. 1972: Monumenta Nipponica Monographs.

____. "The Japanese Labor Movement, 1912-1919: Suzuki Bunji and the Yuaikai," *Journal of Asian Studies* 29.3 (1970), 559-579.

. G. Notehelfer. "Between Tradition and Modernity: Labor and the Ashio Copper Mine," *Monumenta Nipponica* 39.1 (1984), 11-24.

George O. Totten. "Japanese Industrial Relations at the Crossroads: The Great Noda Strike of 1927-1928," in B. Silberman & H. Harootunian, eds. JAPAN IN CRISIS (1974: Princeton University Press), 398-436.

huichi Harada. LABOR CONDITIONS IN JAPAN. 1928: Columbia University Press.

Robert E. Cole. JAPANESE BLUE COLLAR: THE CHANGING TRADITION. 1971: University of California Press.

Ronald P. Dore. BRITISH FACTORY--JAPANESE FACTORY: THE ORIGINS OF NATIONAL DIVERSITY IN EMPLOYMENT RELATIONS. 1973: University of California Press.

olomon B. Levine. INDUSTRIAL RELATIONS IN POSTWAR JAPAN. 1958: University of Illinois Press.

ames C. Abegglen. MANAGEMENT AND WORKER: THE JAPANESE SOLUTION. 1973: Sophia University & Kodansha International. Revision of the author's THE JAPANESE FACTORY (1958).

itaro Kishimoto. "The Characteristics of Labor-Management Relations in Japan and Their Historical Formation," *Kyoto University Economic Review* 35.2 (1965), 33-55.

Kenji Okuda. "Managerial Evolution in Japan," *Management Japan* 5.3 (1971), 13-19; 5.4 (1972), 15-23; 6.1 (1972), 28-35.

Masumi Tsuda. "Study of Japanese Management Development Practices," *Hitotsubashi Journal of Social Studies* 9.1 (1977), 1-12.

Osamu Mano. "Recent Research on the Japanese Personnel Management System in Japan: A Comparative Perspective," *Hokudai Economic Papers* 9 (1979-1980), 1-23.

John W. Bennet & I. Ishino. PATERNALISM IN THE JAPANESE ECONOMY: ANTHROPOLOGICAL STUDIES OF OYABUN-KOBUN PATTERNS. 1963: University of Minnesota Press.

Michael Yoshino. JAPAN'S MANAGERIAL SYSTEM: TRADITION AND INNOVATION. 1968: Massachusetts Institute of Technology Press.

N. Noda. "How Japan Absorbed American Management Methods," in British Institute of Management, MODERN JAPANESE MANAGEMENT (1970: Publications Ltd., for British Institute of Management), 29-66.

Keiichiro Nakagawa, ed. LABOR AND MANAGEMENT. 1979: University of Tokyo Press.

LANDLORD, TENANT & THE RURAL SECTOR

dashi Fukutake. JAPANESE RURAL SOCIETY. R. P. Dore, transl. 1967: Cornell University Press. See the bibliographies to each chapter in this work.

chard K. Beardsley, John W. Hall & Robert E. Ward. VILLAGE JAPAN. 1959: University of Chicago Press.

keo Yazaki. SOCIAL CHANGE AND THE CITY IN JAPAN: FROM EARLIEST TIMES THROUGH THE INDUSTRIAL REVOLUTION. 1968: Japan Publications.

bert J. Smith. KURUSU: A JAPANESE VILLAGE, 1951-1975. 1978: Stanford University Press.

ie Nakane. KINSHIP AND ECONOMIC ORGANIZATION IN RURAL JAPAN. 1967: Athlone.

hn William Robertson-Scott. THE FOUNDATIONS OF JAPAN. 1922: Appleton.

hn F. Embree. SUYE MURA, A JAPANESE VILLAGE. 1939: University of Chicago Press.

iroshi Nasu. ASPECTS OF JAPANESE AGRICULTURE. 1941: Institute of Pacific Relations.

omas C. Smith. THE AGRARIAN ORIGINS OF MODERN JAPAN. 1959: Stanford University Press.

____. "The Japanese Village in the Seventeenth Century" (1952) and "The Land Tax in the Tokugawa Period" (1958), both reprinted in John W. Hall & Marius B. Jansen, eds. STUDIES IN THE INSTITUTIONAL HISTORY OF EARLY MODERN JAPAN (1968: Princeton University Press), 263-299.

____. "Landlords and Rural Capitalists in the Modernization of Japan," *Journal of Economic History* 16.2 (1956), 165-181.

____. "Landlords' Sons in the Business Elite," *Economic Development and Cultural Change* 9.1, part 2 (1960), 93-108.

illiam Chambliss. CHIARAIJIMA VILLAGE: LAND TENURE, TAXATION, AND LOCAL TRADE, 1811-1884. 1965: University of Arizona Press.

ugh Borton. PEASANT UPRISINGS IN JAPAN OF THE TOKUGAWA PERIOD. 1968: Paragon. Reprint of study originally published in *Transactions, Asiatic Society of Japan*, 1938.

. H. Norman. SOLDIER AND PEASANT IN JAPAN: THE ORIGINS OF CONSCRIPTION. 1965: Institute of Pacific Relations. Reprint of two-part article orignally published in *Pacific Affairs*, March & June 1943.

____. JAPAN'S EMERGENCE AS A MODERN STATE (1940: Institute of Pacific Relations), chapter 5. Reprinted in J. W. Dower, ed. ORIGINS OF THE MODERN JAPANESE STATE. 1979: Pantheon.

win Scheiner. "The Mindful Peasant: Sketches for a Study of Rebellion," *Journal of Asian Studies* 32.4 (1973), 579-591.

ikiso Hane. PEASANTS, REBELS, AND OUTCASTES: THE UNDERSIDE OF MODERN JAPAN. 1982: Pantheon.

arrington Moore, Jr. SOCIAL ORIGINS OF DICTATORSHIP AND DEMOCRACY: LORD AND PEASANT IN THE MAKING OF THE MODERN WORLD. 1966: Beacon. See 228-313 on Japan.

onald P. Dore. LAND REFORM IN JAPAN. 1959: Oxford University Press. 1-125 on prewar.

____. "Making Sense of History," *Archives Europiennes de Sociologie* 10.2 (1969), 295-305. Review of Barrington Moore.

_____ & Tsutomu Ouchi. "Rural Origins of Japanese Fascism," in James Morley, ed. DILEMMAS OF GROWTH IN PREWAR JAPAN (1971: Princeton University Press), 181-209. Critique of Barrington Moore.

_____. "The Meiji Landlord: Good or Bad?" *Journal of Asian Studies* 18.3 (1959), 343-355.

_____. "Agricultural Improvement in Japan," *Economic Development and Cultural Change* 9.1 part 2 (1960), 69-92.

_____. "Land Reform and Japan's Economic Development," *Developing Economies* 3.4 (1965), 487-496.

_____. SHINOHATA: A PORTRAIT OF A JAPANESE VILLAGE. 1980: Pantheon.

Morris D. Morris. "The Problem of the Peasant Agriculturist in Meiji Japan, 1873-1885," *Far Eastern Quarterly* 15.3 (1956), 357-370.

Kunio Niwa. "The Reform of the Land Tax and the Government Programme for the Encouragement of Industry," *Developing Economies* 4.4 (1966), 567-593.

Penelope Francks. TECHNOLOGY AND AGRICULTURAL DEVELOPMENT IN PRE-WAR JAPAN. 1984: Yale University Press.

Richard J. Smethurst. AGRICULTURAL DEVELOPMENT AND TENANCY DISPUTES IN JAPAN, 1870-1940. 1986 Princeton University Press.

Ann Waswo. JAPANESE LANDLORDS: THE DECLINE OF A RURAL ELITE. 1977: University of California Press.

_____. "The Origins of Tenant Unrest," in B. Silberman & H. Harootunian, eds. JAPAN IN CRISIS (1974: Princeton University Press), 374-397.

Kenneth Pyle. "The Technology of Japanese Nationalism: The Local Improvement Movement, 1900-1918," *Journal of Asian Studies* 33.1 (1973), 51-65.

Tsutomu Ouchi. "Agricultural Depression and Japanese Villages," *Developing Economies* 5.4 (1967), 597-627.

Shobei Shiota. "The Rice Riots and the Social Problem," *Developing Economies* 4.4 (1966), 516-534.

Shuzo Teruoka. "Japanese Capitalism and Its Agricultural Problems--Culminating in the Rice Riots," *Developing Economies* 4.4 (1966), 472-498.

George O. Totten. "Labor and Agrarian Disputes in Japan Following World War I," *Economic Development and Cultural Change* 9.1 part 2 (1960), 187-212.

Miriam S. Farley. "Japan's Unsolved Tenancy Problem," *Far Eastern Survey* 6.14 (1937), 153-159.

Galen M. Fisher. "The Landlord-Peasant Struggle in Japan," *Far Eastern Survey* 6.18 (1937), 201-206.

W. Ladejinsky. "Farm Tenancy and Japanese Agriculture," *Foreign Agriculture* (Bureau of Agricultural Economics, U. S. Department of Agriculture) 1.9 (1937), 425-446.

Seiyei Wakukawa. "The Japanese Farm-Tenancy System," in Douglas G. Haring, ed. JAPAN'S PROSPECT (1946: Harvard University Press), 115-173.

Thomas R. H. Havens. FARM AND NATION IN MODERN JAPAN: AGRARIAN NATIONALISM, 1870-1940. 1974: Princeton University Press.

_____. "Two Popular Views of Rural Self-Rule in Modern Japan," in Japan P. E. N. Club, ed. STUDIES ON
JAPANESE CULTURE, volume 2 (1973: The Japan P. E. N. Club), 249-255.

ichard J. Smethurst. A SOCIAL BASIS FOR PREWAR JAPANESE MILITARISM: THE ARMY AND THE RURAL
COMMUNITY. 1974: University of California Press.

_____. "The Creation of the Imperial Military Reserve Association in Japan," *Journal of Asian Studies* 30.4
(1971), 815-828.

enry D. Smith II. Review of preceding two books by Havens and Smethurst, *Journal of Japanese Studies* 2.1
(1976), 131-147.

aikichi Irokawa. "The Survival Struggle of the Japanese Community," *Japan Interpreter* 9.4 (1975), 466-494.

sutomu Takizawa. "Historical Background of Agricultural Land Reform in Japan," *Developing Economies* 10.3
(1972), 290-310.

arol Gluck. "The People in History: Recent Trends in Japanese Historiography," *Journal of Asian Studies* 38.1
(1978), 25-50.

"TAISHO DEMOCRACY"

Peter Duus. "Taisho and Early Showa History (1912-1945)," KODANSHA ENCYCLOPEDIA OF JAPAN 3: 197-203.

R. Tsunoda et al. SOURCES OF JAPANESE TRADITION. 1958: Columbia University Press. See Chapter 26, "The High Tide
of Prewar Liberalism," for basic documents.

Thorstein Veblen. "The Opportunity of Japan," 1915; reprinted in his ESSAYS IN OUR CHANGING ORDER (1934: Viking), 248-266.

John Dewey. CHARACTERS AND EVENTS, volume 1, 1929: Holt. Contains three pertinent essays: "Liberalism in Japan" (1919); "On the Two Sides of the Eastern Sea" (1919); and "Japan Revisited: Two Years Later" (1921).

Yusuke Tsurumi. PRESENT DAY JAPAN. 1926: Columbia University Press.

A. Morgan Young. JAPAN IN RECENT TIMES, 1912-1926. 1929: Morrow.

_____. IMPERIAL JAPAN, 1926-1938. 1938: Morrow.

Shigeki Toyama. "Politics, Economics, and the International Environment in the Meiji and Taisho Periods," *Developing Economies* 4.4 (1966), 419-446.

John K. Fairbank, Edwin O. Reischauer & Albert M. Craig. EAST ASIA: THE MODERN TRANSFORMATION. 1965: Houghton Mifflin. See Chapter 7 on "Imperial Japan."

Arthur E. Tiedemann. "Taisho and Early Showa Japan," in his AN INTRODUCTION TO JAPANESE CIVILIZATION (1974: Heath), 217-245.

Takayoshi Matsuo. "The Development of Democracy in Japan--Taisho Democracy, Its Flowering and Breakdown," *Developing Economies* 4.4 (1966), 612-637.

Kenneth Pyle. "Advantages of Followership: German Economics and Japanese Bureaucrats, 1890-1925," *Journal of Japanese Studies* 1.1 (1974), 127-164.

_____. "State and Society in the Interwar Years," *Journal of Japanese Studies* 3.2 (1977), 421-430. A review essay.

Robert A. Scalapino. DEMOCRACY AND THE PARTY MOVEMENT IN PREWAR JAPAN: THE FAILURE OF THE FIRST ATTEMPT. 1953: University of California Press.

George O. Totten, ed. DEMOCRACY IN PREWAR JAPAN: GROUNDWORK OR FACADE? 1965: Yale University Press.

Gino K. Piovesana. "Men and Social Ideas of the Early Taisho period," *Monumenta Nipponica* 19.1-2 (1964), 111-129.

Yoshitake Oka. FIVE POLITICAL LEADERS OF MODERN JAPAN. 1985: University of Tokyo Press. Contains essays on Hara Takashi, Inukai Tsuyoshi, and Saionji Kimmochi.

Tetsuo Najita. HARA KEI IN THE POLITICS OF COMPROMISE, 1905-1915. 1967: Harvard University Press.

Peter Duus. PARTY RIVALRY AND POLITICAL CHANGE IN TAISHO JAPAN. 1968: Harvard University Press.

_____. "The Era of Party Rule: Japan, 1905-1932," in James B. Crowley, ed. MODERN EAST ASIA: ESSAYS IN INTERPRETATION (1970: Harcourt Brace & World), 180-206.

_____. "Liberal Intellectuals and Social Conflict in Taisho Japan," in T. Najita & J. V. Koschmann, eds. CONFLICT IN MODERN JAPANESE HISTORY (1982: Princeton University Press), 412-440.

_____. "Yoshino Sakuzo: the Christian as Political Critic," *Journal of Japanese Studies* 4.2 (1978), 301-326.

_____. "Nagai Ryutaro and the 'White Peril', 1905-1944," *Journal of Asian Studies* 31.1 (1971), 41-48.

Bernard S. Silberman & H. D. Harootunian, eds. JAPAN IN CRISIS: ESSAYS ON TAISHO DEMOCRACY. 1974: Princeton University Press. Fifteen contributions by leading scholars. Includes general interpretative essays by the editors; case studies of Yoshino Sakuzo, Natsume Soseki, and Kawakami Hajime; essays on both leftwing and nationalist thought; economic analyses; and a study of the bureaucracy after 1900.

J. Victor Koschmann, ed. AUTHORITY AND THE INDIVIDUAL IN JAPAN: CITIZEN PROTEST IN HISTORICAL PERSPECTIVE. 1978: University of Tokyo Press.

Tatsuo Arima. THE FAILURE OF FREEDOM: A PORTRAIT OF MODERN JAPANESE INTELLECTUALS. 1969: Harvard University Press. Includes essays on Uchimura Kanzo, Arishima Takeo, Akutagawa Ryunosuke, anarchists, literary "naturalists," proletarian writers, and the "White Birch" group.

Frank O. Miller. MINOBE TATSUKICHI: INTERPRETER OF CONSTITUTIONALISM IN JAPAN. 1965: University of California Press.

Richard Minear. JAPANESE TRADITION AND WESTERN LAW: EMPEROR, STATE, AND LAW IN THE THOUGHT OF HOZUMI YATSUKA. 1970: Harvard University Press.

Roger F. Hackett. YAMAGATA ARITOMO IN THE RISE OF MODERN JAPAN, 1838-1922. 1971: Harvard University Press.

Sharon Minichiello. RETREAT FROM REFORM: PATTERNS OF POLITICAL BEHAVIOR IN INTERWAR JAPAN. 1984: University of Hawaii Press.

Toru Takemoto. FAILURE OF LIBERALISM IN JAPAN: SHIDEHARA KIJURO'S ENCOUNTER WITH ANTI-LIBERALS. 1979: University Press of America.

Sharon H. Nolte. LIBERALISM IN MODERN JAPAN: ISHIBASHI TANZAN AND HIS TEACHERS, 1905-1960. 1986: University of California Press.

Shumpei Okamoto. "The Emperor and the Crowd: The Historical Significance of the Hibiya Riot," in Najita & Koschmann, CONFLICT IN MODERN JAPANESE HISTORY (1982: Princeton University Press), 258-275.

Noel F. Bush. TWO MINUTES TO NOON. 1962: Simon & Schuster. Concerns the great Kanto earthquake of 1923.

Donald T. Roden. SCHOOLDAYS IN IMPERIAL JAPAN: A STUDY IN THE CULTURE OF A STUDENT ELITE. 1980: University of California Press.

Masao Maruyama. "Patterns of Individuation and the Case of Japan: A Conceptual Scheme," in M. Jansen, ed. CHANGING JAPANESE ATTITUDES TOWARD MODERNIZATION (1965: Princeton University Press), 489-531.

Yutaka Arase. "Mass Communication Between the Two World Wars," *Developing Economies* 5.4 (1967), 748-766.

Akira Fujitake. "The Formation and Development of Mass Culture," *Developing Economies* 5.4 (1967), 767-782.

Harris I. Martin. "Popular Music and Social Change in Prewar Japan," *Japan Interpreter* 7.3-4 (1972), 332-352.

Brian Powell. "Japan's First Modern Theater: The Tsukiji Shogekijo and Its Company, 1924-26," *Monumenta Nipponica* 30.1 (1975), 69-86.

Donald Richie. JAPANESE CINEMA: FILM STYLE AND NATIONAL CHARACTER. 1984: Anchor.

Joseph L. Anderson & Donald Richie. THE JAPANESE FILM: ART AND INDUSTRY. 1959; expanded edition, 1982: Princeton University Press.

Hidetoshi Kato. "Service-Industry Business Complexes--The Growth and Development of 'Terminal Culture'," *Japan Interpreter* 7.3-4 (1972), 376-382.

_____. "The Trend Toward Affirmation of War: Norakuro," *Japan Interpreter* 7.2 (1972), 179-186.

Shuichi Kato. "Taisho Democracy as the Pre-Stage for Japanese Militarism," in B. Silberman & H. Harootunian, eds. JAPAN IN CRISIS (1974: Princeton University Press), 217-236.

Seizaburo Shinobu. "From Party Politics to Military Dictatorship," *Developing Economies* 5.4 (1967), 666-684.

Marius B. Jansen. "From Hatoyama to Hatoyama," *Far Eastern Quarterly* 14.1 (1954), 65-79. Review of *Taisho Seiji Shi* , 4 volumes, by Shinobu Seizaburo.

Edward Seidensticker. LOW CITY, HIGH CITY: TOKYO FROM EDO TO THE EARTHQUAKE: HOW THE SHOGUN'S ANCIENT CAPITAL BECAME A GREAT MODERN CITY, 1867-1923. 1983: Knopf.

Henry D. Smith, II. "Tokyo as an Idea: An Exploration of Japanese Urban Thought Until 1945," *Journal of Japanese Studies* 4.1 (1978), 45-80.

James W. White. "Internal Migration in Prewar Japan," *Journal of Japanese Studies* 4.1 (1978), 81-124.

THE POLITICAL LEFT

R. Tsunoda et al. SOURCES OF JAPANESE TRADITION. 1958: Columbia University Press. See Chapter 28, "The Japanese Social Movement," for documents.

Roger Bowen. REBELLION AND DEMOCRACY IN MEIJI JAPAN: COMMONERS IN THE POPULAR RIGHTS MOVEMENT. 1980: University of California Press.

_____."Rice Roots Democracy & Popular Rebellion in Meiji Japan,"*Journal of Peasant Studies* 6.1 (1978), 1-39.

_____. "Political Protest in Prewar Japan: The Case of Fukushima Prefecture," *Bulletin of Concerned Asian Scholars* 16.2 (1984), 23-32.

Nobutake Ike. THE BEGINNINGS OF POLITICAL DEMOCRACY IN JAPAN. 1950: Johns Hopkins.

John Crump. THE ORIGINS OF SOCIALIST THOUGHT IN JAPAN. 1983: St. Martin's.

Stefano Bellieni. "Notes on the History of the Left-Wing Movement in Meiji Japan," Instituto Orientale di Napoli (1979).

Jon Halliday. "The Beginnings of the Left," in his A POLITICAL HISTORY OF JAPANESE CAPITALISM (1975: Pantheon), 62-81.

Hyman Kublin. ASIAN REVOLUTIONARY: THE LIFE OF SEN KATAYAMA. 1964: Princeton University Press.

_____."The Japanese Socialists and the Russo-Japanese War,"*Journal of Modern History* 22.4 (1950), 322-339.

Iso Abe. "Socialism in Japan," in Shigenobu Okuma, comp. FIFTY YEARS OF NEW JAPAN (1910: Dutton), 494-512.

Marius B. Jansen. THE JAPANESE AND SUN YAT-SEN. 1954: Harvard University Press.

_____. "Oi Kentaro's Radicalism and Chauvinism," *Far Eastern Quarterly* 11.3 (1952), 305-316.

F. G. Notehelfer. KOTOKU SHUSHI: PORTRAIT OF A JAPANESE RADICAL. 1971: Cambridge University Press.

George Elison. "Kotoku Shusui: The Change in Thought," *Monumenta Nipponica* 22.3-4 (1967), 437-467. Accompanied by a translation of Kotoku's 1910 "Discussion of Violent Revolution from a Jail Cell," 468-481.

J. Victor Koschmann, ed. AUTHORITY AND THE INDIVIDUAL IN JAPAN: CITIZEN PROTEST IN HISTORICAL PERSPECTIVE. 1977: University of Tokyo Press.

Kenneth Strong. OX AGAINST THE STORM: A BIOGRAPHY OF TANAKA SHOZO--JAPAN'S CONSERVATIONIST PIONEER. 1978: University of British Columbia Press.

Symposium: The Ashio Copper Mine Pollution Incident," *Journal of Japanese Studies* 1.2 (1975), 347-408. Articles by K. Pyle, F. Notehelfer, and A. Stone.

Irwin Scheiner. CHRISTIAN CONVERTS AND SOCIAL PROTEST IN MEIJI JAPAN. 1970: University of California.

Nobuya Bamba & John F. Howes, eds. PACIFISM IN JAPAN: THE CHRISTIAN AND SOCIALIST TRADITION. 1978: University of British Columbia Press. Includes essays on Kitamura Tokoku, Kinoshita Naoe, Uchimura Kanzo, Kotoku Shusui, Abe Isoo, Kagawa Toyohiko, Yanaihara Tadao, and Tabata Shinobu.

George B. Bickle, Jr. THE NEW JERUSALEM: ASPECTS OF UTOPIANISM IN THE THOUGHT OF KAGAWA TOYOHIKO. 1976: University of Arizona Press.

Gail Lee Bernstein. JAPANESE MARXIST: A PORTRAIT OF KAWAKAMI HAJIME, 1879-1946. 1976: Harvard University Press.

_____. "Kawakami Hajime: A Japanese Marxist in Search of the Way," in Bernard Silberman & H. Harootunian, eds. JAPAN IN CRISIS (1974: Princeton University Press), 86-109.

Henry D. Smith, II. JAPAN'S FIRST STUDENT RADICALS. 1972: Harvard University Press.

George O. Totten. THE SOCIAL DEMOCRATIC MOVEMENT IN PREWAR JAPAN. 1966: Yale University Press.

_____. "Labor and Agrarian Disputes in Japan Following World War One," *Economic Development and Cultural Change* 9.1, part 2 (1960), 187-212.

_____. "Japanese Industrial Relations at the Crossroads: the Great Noda Strike of 1927-1928," in Bernard Silberman & H. D. Harootunian, eds. JAPAN IN CRISIS (1974: Princeton University Press), 398-436.

A. Morgan Young. THE SOCIALIST AND LABOR MOVEMENT IN JAPAN, BY AN AMERICAN SOCIOLOGIST. 1921: Japan Chronicle.

E. Colbert. THE LEFT WING IN JAPANESE POLITICS. 1952: Institute of Pacific Relations.

Stephen S. Large. THE YUAIKAI, 1912-19: THE RISE OF LABOR IN JAPAN. 1972: Monumenta Nipponica Monographs.

_____. ORGANIZED WORKERS & SOCIALIST POLITICS IN INTERWAR JAPAN. 1981: Cambridge University.

_____. "The Japanese Labor Movement, 1912-1919: Suzuki Bunji and the Yuaikai," *Journal of Asian Studies* 29.3 (1970), 559-579.

_____. "Nishio Suehiro and the Japanese Social Democratic Movement, 1920-1940," *Journal of Asian Studies* 36.1 (1976), 37-56.

_____. "Revolutionary Worker: Watanabe Masanosuke and the Japanese Communist Party," *Asian Profile* 3.4 (1975), 371-390.

_____. "The Romance of Revolution in Japanese Anarchism and Communism During the Taisho Period," *Modern Asian Studies* 2.3 (1977), 441-467.

Peter Duus. "Oyama Ikuo and the Search for Democracy," in James Morley, ed. DILEMMAS OF GROWTH IN PREWAR JAPAN (1971: Princeton University Press), 423-458.

Thomas A. Stanley. OSUGI SAKAE, ANARCHIST IN TAISHO JAPAN: THE CREATIVITY OF THE EGO. 1982: Harvard East Asian Monographs.

Bradford Simcock. "The Anarcho-Syndicalist Thought and Activity of Osugi Sakae, 1885-1923," *Harvard University Papers on Japan* (1970), 31-54.

Tatsuo Arima. "The Anarchists: The Negation of Politics," in his THE FAILURE OF FREEDOM: A PORTRAIT OF MODERN JAPANESE INTELLECTUALS (1969: Harvard University Press), 51-69.

Victor Garcia & Wat Tyler. MUSEIFUSHUGI: THE REVOLUTIONARY IDEA IN JAPAN. 1981: Cienfuegos.

George Beckmann & Genji Okubo. THE JAPANESE COMMUNIST PARTY, 1922-1945. 1969: Stanford University.

George Beckmann. "Japanese Adaptations of Marx-Leninism," *Asian Cultural Studies* 3 (1962), 103-114.

_____. "The Radical Left and the Failure of Communism," in James Morley, ed. DILEMMAS OF GROWTH IN PREWAR JAPAN (1971: Princeton University Press), 139-178.

Yoshitomo Takeuchi. "The Role of Marxism in Japan," *Developing Economies* 5.4 (1969), 927-947.

THE POLITICAL LEFT--III

Yasukichi Yasuba. "Anatomy of the Debate on Japanese Capitalism," *Journal of Japanese Studies* 2.1 (1975), 63-82.

Robert Scalapino. THE JAPANESE COMMUNIST MOVEMENT, 1920-1966. 1967: University of California Press.

Central Committee, Communist Party of Japan. THE FIFTY YEARS OF THE COMMUNIST PARTY OF JAPAN. 1973: Central Committee, Communist Party of Japan (Nihon Kyosanto).

A. Roger Swearingen & Paul Langer. RED FLAG IN JAPAN: INTERNATIONAL COMMUNISM IN ACTION, 1919-1951. 1952: Harvard University Press.

Paul Langer. COMMUNISM IN JAPAN: A CASE OF POLITICAL NATURALIZATION. 1972: Hoover Institution Press.

Hiroaki Matsuzawa. "'Theory' and 'Organization' in the Japan Communist Party," in J. Victor Koschmann, ed. AUTHORITY AND THE INDIVIDUAL IN JAPAN (1978: University of Tokyo Press), 108-127.

Patricia G. Steinhoff. "Tenko: Ideology and Social Integration in Prewar Japan," 1969: Ph.D. dissertation in Sociology, Harvard University.

Kazuko Tsurumi. "Six Types of Change in Personality: Case Studies of Ideological Conversion in the 1930's," in her SOCIAL CHANGE AND THE INDIVIDUAL (1966: Princeton University Press), 29-79.

Ian Neary. "Tenko of an Organization: the Suiheisha in the Late 1930's," *Proceedings of the British Association for Japanese Studies*, volume 2, part 2 (1977), 64-76.

Shigeharu Nakano. "The House in the Village," in Brett de Bary, transl. THREE WORKS BY NAKANO SHIGEHARU, *Cornell University East Asian Papers* 21 (1979), 21-73.

John Boyle. "The Role of the Radical Left Wing in the Japanese Suffrage Movement," *Studies on Asia* 6 (1965), 81-96.

Bunso Hashikawa. "Antiwar Values--the Resistance in Japan," *Japan Interpreter* 9.1 (1974), 86-97.

_____. "The 'Civil Society' Ideal and Wartime Resistance," in Koschmann, AUTHORITY AND THE INDIVIDUAL IN JAPAN (1978: University of Tokyo Press), 128-142.

Chalmers Johnson. AN INSTANCE OF TREASON: OZAKI HOTSUMI AND THE SORGE SPY RING. 1964: Stanford University Press.

F. W. Deakin & G. R. Storry. THE CASE OF RICHARD SORGE. 1966: Chatto & Windus.

G. T. Shea. LEFTWING LITERATURE IN JAPAN. 1964: University of Tokyo Press.

Yoshio Iwamoto. "Aspects of the Proletarian Literary Movement in Japan," in Silberman & Harootunian, JAPAN IN CRISIS (1974: Princeton University Press), 156-182.

Tatsuo Arima. "Proletarian Literature: The Tyranny of Politics," in his THE FAILURE OF FREEDOM (1969: Harvard University Press), 173-213.

Donald Keene. "Proletarian Literature of the 1920s" and "Tenko Literature: the Writings of Ex-Communists," in his DAWN TO THE WEST: JAPANESE LITERATURE OF THE MODERN ERA (1984: Holt, Rinehart & Winston), 594-628 and 846-905.

Vlasta Hilska. "Japanese Proletarian Literature," in Vlasta Hilska & Zdenka Vasiljevova, PROBLEMS OF MODERN JAPANESE SOCIETY (1971: Universita Karlova), 11-52.

Naoe Kinoshita. PILLAR OF FIRE. 1972: Allen & Unwin. Translation by Kenneth Strong of 1904 novel by one of the pioneers of socialism in Japan.

Takiji Kobayashi. "THE FACTORY SHIP" AND "THE ABSENTEE LANDLORD". 1973: University of Washington Press. Translation by Frank Motofuji of two works by the most famous proletarian writer.

93

NATIONALISM & THE EMPEROR SYSTEM

R. Tsunoda et al. SOURCES OF JAPANESE TRADITION. 1958: Columbia University Press. See Chapter 27 for documents pertaining to "The Rise of Revolutionary Nationalism."

Robert K. Hall. SHUSHIN: THE ETHICS OF A DEFEATED NATION. 1949: Teachers College, Columbia University. Includes extensive translations from ethics textbooks of 1936-1940.

Japanese Ministry of Education. KOKUTAI NO HONGI: CARDINAL PRINCIPLES OF THE NATIONAL ENTITY OF JAPAN. Translated by John Gauntlett and edited by Robert K. Hall. 1949: Harvard University Press. The consummate official explanation of the Japanese national polity (kokutai), originally published in 1937.

_____. "The Way of the Subject" (Shinmin no Michi), reprinted in Otto Tolischus, TOKYO RECORD (1943: Reynal & Hitchcock), 405-427.

Masao Maruyama. THOUGHT AND BEHAVIOR IN MODERN JAPANESE POLITICS. 1963: Oxford University Press. Pioneer essays on nationalism and fascism in modern Japan.

_____. Introduction to Ivan Morris, NATIONALISM AND THE RIGHT-WING IN JAPAN: A STUDY OF POSTWAR TRENDS (1960: Oxford University Press), xvii-xxvii.

Kazuko Tsurumi. SOCIAL CHANGE AND THE INDIVIDUAL: JAPAN BEFORE AND AFTER DEFEAT IN WORLD WAR II. 1966: Princeton University Press. Excellent essays on indoctrination and "socialization for death."

Masanori Nakamura. "The Emperor System of the 1900's," Bulletin of Concerned Asian Scholars 16.2 (1984), 2-11.

Jiro Kamishima. "Mental Structure of the Emperor System," Developing Economies 5.4 (1967), 702-726.

Noboru Kojima. "Militarism and the Emperor System," Japan Interpreter 8.2 (1973), 219-227.

Michio Takeyama. "The Emperor System," Journal of Social and Political Ideas in Japan 2.2 (1964), 21-27.

John W. Hall. "A Monarch for Modern Japan," in Robert E. Ward, ed. POLITICAL DEVELOPMENT IN MODERN JAPAN (1965: Princeton University Press), 11-64.

Byron K. Marshall. CAPITALISM AND NATIONALISM IN PREWAR JAPAN: THE IDEOLOGY OF THE BUSINESS ELITE, 1868-1941. 1967: Stanford University Press.

Daniel C. Holtom. THE NATIONAL FAITH OF JAPAN: A STUDY IN MODERN SHINTO. 1938: Dutton.

_____. MODERN JAPAN AND SHINTO NATIONALISM. Revised edition. 1947: University of Chicago Press.

Nobushige Hozumi. ANCESTOR WORSHIP AND JAPANESE LAW. 6th edition. 1940: Maruzen.

John Paul Reed. KOKUTAI: A STUDY OF CERTAIN SACRED AND SECULAR ASPECTS OF JAPANESE NATIONALISM. 1940: University of Chicago Press.

Carol Gluck. JAPAN'S MODERN MYTHS: IDEOLOGY IN THE LATE MEIJI PERIOD. 1985: Princeton University Press.

Tetsuo Najita. JAPAN: THE INTELLECTUAL FOUNDATIONS OF MODERN JAPANESE POLITICS. 1974; 1980: University of Chicago Press.

_____. "Nakano Seigo and the Spirit of the Meiji Restoration," in James Morley, ed. DILEMMAS OF GROWTH IN PREWAR JAPAN (1971: Princeton University Press), 375-421.

Leslie Oates. NAKANO SEIGO (1886-1943). 1982: University of Queensland Press.

NATIONALISM & THE EMPEROR SYSTEM--II

Delmer M. Brown. NATIONALISM IN JAPAN: AN INTRODUCTORY HISTORICAL ANALYSIS. 1955: University of California Press.

Marlene Mayo, ed. THE EMERGENCE OF IMPERIAL JAPAN: SELF DEFENSE OR CALCULATED AGGRESSION? 1970: Heath. See especially essays by Yoshitake Oka and Sannosuke Matsumoto.

Kimitada Miwa. "The Rejection of Localism: An Origin of Ultranationalism in Japan," *Japan Interpreter* 9.1 (1974), 68-79.

Grant Goodman, ed. IMPERIAL JAPAN AND ASIA--A REASSESSMENT. 1967: Occasional Papers of the East Asia Institute, Columbia University.

Wilbur M. Fridell. "Government Ethics Textbooks in Late Meiji Japan," *Journal of Asian Studies* 29.4 (1970), 823-834.

Harold J. Wray. "A Study in Contrasts: Japanese School Textbooks, 1903 and 1941-1945," *Monumenta Nipponica* 27.1 (1973), 69-86.

Kenneth B. Pyle. "The Technology of Japanese Nationalism: The Local Improvement Movement, 1900-1918," *Journal of Asian Studies* 33.1 (1973), 51-65.

Mikiso Hane. "Nationalism and the Decline of Liberalism in Meiji Japan," *Studies on Asia* 4 (1963), 69-80.

Osamu Kuno. "The Meiji State, Minponshugi and Ultranationalism," in J.V. Koschmann, ed. AUTHORITY & THE INDIVIDUAL IN JAPAN (1978: University of Tokyo Press), 60-80.

Kimitada Miwa. "Fukuzawa Yukichi's 'Departure from Asia': A Prelude to the Sino-Japanese War," in Edmund Skrzypczak, ed. JAPAN'S MODERN CENTURY (1968: Tuttle), 1-26.

Albert M. Craig. "Fukuzawa Yukichi: The Philosophical Foundations of Meiji Nationalism," in Robert Ward, ed. POLITICAL DEVELOPMENT IN MODERN JAPAN (1965: Princeton University Press), 99-148.

Symposium on Japanese Nationalism, *Journal of Asian Studies* 31.1 (1971). Kenneth Pyle, "Some Recent Approaches to Japanese Nationalism" (5-16); Tetsuo Najita, "Restorationism in the Political Thought of Yamagata Daini (1725-1767)" (17-30); Fred Notehelfer, "Kotoku Shusui & Nationalism" (31-40); Peter Duus, "Nagai Ryutaro & the 'White Peril,' 1905-1944" (41-48); Sannosuke Matsumoto, "The Significance of Nationalism in Modern Japanese Thought" (49-56); Harry Harootunian, "Nationalism as Intellectual History" (57-62).

Donald Keene. "The Sino-Japanese War of 1894-95 and Japanese Culture," in his LANDSCAPES AND PORTRAITS: APPRECIATIONS OF JAPANESE CULTURE (1971: Kodansha International), 259-299.

E. H. Norman. "The Genyosha: A Study in the Origins of Japanese Imperialism," *Pacific Affairs* 17 (1944), 261-284.

Inazo Nitobe. BUSHIDO: THE SOUL OF JAPAN. 1899; reprinted 1969: Tuttle.

George M. Wilson. RADICAL NATIONALIST IN JAPAN: KITA IKKI, 1883-1937. 1969: Harvard University Press.

Koichi Nomura. "Kita Ikki," *Developing Economies* 4.2 (1966), 231-244.

Thomas R. H. Havens. FARM AND NATION IN MODERN JAPAN: AGRARIAN NATIONALISM, 1870-1940. 1974: Princeton University Press.

Richard J. Smethurst. A SOCIAL BASIS FOR PREWAR JAPANESE MILITARISM: THE ARMY AND THE RURAL COMMUNITY. 1974: University of California Press.

NATIONALISM & THE EMPEROR SYSTEM--III

Henry D. Smith, II. Review of preceding two books by Havens and Smethurst, *Journal of Japanese Studies* 2.1 (1976), 131-147.

Herbert P. Bix. "Rethinking 'Emperor-System Fascism': Ruptures and Continuities in Modern Japanese History," *Bulletin of Concerned Asian Studies* 14.2 (1982), 2-19.

_____. "Emperor-System Fascism: A Study of the Shift Process in Japanese Politics," *Shakai Rodo Kenkyu* 27.2 and 27.3-4 (1981), 1-14, 99-129.

Ben-Ami Shillony. REVOLT IN JAPAN: THE YOUNG OFFICERS AND THE FEBRUARY 26, 1936 INCIDENT. 1972: Princeton University Press.

_____. POLITICS AND CULTURE IN WARTIME JAPAN. 1982: Oxford University Press.

George M. Wilson, ed. CRISIS POLITICS IN PREWAR JAPAN. 1970: Monumenta Nipponica Monographs.

Richard Storry. THE DOUBLE PATRIOTS: A STUDY OF JAPANESE NATIONALISM. 1957: Houghton Mifflin.

Donald Keene. "Japanese Literature and Politics in the 1930s," *Journal of Japanese Studies* 2.2 (1976), 225-248.

_____. "Japanese Writers and the Greater East Asia War," in his LANDSCAPES AND PORTRAITS (1971: Kodansha International), 300-321; article originally published in 1964.

_____. "The Barren Years: Japanese War Literature," *Monumenta Nipponica* 33.1 (1978), 67-112.

_____. "War Literature," in his DAWN TO THE WEST: JAPANESE LITERATURE OF THE MODERN ERA (1984: Holt, Rinehart & Winston), 906-961.

Louis Allen. "Japanese Literature of the Second World War," *Proceedings of the British Association for Japanese Studies*, volume 2, part 1 (1977), 117-152.

James B. Crowley. "A New Asian Order: Some Notes on Prewar Japanese Nationalism," in Bernard Silberman & H. Harootunian, eds. JAPAN IN CRISIS (1974: Princeton University Press), 270-298.

_____. "Intellectuals as Visionaries of the New Asian Order," in James Morley, ed. DILEMMAS OF GROWTH IN PREWAR JAPAN (1971: Princeton University Press), 319-373.

_____. "A New Deal for Japan and Asia: One Road to Pearl Harbor," in his MODERN EAST ASIA: ESSAYS IN INTERPRETATION (1970: Harcourt Brace & World), 235-264.

Ivan Morris. "If Only We Might Fall . . . ," an essay on the kamikaze pilots in his THE NOBILITY OF FAILURE: TRAGIC HEROES IN THE HISTORY OF JAPAN (1975: Holt, Rinehart & Winston), 276-334.

Otto D. Tolischus, ed. THROUGH JAPANESE EYES. 1945: Reynal & Hitchcock. Quotations by Japanese ideologues.

Shinichi Fujii. TENNO SEIJI: DIRECT IMPERIAL RULE. 1944: Yuhikaku.

Joshua A. Fogel. POLITICS AND SINOLOGY: THE CASE OF NAITO KONAN (1866-1934). 1984: Harvard East Asian Monographs.

"FASCISM," MILITARISM & THE SHOWA CRISIS

Masao Maruyama. THOUGHT AND BEHAVIOR IN MODERN JAPANESE POLITICS. Ivan Morris, ed. 1963: Oxford University Press. Classic early postwar essays. See especially "The Ideology and Dynamics of Japanese Fascism" (1947).

Tetsuo Najita & J. Victor Koschmann, eds. CONFLICT IN MODERN JAPANESE HISTORY: THE NEGLECTED TRADITION. 1982: Princeton University Press.

Peter Duus & Daniel Okimoto. "Fascism and the History of Pre-War Japan: The Failure of a Concept," *Journal of Asian Studies* 39.1 (1979), 65-76.

Gordon M. Berger. "Changing Historiographical Perspectives on Early Showa Politics: 'The Second Approach'," *Journal of Asian Studies* 34.2 (1975), 473-484.

W. Miles Fletcher. "Intellectuals and Fascism in Early Showa Japan," *Journal of Asian Studies* 39.1 (1979), 39-63.

_____. THE SEARCH FOR A NEW ORDER: INTELLECTUALS AND FASCISM IN PREWAR JAPAN. 1982: University of North Carolina Press.

Germaine Hoston. "Marxism and Japanese Expansionism: Takahashi Kamekichi and the Theory of Petty Imperialism," *Journal of Asian Studies* 10.1 (1984), 1-30.

Jon Halliday. A POLITICAL HISTORY OF JAPANESE CAPITALISM. 1975: Pantheon. See especially 133-140 on "The Question of Japanese 'Fascism'."

E. J. Hobsbawn. "Vulnerable Japan," *New York Review of Books* 22 (1975), 26-32.

George M. Wilson. "A New Look at the Problem of 'Japanese Fascism'," *Comparative Studies in Society and History* 10.4 (1968), 401-412.

Barrington Moore, Jr. SOCIAL ORIGINS OF DICTATORSHIP AND DEMOCRACY (1966: Beacon), 228-313.

Ronald Dore. "Making Sense of History," *Archives Europeennes de Sociologie* 10.2 (1969), 295-305. Review of Barrington Moore's SOCIAL ORIGINS.

_____ & Tsutomu Ouchi. "Rural Origins of Japanese Fascism," in James Morley, ed. DILEMMAS OF GROWTH IN PREWAR JAPAN (1971: Princeton University Press), 181-209. Critique of Barrington Moore.

Shuichi Kato. "Taisho Democracy As the Pre-Stage for Japanese Militarism," in B. Silberman & H. Harootunian, eds. JAPAN IN CRISIS (1974: Princeton University Press), 217-236.

Seizaburo Shinobu. "From Party Politics to Military Dictatorship," *Developing Economies* 5.4 (1967), 666-684.

Sannosuke Matsumoto. "The Roots of Political Disillusionment: 'Public' and 'Private' in Japan," in J. Victor Koschmann, ed. AUTHORITY AND THE INDIVIDUAL IN JAPAN (1978: Tokyo University Press), 31-51.

Herbert Bix. "Kawakami Hajime and the Organic Law of Japanese Fascism," *Japan Interpreter* 12.1 (1978), 118-133.

_____. "Rethinking 'Emperor-System Fascism': Ruptures and Continuities in Modern Japanese History," *Bulletin of Concerned Asian Scholars* 14.2 (1982), 2-19.

_____. "Emperor-System Fascism: A Study of the Shift Process in Japanese Politics," *Shakai Rodo Kenkyu* 27.2 and 27.3-4 (1981), 1-14, 99-129.

Gavan McCormack. "Nineteen-Thirties Japan: Fascism?" *Bulletin of Concerned Asian Scholars* 14.2 (1982), 20-32.

97

"FASCISM," MILITARISM & THE SHOWA CRISIS--II

Gregory Kasza. "Fascism From Below? A Comparative Perspective on the Japanese Right, 1931- 1936," *Journal of Contemporary History* 19.4 (1984), 607-630.

Takeshi Ishida. "Elements of Tradition and 'Renovation' in Japan During the 'Era of Fascism'," *Social Science Abstracts* 17 (Shakai Kagaku Kenkyujo, Tokyo University, 1976), 111-140.

Jiro Kamishima. "Mental Structure of the Emperor System," *Developing Economies* 5.4 (1967), 702-726.

Noboru Kojima. "Militarism and the Emperor System," *Japan Interpreter* 8.2 (1973), 219-227.

Chihiro Hosoya. "The Military and the Foreign Policy of Prewar Japan," *Hitotsubashi Journal of Law and Politics* 7
(1974), 1-7.

Ivan Morris, ed. JAPAN 1931-1945: MILITARISM, FASCISM, JAPANISM? 1963: Heath.

Heinz Lubasz, ed. FASCISM: THREE MAJOR REGIMES. 1973: Wiley. Excerpts from Richard Storry, Robert Scalapino, Masao Maruyama, Fairbank-Reischauer-Craig text, plus statements by Kita Ikki, Prince Konoe, and General Araki.

Y. M. Zhukov, ed. THE RISE AND FALL OF THE GUNBATSU: A STUDY IN MILITARY HISTORY. 1975: Progress. An orthodox Soviet analysis.

Sakuzo Yoshino. "Fascism in Japan," *Contemporary Japan* 1.2 (1932), 185-197.

O. Tanin & E. Yohan. MILITARISM AND FASCISM IN JAPAN. 1934: International. Marxist analysis, with introduction by Karl Radek.

Emil Lederer. "Fascist Tendencies in Japan," *Pacific Affairs* 7 (1934), 373-385.

Toshio Shiratori. "Fascism versus Popular Front," *Contemporary Japan* 6.4 (1938), 581-589.

Otto Koellreutter. "National Socialism and Japan," *Contemporary Japan* 8.2 (1939), 194-202.

Victor A. Yakhontoff. "The Fascist Movement in Japan," *Science and Society* 3.1 (1939), 28-41.

Saburo Ienaga. THE PACIFIC WAR, 1931-1945. 1968; transl. 1978: Pantheon.

Gordon M. Berger. PARTIES OUT OF POWER IN JAPAN, 1931-1941. 1977: Princeton University Press. See also review by M. Peattie in *Journal of Japanese Studies* 4.1 (1978), 198-208.

_____. "Imperial Rule Assistance Association," KODANSHA ENCYCLOPEDIA OF JAPAN 3: 280-281.

Richard J. Smethurst. A SOCIAL BASIS FOR PREWAR JAPANESE MILITARISM: THE ARMY AND THE RURAL COMMUNITY. 1974: University of California Press.

Richard H. Mitchell. THOUGHT CONTROL IN PREWAR JAPAN. 1976: Cornell University Press. See also the critique of this study by Herbert Bix in *Japan Interpreter* 12.1 (1978), 118-133.

_____. "Japan's Peace Preservation Law of 1925, Its Origin and Significance," *Monumenta Nipponica* 28.3 (1973), 317-346.

_____. CENSORSHIP IN IMPERIAL JAPAN. 1984: Princeton University Press.

Richard Deacon. KEMPEITAI: A HISTORY OF THE JAPANESE SECRET SERVICE. 1983: Beaufort.

"FASCISM," MILITARISM & THE SHOWA CRISIS--III

George M. Wilson. RADICAL NATIONALIST IN JAPAN: KITA IKKI, 1883-1937. 1969: Harvard University Press.

Sharon Minichiello. RETREAT FROM REFORM: PATTERNS OF POLITICAL BEHAVIOR IN INTERWAR JAPAN. 1984: University of Hawaii Press.

Robert Scalapino. DEMOCRACY AND THE PARTY MOVEMENT IN PREWAR JAPAN. 1953: University of California Press.

Hugh Borton. JAPAN SINCE 1931: ITS POLITICAL AND SOCIAL DEVELOPMENT. 1940: Institute of Pacific Relations.

James W. Morley, ed. DILEMMAS OF GROWTH IN PREWAR JAPAN. 1971: Princeton University Press.

George M. Wilson, ed. CRISIS POLITICS IN PREWAR JAPAN: INSTITUTIONAL AND IDEOLOGICAL PROBLEMS OF THE 1930S. 1970: Monumenta Nipponica Monographs. Articles by Wilson on "renovation," Ben-Ami Shillony on military radicals, and Robert Spaulding on renovationist bureaucrats.

James B. Crowley. JAPAN'S QUEST FOR AUTONOMY: NATIONAL SECURITY AND FOREIGN POLICY, 1930-1938. 1966: Princeton University Press.

Mark R. Peattie. ISHIWARA KANJI AND JAPAN'S CONFRONTATION WITH THE WEST. 1975: Princeton University Press.

Saburo Shiroyama. WAR CRIMINAL: THE LIFE AND DEATH OF HIROTA KOKI. 1974; transl. 1977: Kodansha International.

Yoshitake Oka. KONOE FUMIMARO: A POLITICAL BIOGRAPHY. Shumpei Okamoto & Patricia Murray, transl. 1983: University of Tokyo Press.

Gordon M. Berger. "Japan's Young Prince: Konoe Fumimaro's Early Political Career, 1916-31," *Monumenta Nipponica* 29.4 (1974), 451-476.

Ben-Ami Shillony. REVOLT IN JAPAN: THE YOUNG OFFICERS AND THE FEBRUARY 26, 1936 INCIDENT. 1973: Princeton University Press.

_____. "The February 26 Affair: Politics of a Military Insurrection," in George Wilson, ed. CRISIS POLITICS IN PREWAR JAPAN (1970: Monumenta Nipponica Monographs), 25-50.

_____. "Myth and Reality in Japan of the 1930s," in W. J. Beasley, ed. MODERN JAPAN: ASPECTS OF HISTORY, LITERATURE AND SOCIETY (1975: Allen & Unwin), 81-88.

_____. "Japanese Intellectuals During the Pacific War," *Proceedings of the British Association for Japanese Studies,* volume 2, part 1 (1977), 90-99.

_____. POLITICS AND CULTURE IN WARTIME JAPAN. 1982: Oxford University Press.

Richard Rice. "Economic Mobilization in Wartime Japan: Business, Bureaucracy, and Military in Conflict," *Journal of Asian Studies* 38.4 (1979), 689-706.

Chalmers Johnson. MITI AND THE JAPANESE MIRACLE. 1982: Stanford University Press. See especially chapters on pre-1945 Ministry of Commerce and Industry & Munitions Ministry.

Ernest J. Notar. "Japan's Wartime Labor Policy: A Search for Method," *Journal of Asian Studies* 44.2 (1985), 311-328.

Zdenka Vasiljevova. "The Industrial Patriotic Movement: A Study on the Structure of Fascist Dictatorship in Wartime Japan," in Vdasta Hilska & Zdenka Vasiljevova, PROBLEMS OF MODERN JAPANESE SOCIETY (1971: Universita Karlova, Praha), 65-157.

Robert J. C. Butow. TOJO AND THE COMING OF THE WAR. 1961: Princeton University Press.

David Anson Titus. PALACE AND POLITICS IN PREWAR JAPAN. 1974: Columbia University Press.

David Bergamini. JAPAN'S IMPERIAL CONSPIRACY. 1971: Morrow.

Charles D. Sheldon. "Japan's Aggression and the Emperor, 1931-1941, from Contemporary Diaries," *Modern Asian Studies* 10.1 (1976), 1-40.

Mikiso Hane, transl. EMPEROR HIROHITO AND HIS CHIEF AIDE-DE-CAMP: THE HONJO DIARY, 1933-36. 1983: University of Tokyo Press.

Sei-ichi Imai. "Cabinet, Emperor and Senior Statesmen," in Dorothy Borg & Shumpei Okamoto, eds. PEARL HARBOR AS HISTORY (1973: Columbia University Press), 53-79.

Tessa Morris-Suzuki. SHOWA: AN INSIDE HISTORY OF HIROHITO'S JAPAN. 1984: Athlone.

Mainichi Daily News. FIFTY YEARS OF LIGHT AND DARK: THE HIROHITO ERA. 1975: Mainichi Newspapers.

Thomas Havens. VALLEY OF DARKNESS: THE JAPANESE PEOPLE AND WORLD WAR TWO. 1978: Norton.

IMPERIALISM, COLONIALISM & WAR [see also the "Japan Abroad" bibliography, pp. 117-174 below]

Paul H. Clyde & Burton F. Beers. THE FAR EAST: A HISTORY OF THE WESTERN IMPACT AND THE EASTERN RESPONSE. 5th edition. 1971: Prentice-Hall.

James W. Morley, ed. JAPAN'S FOREIGN POLICY, 1868-1941: A RESEARCH GUIDE. 1974: Columbia University Press.

Ian Nish. JAPANESE FOREIGN POLICY, 1869-1942. 1977: Routledge & Kegan Paul.

Robert A. Scalapino, ed. THE FOREIGN POLICY OF MODERN JAPAN. 1977: University of California Press.

Michael Blaker. JAPANESE INTERNATIONAL NEGOTIATING STYLE. 1977: Columbia University Press.

Kazuo Shibagaki. The Logic of Japanese Imperialism," *Social Science Abstracts* 14 (Shakai Kagaku Kenkyujo, Tokyo University, 1973), 70-87.

Richard Storry. JAPAN AND THE DECLINE OF THE WEST IN ASIA. 1979: Macmillan.

Frances V. Moulder. JAPAN, CHINA AND THE MODERN WORLD ECONOMY: TOWARD A REINTERPRETATION OF EAST ASIAN DEVELOPMENT, ca. 1600 to ca. 1918. 1977: Cambridge University Press.

James B. Crowley. "Japan's Foreign Military Policies," in James W. Morley, ed. JAPAN'S FOREIGN POLICY (1974: Columbia University Press), 3-117.

Akira Iriye. "The Historical Background," in his THE COLD WAR IN ASIA: A HISTORICAL INTRODUCTION (1974: Prentice-Hall), 8-46.

_____. PACIFIC ESTRANGEMENT: JAPANESE AND AMERICAN EXPANSION, 1897-1911. 1972: Harvard University Press.

Grant Goodman, ed. IMPERIAL JAPAN AND ASIA--A REASSESSMENT. 1967: Occasional Papers for the East Asia Institute, Columbia University.

Marius B. Jansen. "Modernization and Foreign Policy in Meiji Japan," in Robert Ward, ed. POLITICAL DEVELOPMENT IN MODERN JAPAN (1968: Princeton University Press), 149-188.

_____. "Japanese Views of China During the Meiji Period," in Albert Feuerwerker et al. APPROACHES TO MODERN CHINESE HISTORY (1967: University of California Press), 163-189.

_____. JAPAN AND CHINA: FROM WAR TO PEACE, 1894-1972. 1975: Rand McNally.

Joshua Fogel. POLITICS AND SINOLOGY: THE CASE OF NAITO KONAN. 1984: Harvard East Asian Monographs.

Munemitsu Mutsu. KENKENROKU: A DIPLOMATIC RECORD OF THE SINO-JAPANESE WAR, 1894-1895. Gordon M. Berger, transl. 1982: Princeton University Press.

Shumpei Okamoto. THE JAPANESE OLIGARCHY AND THE RUSSO-JAPANESE WAR. 1971: Columbia University Press.

F. Hilary Conroy. THE JAPANESE SEIZURE OF KOREA, 1868-1910: A STUDY OF REALISM AND IDEALISM IN INTERNATIONAL RELATIONS. 1960: University of Pennsylvania Press.

Andrew C. Nahm, ed. KOREA UNDER JAPANESE COLONIAL RULE: STUDIES OF THE POLICY AND TECHNIQUES OF JAPANESE COLONIALISM. 1973: Center for Korean Studies, Institute of International and Area Studies, Western Michigan University.

Ramon H. Myers & Mark R. Peattie, eds. THE JAPANESE COLONIAL EMPIRE 1895-1945. 1984: Princeton University Press.

101

E. Patricia Tsurumi. JAPANESE COLONIAL EDUCATION IN TAIWAN, 1895-1945. 1977: Harvard University Press.

Ian Nish. THE ANGLO-JAPANESE ALLIANCE: THE DIPLOMACY OF TWO ISLAND EMPIRES, 1894-1907. 1966: Athlone.

_____. ALLIANCE IN DECLINE: A STUDY IN ANGLO-JAPANESE RELATIONS, 1908-1923. 1972: Athlone.

Roger Dingman. POWER IN THE PACIFIC: THE ORIGINS OF NAVAL ARMS LIMITATION, 1914-1922. 1976: University of Chicago Press.

James Morley. THE JAPANESE THRUST INTO SIBERIA, 1918. 1957: Columbia University Press.

Takashi Saito. "Japan's Foreign Policy in the International Environment of the Nineteen-Twenties," *Developing Economies* 5.4 (1967), 685-701.

Akira Iriye. AFTER IMPERIALISM: THE SEARCH FOR A NEW ORDER IN THE FAR EAST, 1921-1931. 1965: Harvard University Press.

_____. "The Failure of Economic Expansion: 1918-1931," in B. Silberman & H. Harootunian, eds. JAPAN IN CRISIS (1974: Princeton University Press), 237-269.

_____. "The Failure of Military Expansionism," in James Morley, ed. DILEMMAS OF GROWTH IN PREWAR JAPAN (1971: Princeton University Press), 107-138.

Nobuya Bamba. JAPANESE DIPLOMACY IN A DILEMMA: NEW LIGHT ON JAPAN'S CHINA POLICY, 1924-1929. 1972: University of British Columbia Press.

Richard Storry. "The Road to War: 1931-1945," in Arthur E. Tiedemann, ed. AN INTRODUCTION TO JAPANESE CIVILIZATION (1974: Heath), 247-276.

Sadako Ogata. DEFIANCE IN MANCHURIA: THE MAKING OF JAPANESE FOREIGN POLICY, 1931-1932. 1964: University of California Press.

Mark Peattie. ISHIWARA KANJI AND JAPAN'S CONFRONTATION WITH THE WEST. 1975: Princeton University Press.

Christopher Thorne. THE LIMITS OF FOREIGN POLICY: THE WEST, THE LEAGUE AND THE FAR EASTERN CRISIS OF 1931-1933. 1973: Oxford University Press.

Gordon Berger. "The Three-dimensional Empire: Japanese Attitudes and the New Order in Asia, 1937-1945," *Japan Interpreter* 12.3-4 (1979), 355-383.

James B. Crowley. JAPAN'S QUEST FOR AUTONOMY: NATIONAL SECURITY AND FOREIGN POLICY, 1930-1938. 1968: Princeton University Press.

_____. "A New Asian Order: Some Notes on Prewar Japanese Nationalism," in Silberman & Harootunian, JAPAN IN CRISIS (1974: Princeton University Press), 270-298.

_____. "Intellectuals as Visionaries of the New Asian Order," in Morley, DILEMMAS OF GROWTH IN PREWAR JAPAN (1971: Princeton University Press), 319-373.

_____. "A New Deal for Japan and Asia: One Road to Pearl Harbor," in Crowley, MODERN EAST ASIA: ESSAYS IN INTERPRETATION (1970: Harcourt Brace & World), 235-264.

James Morley, ed. JAPAN ERUPTS: THE LONDON NAVAL CONFERENCE & THE MANCHURIAN INCIDENT, 1928-1932. 1984: Columbia University Press. First in a projected 5-volume version of the 1962-1963 Japanese series *Taiheiyo Senso e no Michi* (Road to the Pacific War).

_____. THE CHINA QUAGMIRE: JAPAN'S EXPANSION ON THE ASIAN CONTINENT, 1933-1941. 1983: Columbia University Press.

_____. DETERRENT DIPLOMACY: JAPAN, GERMANY, AND THE USSR, 1935-1940. 1976: Columbia University Press.

_____. THE FATEFUL CHOICE: JAPAN'S ADVANCE INTO SOUTHEAST ASIA, 1939-1941. 1980: Columbia University Press.

Stephen Pelz. RACE TO PEARL HARBOR: THE FAILURE OF THE SECOND LONDON NAVAL CONFERENCE AND THE ONSET OF WORLD WAR II. 1974: Harvard University Press.

Saburo Shiroyama. WAR CRIMINAL: THE LIFE AND DEATH OF HIROTA KOKI. 1974: Kodansha International.

Hiroyuki Agawa. THE RELUCTANT ADMIRAL: YAMAMOTO AND THE IMPERIAL NAVY. 1979: Kodansha International.

Robert J. C. Butow. TOJO AND THE COMING OF THE WAR. 1961: Stanford University Press.

J. W. Dower. EMPIRE AND AFTERMATH: YOSHIDA SHIGERU AND THE JAPANESE EXPERIENCE, 1878-1954. 1979: Harvard East Asian Monographs.

F. C. Jones. JAPAN'S NEW ORDER IN EAST ASIA: ITS RISE AND FALL, 1937-45. 1954: Oxford University Press.

Richard Deacon. KEMPEITAI: A HISTORY OF THE JAPANESE SECRET SERVICE. 1983: Beaufort.

Nobutake Ike, transl. JAPAN'S DECISION FOR WAR: RECORDS OF THE 1941 POLICY CONFERENCES. 1967: Stanford University Press.

Louis Morton. "Japan's Decision for War," in K. R. Greenfield, ed. COMMAND DECISIONS (1959: Harcourt Brace), 63-87.

John McKechney, S. J. "The Pearl Harbor Controversy: A Debate Among Historians," *Monumenta Nipponica* 18.1-4 (1963), 45-88.

Dorothy Borg & Shumpei Okamoto, eds. PEARL HARBOR AS HISTORY: JAPANESE-AMERICAN RELATIONS, 1931-1941. 1973: Columbia University Press.

Gordon W. Prange. AT DAWN WE SLEPT: THE UNTOLD STORY OF PEARL HARBOR. 1981: Penguin.

H. P. Willmott. EMPIRES IN THE BALANCE: JAPANESE AND ALLIED PACIFIC STRATEGIES TO APRIL 1942. 1982: Naval Institute Press.

John J. Stephan. HAWAII UNDER THE RISING SUN: JAPAN'S PLANS FOR CONQUEST AFTER PEARL HARBOR. 1984: University of Hawaii Press.

Saburo Ienaga. THE PACIFIC WAR, 1931-1945. 1978: Pantheon.

John Costello. THE PACIFIC WAR, 1941-1945. 1982: Quill.

Ronald H. Spector. EAGLE AGAINST THE SUN: THE AMERICAN WAR WITH JAPAN. 1984: Free Press.

John Toland. THE RISING SUN: THE DECLINE AND FALL OF THE JAPANESE EMPIRE, 1936-1945. 1970: Random House.

David Bergamini. JAPAN'S IMPERIAL CONSPIRACY. 1971: Morrow.

Joyce Lebra, ed. JAPAN'S GREATER EAST ASIA CO-PROSPERITY SPHERE IN WORLD WAR II: SELECTED READINGS AND DOCUMENTS. 1975: Oxford University Press.

_____. JAPANESE-TRAINED ARMIES IN SOUTHEAST ASIA: INDEPENDENCE AND VOLUNTEER FORCES IN WORLD WAR II. 1977: Columbia University Press.

_____. JUNGLE ALLIANCE: JAPAN AND THE INDIAN NATIONAL ARMY. 1971: Donald Moore.

"The War and Japan: Revisionist Views," Special Issue of *Japan Echo* 11 (1984). Articles by Japanese writers.

Akira Iriye. POWER AND CULTURE: THE JAPANESE-AMERICAN WAR, 1941-1945. 1981: Harvard University Press.

John W. Dower. "Rethinking World War Two in Asia," *Reviews in American History* 12.2 (1984), 155-169.

_____. WAR WITHOUT MERCY: RACE AND POWER IN THE PACIFIC WAR. 1986: Pantheon.

SOCIETY, CULTURE & LAW

Irene Tauber. THE POPULATION OF JAPAN. 1958: Princeton University Press.

Tadashi Fukutake. THE JAPANESE SOCIAL STRUCTURE: ITS EVOLUTION IN THE MODERN CENTURY. Ronald Dore, transl. 1982: Columbia University Press & University of Tokyo Press.

_____. JAPANESE SOCIETY TODAY. 1974: University of Tokyo Press.

_____. JAPANESE RURAL SOCIETY. 1967: Cornell University Press.

_____. MAN AND SOCIETY IN JAPAN. 1962: University of Tokyo Press.

H. Paul Varley. JAPANESE CULTURE: A SHORT HISTORY. 3rd edition. 1984: University of Hawaii Press.

Takie Sugiyama Lebra. JAPANESE PATTERNS OF BEHAVIOR. 1976: University of Hawaii Press.

_____ & William P. Lebra, eds. JAPANESE CULTURE AND BEHAVIOR: SELECTED READINGS. 1974: University of Hawaii Press.

Robert J. Smith. JAPANESE SOCIETY: TRADITION, SELF AND THE SOCIAL ORDER. 1985: Cambridge University Press.

Chie Nakane. JAPANESE SOCIETY. 1970: University of California Press.

Takeshi Ishida. JAPANESE SOCIETY. 1972: University Press of America.

Hajime Nakamura. WAYS OF THINKING OF EASTERN PEOPLES: INDIA, CHINA, TIBET, JAPAN. 1964: University of Hawaii Press.

Hiroshi Minami. PSYCHOLOGY OF THE JAPANESE PEOPLE. 1971: University of Toronto Press.

Takeo Doi. THE ANATOMY OF DEPENDENCE. 1973: Kodansha International.

George A. DeVos. SOCIALIZATION FOR ACHIEVEMENT: ESSAYS ON THE CULTURAL PSYCHOLOGY OF THE JAPANESE. 1973: University of California Press.

Donald Roden. "Forays into Japanese Cultural Psychology," *Bulletin of Concerned Asian Scholars* 6.2 (1974), 27-32. Critique of DeVos.

Bradley M. Richardson. THE POLITICAL CULTURE OF JAPAN. 1974: University of California Press.

Arthur E. Tiedemann, ed. AN INTRODUCTION TO JAPANESE CIVILIZATION. 1974: Heath. Includes survey essays on society (Koya Azumi), religion (Wm. Theodore DeBary), law (Dan Fenno Henderson), literature (Donald Keene), and art (Hugo Munsterberg).

John W. Hall & Richard Beardsley, eds. TWELVE DOORS TO JAPAN. 1965: McGraw-Hill. Includes survey essays from various disciplinary perspectives.

R. K. Beardsley, J. W. Hall & R. E. Ward. VILLAGE JAPAN. 1959: University of Chicago Press.

Kurt Steiner. LOCAL GOVERNMENT IN JAPAN. 1965: Stanford University Press.

John Embree. SUYE MURA. 1939: University of Chicago Press. The only prewar anthropological study in English based on field work in Japan.

Robert J. Smith & Ella Lury Wiswell. THE WOMEN OF SUYE MURA. 1982: University of Chicago Press. Based on fieldwork conducted in the 1930s in conjunction with the preceding project.

SOCIETY, CULTURE & LAW--II

Kunio Yanagita. ABOUT OUR ANCESTORS: THE JAPANESE FAMILY SYSTEM. 1970: Japan Society for the Promotion of Science. Translation by Fanny Hagin Mayer & Yasuyo Ishiwara of essays by Japan's most eminent ethnologist.

J. Victor Koschmann, Keibo Oiwa & Shinji Yamashita, eds. INTERNATIONAL PERSPECTIVES ON YANAGITA KUNIO AND JAPANESE FOLKLORE STUDIES. 1985: China-Japan Program, Cornell University.

Kazuko Tsurumi. "Yanagita Kunio's Work as a Model of Endogenous Development," *Japan Quarterly* 22.3 (1975), 223-238.

Ronald Morse. "Personalities and Issues in Yanagita Kunio Studies," *Japan Quarterly* 22.3 (1975), 239-254.

_____. "The Search for Japan's National Character and Distinctiveness: Yanagita Kunio (1875-1962) and the Folklore Movement." 1975: Ph.D. dissertation in History, Princeton University.

_____, transl. LEGENDS OF TONO. 1975: Japan Foundation. An important transcription of local legends from Iwate prefecture by Yanagita.

Nyozekan Hasegawa. THE JAPANESE CHARACTER: A CULTURAL PROFILE. 1965: Kodansha International.

Kurt Singer. MIRROR, SWORD AND JEWEL: THE GEOMETRY OF JAPANESE LIFE. 1981: Kodansha International.

Ruth Benedict. THE CHRYSANTHEMUM AND THE SWORD. 1946: Houghton Mifflin. A famous study based on World War Two research on the Japanese "national character."

Lafcadio Hearn. JAPAN: AN ATTEMPT AT INTERPRETATION. 1913: Macmillan.

Carol Gluck. "The People in History: Recent Trends in Japanese Historiography," *Journal of Asian Studies* 38.1 (1978), 25-50.

Takeo Yazaki. SOCIAL CHANGE AND THE CITY IN JAPAN: FROM EARLIEST TIMES THROUGH THE CULTURAL REVOLUTION. 1968: Japan Publications.

Mikiso Hane. PEASANTS, REBELS, AND OUTCASTES: THE UNDERSIDE OF MODERN JAPAN. 1982: Pantheon.

Hugh Patrick, ed. JAPANESE INDUSTRIALIZATION AND ITS SOCIAL CONSEQUENCES. 1976: University of California Press.

Gary D. Allinson. JAPANESE URBANISM: INDUSTRY AND POLITICS IN KARIYA, 1872-1972. 1975: University of California Press.

Tetsuo Najita & J. Victor Koschmann, eds. CONFLICT IN MODERN JAPAN: THE NEGLECTED TRADITION. 1982: Princeton University Press.

J. Victor Koschmann, ed. AUTHORITY AND THE INDIVIDUAL IN JAPAN. 1978: University of Tokyo Press.

Kazuko Tsurumi. SOCIAL CHANGE AND THE INDIVIDUAL: JAPAN BEFORE AND AFTER DEFEAT IN WORLD WAR TWO. 1970: Princeton University Press.

Robert Bellah. "Values and Social Change in Modern Japan," *Asian Cultural Studies* 3 (International Christian University, 1962), 13-56.

____. BEYOND BELIEF: ESSAYS ON RELIGION IN A POST-TRADITIONAL WORLD. 1970: Harper & Row. Includes revised version of preceding article.

____. "Japan's Cultural Identity: Some Reflections on the Work of Watsuji Tetsuro," *Journal of Asian Studies* 24.4 (1965), 573-594.

Iarius B. Jansen, ed. CHANGING JAPANESE ATTITUDES TOWARD MODERNIZATION. 1965: Princeton University Press.

onald Dore, ed. ASPECTS OF SOCIAL CHANGE IN MODERN JAPAN. 1967: Princeton University Press.

onald Shivley, ed. TRADITION AND MODERNIZATION IN JAPANESE CULTURE. 1971: Princeton University Press.

zra F. Vogel, ed. MODERN JAPANESE ORGANIZATION AND DECISION-MAKING. 1975: University of California Press.

Ibert M. Craig, ed. JAPAN: A COMPARATIVE VIEW. 1979: Princeton University Press.

akeo Kuwabara. JAPAN AND WESTERN CIVILIZATION: ESSAYS ON COMPARATIVE CULTURE. Hidetoshi Kato, ed. 1984: University of Tokyo Press.

win Scheiner, ed. MODERN JAPAN: AN INTERPRETIVE ANTHOLOGY. 1974: Macmillan.

onald Keene. LANDSCAPES AND PORTRAITS: AN APPRECIATION OF JAPANESE CULTURE. 1971: Kodansha International.

V. G. Beasley, ed. MODERN JAPAN: ASPECTS OF HISTORY, LITERATURE AND SOCIETY. 1976: University of California Press.

George K. Yamamoto & Tsuyoshi Ishida, eds. SELECTED READINGS ON MODERN JAPANESE SOCIETY. 1971: McCutchan.

asushi Kuyama & Nobuo Kobayashi, eds. MODERNIZATION AND TRADITION IN JAPAN. 1969: International Institute for Japan Studies (Nishinomiya).

. J. Smith & R. K. Beardsley, eds. JAPANESE CULTURE: ITS DEVELOPMENT AND CHARACTERISTICS. 1962: Aldine.

ernard Silberman, ed. JAPANESE CHARACTER AND CULTURE. 1962: University of Arizona Press.

____. "*Ringisei*--Traditional Values or Organizational Imperatives in the Japanese Upper Civil Service, 1868-1945," *Journal of Asian Studies* 32.2 (1973), 251-264.

____ & H. Harootunian, eds. MODERN JAPANESE LEADERSHIP: TRANSITION AND CHANGE. 1966: Princeton University Press.

oseph Roggendorf, ed. STUDIES IN JAPANESE CULTURE. 1965: Monumenta Nipponica Monographs.

harles G. Cleaver. JAPANESE AND AMERICANS: CULTURAL PARALLELS AND PARADOXES. 1976: University of Minnesota Press.

ewis Austin, ed. JAPAN--THE PARADOX OF PROGRESS. 1976: Yale University Press.

. G. O'Neill, ed. TRADITION AND MODERN JAPAN. 1982: University of British Columbia Press.

107

SOCIETY, CULTURE & LAW--IV

Ivan Morris. THE NOBILITY OF FAILURE: TRAGIC HEROES IN THE HISTORY OF JAPAN. 1975: Holt, Rinehart & Winston.

Robert Jay Lifton et al. SIX LIVES, SIX DEATHS: PORTRAITS FROM MODERN JAPAN. 1979: Yale University Press.

Agnes N. Keith. BEFORE THE BLOSSOMS FALL: LIFE AND DEATH IN JAPAN. 1975: Little, Brown.

Stuart Picken. DEATH AND THE JAPANESE. 1985: Athlone.

David W. Plath. LONG ENGAGEMENTS: MATURITY IN MODERN JAPAN. 1980: Stanford University Press.

Albert Craig & Donald Shively, eds. PERSONALITY IN JAPANESE HISTORY. 1970: University of California Press.

Frank Gibney. FIVE GENTLEMEN OF JAPAN: THE PORTRAIT OF A NATION'S CHARACTER. 1953: Farrar, Straus & Young.

Joseph L. Anderson & Donald Richie. THE JAPANESE FILM: ART AND INDUSTRY. Expanded edition. 1984: Princeton University Press.

Donald Richie. THE JAPANESE MOVIE. 1982: Kodansha International.

_____. OZU: HIS LIFE AND FILMS. 1974: University of California Press.

_____. THE FILMS OF AKIRA KUROSAWA. Revised edition. 1984: University of California Press.

Noel Burch. TO THE DISTANT OBSERVER: FORM AND MEANING IN THE JAPANESE CINEMA. 1979: University of California Press.

Audie Bock. JAPANESE FILM DIRECTORS. 1978: Kodansha International.

Tadao Sato. CURRENTS IN JAPANESE CINEMA. 1982: Kodansha International.

John W. Dower & Japan Photographers Association, eds. A CENTURY OF JAPANESE PHOTOGRAPHY. 1980: Pantheon. Covers 1840s to 1945, with 514 plates and a survey essay.

Arthur von Mehren, ed. LAW IN JAPAN: THE LEGAL ORDER IN A CHANGING SOCIETY. 1963: Harvard University Press.

Dan Fenno Henderson. CONCILIATION AND JAPANESE LAW, TOKUGAWA AND MODERN. 2 volumes. 1965: University of Washington Press.

Rex Coleman & John Owen Haley, comp. AN INDEX TO JAPANESE LAW: A BIBLIOGRAPHY OF WESTERN LANGUAGE MATERIALS, 1867-1973. 1975: Japanese American Society for Legal Studies, University of Tokyo. Special issue of *Law in Japan: An Annual*.

EDUCATION & SCIENCE

Herbert Passin. SOCIETY AND EDUCATION IN JAPAN. 1965: Teachers College, Columbia University.

Government of Japan, Ministry of Education, ed. JAPAN'S MODERN EDUCATIONAL SYSTEM: A HISTORY OF THE FIRST HUNDRED YEARS. 1980: Ministry of Education.

Tokiomi Kaigo. JAPANESE EDUCATION: ITS PAST AND PRESENT. 1968: Kokusai Bunka Shinkokai.

Michio Nagai. "Westernization and Japanization: The Early Meiji Transformation of Education," in Donald Shively, ed. TRADITION & MODERNIZATION IN JAPANESE CULTURE (1971: Princeton University Press), 35-76.

E. P. Tsurumi. "Meiji Primary School Language and Ethics Textbooks: Old Values for a New Society?" *Modern Asian Studies* 8.2 (1974), 247-261.

Harold J. Wray. "A Study in Contrasts: Japanese School Textbooks of 1903 and 1941-5," *Monumenta Nipponica* 28.1 (1973), 69-86.

Earl H. Kinmonth. THE SELF-MADE MAN IN MEIJI JAPANESE THOUGHT: FROM SAMURAI TO SALARY MAN. 1981: University of California Press.

Donald Roden. SCHOOLDAYS IN IMPERIAL JAPAN: A STUDY IN THE CULTURE OF A STUDENT ELITE. 1980: University of California Press.

_____. "'Monasticism' and the Paradox of the Meiji Higher Schools," *Journal of Asian Studies* 37.3 (1978), 413-425.

_____. "Baseball and the Quest for National Dignity in Meiji Japan," *American Historical Review* 85.3 (1980), 511-534.

Byron K. Marshall. "Professors and Politics: The Meiji Academic Elite," *Journal of Japanese Studies* 3.1 (1977), 71-97.

_____. "Growth and Conflict in Japanese Higher Education, 1905-1930," in Tetsuo Najita & J. Victor Koschmann, eds. CONFLICT IN MODERN JAPANESE HISTORY (1982: Princeton Univ. Press), 276-294.

Toshiaki Okubo. "The Birth of the Modern University in Japan," *Journal of World History* 10.4 (1967), 763-779.

James Bartholomew. "Japanese Modernization and the Imperial Universities, 1876-1920," *Journal of Asian Studies* 37.2 (1978), 251-271.

Michio Nagai. HIGHER EDUCATION IN JAPAN: ITS TAKE-OFF AND CRASH. 1971: Univ. of Tokyo Press.

Thomas P. Rohlen. JAPAN'S HIGH SCHOOLS. 1983: University of California Press.

Shigeru Nakayama, David L. Swain & Eri Yagi, eds. SCIENCE AND SOCIETY IN MODERN JAPAN: SELECTED HISTORICAL SOURCES. 1974: Univ. of Tokyo Press & Massachusetts Institute of Technology Press.

Shigeru Nakayama. ACADEMIC AND SCIENTIFIC TRADITIONS IN CHINA, JAPAN, AND THE WEST. 1984: University of Tokyo Press.

James Bartholomew. "Japanese Culture and the Problem of Modern Science," in Arnold Thackray & Everett Mendelsohn, eds. SCIENCE AND VALUES (1975: Humanities Press), 109-155.

_____. "Science, Bureaucracy, and Freedom in Meiji and Taisho Japan," in Najita & Koschmann, CONFLICT IN MODERN JAPANESE HISTORY (1982: Princeton University Press), 226-257.

PHILOSOPHY & RELIGION

Gino Piovesana. RECENT JAPANESE PHILOSOPHICAL THOUGHT, 1862-1962: A SURVEY. 1968: Enderle.

_____. CONTEMPORARY JAPANESE PHILOSOPHICAL THOUGHT. 1969: St. John's University Press.

Winston Bradley Davis. TOWARD MODERNITY: A DEVELOPMENTAL TYPOLOGY OF POPULAR RELIGIOUS AFFILIATIONS IN JAPAN. 1977: Cornell University East Asia Papers.

Joseph Kitagawa. RELIGION IN JAPANESE HISTORY. 1966: Columbia University Press.

H. Byron Earhart. JAPANESE RELIGION: UNITY AND DIVERSITY. 3rd edition. 1982: Wadsworth.

_____, ed. RELIGION IN THE JAPANESE EXPERIENCE: SOURCES & INTERPRETATIONS. 1974: Duxbury.

_____, ed. THE NEW RELIGIONS OF JAPAN: A BIBLIOGRAPHY OF WESTERN LANGUAGE MATERIALS. 1983: Center for Japanese Studies, University of Michigan.

Shigeyoshi Murakami. JAPANESE RELIGION IN THE MODERN CENTURY. H. Byron Earhart, transl. 1980: University of Tokyo Press.

Edward Norbeck. RELIGION AND SOCIETY IN MODERN JAPAN: CONTINUITY AND CHANGE. 1970: Rice University Press.

Kiyomi Morioka & William H. Newell, eds. THE SOCIOLOGY OF JAPANESE RELIGION. 1968: Brill.

Daniel C. Holtom. THE NATIONAL FAITH OF JAPAN: A STUDY IN MODERN SHINTO. 1938: Dutton.

_____. MODERN JAPAN AND SHINTO NATIONALISM. 1943; revised edition, 1947: Univ. of Chicago Press.

Ichiro Hori, ed. JAPANESE RELIGION. 1972: Kodansha International.

_____. FOLK RELIGION IN JAPAN: CONTINUITY AND CHANGE. 1968: University of Tokyo Press & University of Chicago Press.

Tokutaro Sakurai. "The Major Features and Characteristics of Japanese Folk Belief," in Morioka and Newell, THE SOCIOLOGY OF JAPANESE RELIGION (1968: Brill), 13-24.

Robert J. Smith. ANCESTOR WORSHIP IN CONTEMPORARY JAPAN. 1974: Stanford University Press.

David Plath. "Where the Family of God Is the Family: The Role of the Dead in Japanese Households," _American Anthropologist_ 66.2 (1964), 300-317.

Carman Blacker. THE CATALPA BOW: A STUDY OF SHAMANISTIC PRACTICES IN JAPAN. 1975: Allen & Unwin.

Winston Bradley Davis. DOJO: MAGIC AND EXORCISM IN MODERN JAPAN. 1980: Stanford University Press.

H. Byron Earhart. A RELIGIOUS STUDY OF THE MT. HAGURO SECT OF SHUGENDO: AN EXAMPLE OF JAPANESE MOUNTAIN RELIGION. 1970: Monumenta Nipponica Monographs.

Kiyoko Takeda. "Japanese Christianity: Between Orthodoxy and Heterodoxy," in J. V. Koschmann, ed. AUTHORITY AND THE INDIVIDUAL IN JAPAN (1978: University of Tokyo Press), 82-107.

Irwin Scheiner. CHRISTIAN CONVERTS AND SOCIAL PROTEST IN MEIJI JAPAN. 1970: Univ. of Cal. Press.

Nobuya Bamba & John Howes, eds. PACIFISM IN JAPAN: THE CHRISTIAN AND SOCIALIST TRADITION. 1978: University of British Columbia Press.

George B. Bickle, Jr. THE NEW JERUSALEM: ASPECTS OF UTOPIANISM IN THE THOUGHT OF KAGAWA TOYOHIKO. 1976: University of Arizona Press.

WOMEN

Hesung Chun Koh et al., comp. KOREAN AND JAPANESE WOMEN: AN ANALYTIC BIBLIOGRAPHIC GUIDE. 1982: Greenwood.

Historical Studies

Joyce Ackroyd. "Women in Feudal Japan," *Transactions, Asiatic Society of Japan* (1959), 31-68.

Susan J. Pharr. "Japan: Historical and Contemporary Perspectives," in Janet Giele & Audrey Smock, eds. WOMEN: ROLE AND STATUS IN EIGHT COUNTRIES (1977: Wiley), 219-255.

Ronald P. Loftus. "Japanese Women in History and Society," *Journal of Ethnic Studies* 8.3 (1980), 109-122.

Junko Oguri & Nancy Andrew. "Women in Japanese Religion," KODANSHA ENCYCLOPEDIA OF JAPAN 8: 256-257.

Nancy Andrew. "History of Women in Japan," KODANSHA ENCYCLOPEDIA OF JAPAN 8: 257-260.

Joyce C. Lebra. "Women and Modernization," KODANSHA ENCYCLOPEDIA OF JAPAN 8: 260-261.

Susan J. Pharr. "Women in Contemporary Japan," KODANSHA ENCYCLOPEDIA OF JAPAN 8: 261-263.

Takashi Koyama. THE CHANGING SOCIAL POSITION OF WOMEN IN JAPAN. 1961: UNESCO (Paris).

Mary Beard. THE FORCE OF WOMEN IN JAPANESE HISTORY. 1953: Public Affairs.

Chiyoko Higuchi. HER PLACE IN THE SUN: WOMEN WHO SHAPED JAPAN. 1973: The East.

Mikiso Hane. PEASANTS, REBELS, AND OUTCASTES: THE UNDERSIDE OF MODERN JAPAN. 1982: Pantheon. See especially chapters on rural women (78-101) and poverty and prostitution (206-225) in Japan prior to 1945.

. Yamazaki. "Sandankan No. 8 Brothel," *Bulletin of Concerned Asian Scholars* 7.4 (1975), 52-60.

Alice Mabel Bacon. JAPANESE GIRLS AND WOMEN. 1902: Houghton Mifflin.

Sidney L. Gulick. WORKING WOMEN OF JAPAN. 1915: Missionary Education Movement of the United States and Canada.

Yasue Aoki Kidd. WOMEN WORKERS IN THE JAPANESE COTTON MILLS, 1880-1920. 1978: *Cornell University East Asia Papers*, 20.

. Patricia Tsurumi. "Female Textile Workers and the Failure of Early Trade Unionism in Japan," *History Workshop* 18 (1984), 3-27.

Sharlie Ushioda. "Women and War in Meiji Japan: The Case of Fukuda Hideko," *Peace and Change* 14.3 (1977), 9-12.

Sharon L. Sievers. FLOWERS IN SALT: THE BEGINNINGS OF FEMINIST CONSCIOUSNESS IN MODERN JAPAN. 1983: Stanford University Press. Covers 1868 to early 20th century.

Nancy Andrew. "The Seitosha: An Early Japanese Women's Organization, 1911-1916," *Harvard University Papers on Japan* (1972), 45-69.

Ken Miyamoto. "Ito Noe and the Bluestockings," *Japan Interpreter* 10.2 (Autumn 1975), 190-203.

Dee Ann Vavich. "The Japanese Woman's Movement: Ichikawa Fusae, a Pioneer in Woman's Suffrage," *Monumenta Nipponica* 22.3-4 (1967), 402-436.

WOMEN--II

Patricia Murray. "Ichikawa Fusae and the Lonely Red Carpet," *Japan Interpreter* 10.2 (1975), 171-181.

Chieko Mulhern. "Japan's First Newspaperwoman: Hani Motoko," *Japan Interpreter* 7.3-4 (1979), 310-329.

Motoko Hani. "Stories of My Life," *Japan Interpreter* 7.3-4 (1979), 310-354. Translation with introductory essay.

Robert J. Smith & Ella Lury Wiswell. THE WOMEN OF SUYE MURA. 1982: University of Chicago Press. Based on fieldwork in the 1930s.

Robert J. Smith. "Japanese Village Women: Suye-mura, 1935-1936," *Journal of Japanese Studies* 7.2 (1981), 259-284.

Sharon Nolte. "Women in a Prewar Japanese Village: Suye Mura Revisited," *Journal of Peasant Studies* 7.2 (1981), 259-284.

Kazuko Tsurumi. SOCIAL CHANGE AND THE INDIVIDUAL: JAPAN BEFORE AND AFTER DEFEAT IN WORLD WAR II. 1970: Princeton University Press. Chapters 7 & 8 on women.

T. Havens. "Women and War in Japan, 1937-45," *American Historical Review* 80.4 (1975), 913-934.

First-Hand Accounts

Ekiken (Ekken) Kaibara. "THE WAY OF CONTENTMENT" AND "GREATER LEARNING FOR WOMEN." 1913; reprint edition, 1979: University Publications of America. Translations of two famous essays by a Neo-Confucian scholar who lived from 1630 to 1714.

MEIROKU ZASSHI, JOURNAL OF THE JAPANESE ENLIGHTENMENT. William R. Braisted, transl. 1976: Harvard University Press. This famous intellectual journal of the 1870s contains various articles on women.

Ai Hoshino. "The Education of Women," in Inazo Nitobe, ed. WESTERN INFLUENCE IN MODERN JAPAN (1931: University of Chicago Press), 215-230. The author was president of Tsuda College.

Contemporary Japan, volumes 1 to 10 (1932-1941). This semi-official Japanese publication contains numerous articles on women by Japanese authors.

Shidzue Ishimoto. FACING TWO WAYS: THE STORY OF MY LIFE. 1935: Farrar & Rinehart. See the 1984 edition, with introduction and afterword by Barbara Molony. Baroness Ishimoto was a pioneer in the Japanese women's movement.

Etsu Sugimoto. A DAUGHTER OF THE SAMURAI. 1928: Doubleday.

_____. A DAUGHTER OF THE NARIKIN. 1932: Doubleday.

_____. A DAUGHTER OF THE NOHFU. 1938: Hurst & Blackett.

Yoko Matsuoka. DAUGHTER OF THE PACIFIC. 1952: Harper.

Sumie Mishima. MY NARROW ISLE: THE STORY OF A MODERN WOMAN IN JAPAN. 1941: John Day.

_____. THE BROADER WAY: A WOMAN'S LIFE IN THE NEW JAPAN. 1953: John Day.

Chiyono Sugimoto Kiyooka. BUT THE SHIPS ARE SAILING, SAILING. 1959: Hokuseido. On life in Occupied Japan.

Nobuko Albery. BALLOON TOP. 1978: Pantheon. On growing up in Occupied Japan.

Yasushi Inoue. CHRONICLES OF MY MOTHER. 1982: Kodansha International. Recollections of a famous
novelist.

James Trager. LETTERS FROM SACHIKO: A JAPANESE WOMAN'S VIEW OF LIFE IN THE LAND OF THE
ECONOMIC MIRACLE. 1982: Atheneum.

Tetsuko Kuroyanagi. TOTTO-CHAN: THE LITTLE GIRL AT THE WINDOW. Dorothy Britton, transl. 1982:
Kodansha International. Autobiography of one of Japan's most famous television personalities.

Literature By & About Women

Kenneth Rexroth & Ikuko Atsumi. THE BURNING HEART: WOMEN POETS OF JAPAN. 1977: Seabury.

Robert Lyons Danly. IN THE SHADE OF SPRING LEAVES: THE LIFE AND WRITINGS OF HIGUCHI ICHIYO, A
WOMAN OF LETTERS IN MEIJI JAPAN. 1981: Yale University Press.

Takeo Arishima. A CERTAIN WOMAN. Kenneth Strong, transl. 1978: Columbia University Press.

Sawako Ariyoshi. THE DOCTOR'S WIFE. Wakako Hironaka & Ann Siller Kostant, transl. 1978: Kodansha
International.

_____. THE RIVER KI. Mildred Tahara, transl. 1980: Kodansha International.

Fumiko Enchi. THE WAITING YEARS. John Bester, transl. 1976: Kodansha International.

See also the treatment of women in fiction by Mori Ogai (especially WILD GEESE), Nagai Kafu (especially
GEISHA IN RIVALRY), Natsume Soseki, Kawabata Yasunari, and Tanizaki Junichiro (especially THE
MAKIOKA SISTERS).

Noriko Mizuta Lippit & Kyoko Iriye Selden, transl. STORIES BY CONTEMPORARY JAPANESE WOMEN
WRITERS. 1982: M. E. Sharpe.

Yukiko Tanaka & Elizabeth Hanson, transl. THIS KIND OF WOMAN: TEN STORIES BY JAPANESE WOMEN
WRITERS, 1960-1976. 1982: Stanford University Press.

Phyllis Birnbaum, transl. RABBITS, CRABS, ETC: STORIES BY JAPANESE WOMEN. 1982: University of
Hawaii Press.

Yuko Tsushima. CHILD OF FORTUNE. G. Harcourt, transl. 1983: Kodansha International.

Women in Contemporary Japan

Takie Sugiyama Lebra. JAPANESE WOMEN: CONSTRAINT AND FULFILLMENT. 1984: University of Hawaii
Press.

Joyce Lebra, Joy Paulson & Elizabeth Powers, eds. WOMEN IN CHANGING JAPAN. 1976: Stanford University
Press.

113

WOMEN--IV

Dorothy Robins-Mowry. THE HIDDEN SUN: WOMEN OF MODERN JAPAN. 1983: Westview.

Alice H. Cook & Hiroko Hayashi. WORKING WOMEN IN JAPAN. 1980: Cornell University Press.

Gail Lee Bernstein. HARUKO'S WORLD: A JAPANESE FARM WOMAN AND HER COMMUNITY. 1983: Stanford University Press.

Susan J. Pharr. POLITICAL WOMEN IN JAPAN: THE SEARCH FOR A PLACE IN POLITICAL LIFE. 1981: University of California Press.

Michael Berger. "Japanese Women--Old Images and New Realities," *Japan Interpreter* 11.1 (1976), 56-67.

Takie Sugiyama Lebra. "Sex Equality for Japanese Women," *Japan Interpreter* 10.3-4 (1976), 284-295.

Liza Crihfield Dalby. GEISHA. 1983: University of California Press.

Yuriko Saisho. WOMEN EXECUTIVES IN JAPAN. 1981: Yuri International.

Samuel Coleman. FAMILY PLANNING IN JAPANESE SOCIETY: TRADITIONAL BIRTH CONTROL IN A MODERN URBAN CULTURE. 1984: Princeton University Press.

Keiko Kiguchi. "Japanese Women in Transition," *Japan Quarterly* 29 (1982), 311-318.

INORITY GROUPS: OUTCASTES & KOREANS

orge De Vos. JAPAN'S MINORITIES: BURAKUMIN, KOREANS, AINU AND OKINAWANS. 1983: Minority Rights Group.

_____ & Hiroshi Wagatsuma. JAPAN'S INVISIBLE RACE: CASTE IN CULTURE AND PERSONALITY. 1966: University of California Press.

:iji Nagahara. "The Medieval Origins of the *Eta-Hinin,*" *Journal of Japanese Studies* 5.2 (1979), 385-403.

igeaki Ninomiya. "An Inquiry Concerning the Origin, Development, and Present Situation of the Eta in Relation to the History of Social Classes in Japan," *Transactions, Asiatic Society of Japan,* 2nd series, 10 (1933), 46-154.

lliam Lyman Brooks. "Outcaste Society in Early Modern Japan," 1976: Ph.D. dissertation in History, Columbia University.

1 Neary. "Tenko of an Organization: The Suiheisha in the Late 1930s," *Proceedings of the British Association for Japanese Studies,* volume 2, part 2 (1977), 64-76.

hn D. Donoghue. PARIAH PERSISTANCE IN CHANGING JAPAN. 1977: University Press of America.

son Shimazaki. THE BROKEN COMMANDMENT. Kenneth Strong, transl. 1974: University of Tokyo Press.

raku Kaiho Kenkyujo (Buraku Liberation League). LONG-SUFFERING BROTHERS & SISTERS, UNITE! 1981: Liberation Publishing House.

lward W. Wagner. THE KOREAN MINORITY IN JAPAN. 1951: Institute of Pacific Relations.

chard Mitchell H. THE KOREAN MINORITY IN JAPAN. 1967: University of California Press.

1angsoo Lee & George De Vos, eds. KOREANS IN JAPAN: ETHNIC CONFLICT & ACCOMMODATION. 1981: University of California Press.

115

LITERATURE

** International House of Japan Library, comp. MODERN JAPANESE LITERATURE IN TRANSLATION: A BIBLIOGRAPHY. 1979: Kodansha International. Includes 1,500 authors from 1868-1978.

Donald Keene. JAPANESE LITERATURE: AN INTRODUCTION FOR WESTERN READERS. 1953: Grove.

_____. WORLD WITHIN WALLS: JAPANESE LITERATURE OF THE PRE-MODERN ERA, 1600-1867. 1976: Grove.

_____. DAWN TO THE WEST: JAPANESE LITERATURE OF THE MODERN ERA. 2 volumes. 1984: Holt, Rinehart & Winston.

_____, ed. ANTHOLOGY OF JAPANESE LITERATURE: FROM THE EARLIEST ERA TO THE MID-NINETEENTH CENTURY. 1955: Grove.

_____, ed. MODERN JAPANESE LITERATURE: AN ANTHOLOGY. 1956: Grove.

Shuichi Kato. A HISTORY OF JAPANESE LITERATURE: THE YEARS OF ISOLATION (volume 2) and THE MODERN YEARS (volume 3). 1979: Kodansha International.

Masao Miyoshi. ACCOMPLICES OF SILENCE: THE MODERN JAPANESE NOVEL. 1974: University of California Press.

Makoto Ueda. MODERN JAPANESE WRITERS AND THE NATURE OF LITERATURE. 1976: Stanford Univ. Press

_____. MODERN JAPANESE POETS AND THE NATURE OF LITERATURE. 1983: Stanford University Press.

J. Thomas Rimer. MODERN JAPANESE FICTION AND ITS TRADITIONS: AN INTRODUCTION. 1978: Princeton University Press.

_____ & Robert E. Morrell. GUIDE TO JAPANESE POETRY. 1975: G. K. Hall.

Noriko Mizuta Lippit. REALITY AND FICTION IN MODERN JAPANESE LITERATURE. 1980: M. E. Sharpe.

Hisaaki Yamanouchi. THE SEARCH FOR AUTHENTICITY IN MODERN JAPANESE LITERATURE. 1978: Cambridge University Press.

Arthur G. Kimball. CRISIS IN IDENTITY AND CONTEMPORARY JAPANESE NOVELS. 1972: Tuttle.

Irena Powell. WRITERS AND SOCIETY IN MODERN JAPAN. 1983: Kodansha International.

See in particular translations of works by the following authors (names are given in Japanese order):

Ihara Saikaku	1642-1693
Chikamatsu Monzaemon	1653-1724
Futabatei Shimei	1864-1910
Mori Ogai	1862-1922
Natsume Soseki	1867-1916
Higuchi Ichiyo	1872-1896
Tayama Katai	1871-1930
Shimazaki Toson	1872-1943
Arishima Takeo	1878-1923
Nagai Kafu	1879-1959
Akutagawa Ryunosuke	1892-1927
Shiga Naoya	1883-1971
Tanizaki Junichiro	1886-1965
Kawabata Yasunari	1899-1972
Dazai Osamu	1909-1948

Japan Abroad: Foreign Relations, Empire & War from the Restoration to 1945

JAPAN ABROAD: FOREIGN RELATIONS, EMPIRE & WAR

FROM THE RESTORATION TO 1945

Paul H. Clyde & Burton F. Beers. THE FAR EAST: A HISTORY OF THE WESTERN IMPACT AND THE EASTERN RESPONSE, 1830-1975. 6th edition. 1976: Prentice-Hall.

James Morley, ed. JAPAN'S FOREIGN POLICY, 1868-1941. 1974: Columbia University Press.

Ian Nish. JAPANESE FOREIGN POLICY, 1869-1942. 1976: Routledge & Kegan Paul.

Ramon H. Myers & Mark R. Peattie, eds. THE JAPANESE COLONIAL EMPIRE, 1895-1945. 1984: Princeton University Press.

Richard Storry. JAPAN AND THE DECLINE OF THE WEST IN ASIA, 1894-1942. 1979: St. Martin's.

James B. Crowley, ed. MODERN EAST ASIA: ESSAYS IN INTERPRETATION. 1970: Harcourt Brace & World.

_____. "Historical Prologue to the 1930's," in his JAPAN'S QUEST FOR AUTONOMY: NATIONAL SECURITY AND FOREIGN POLICY, 1930-1938 (1968: Princeton University Press), 3-34.

_____. "Japan's Military Foreign Policies," in James Morley, ed. JAPAN'S FOREIGN POLICY (1974: Princeton University Press), 3-117.

Ikuhiko Hata. "Imperial Japanese Armed Forces," KODANSHA ENCYCLOPEDIA OF JAPAN 1: 86-88.

Shinji Kondo. JAPANESE MILITARY HISTORY. 1983: Garland.

Morinosuke Kajima. THE EMERGENCE OF JAPAN AS A WORLD POWER 1895-1925. 1968: Tuttle.

_____. A BRIEF DIPLOMATIC HISTORY OF MODERN JAPAN. 1965: Tuttle.

J. K. Fairbank, E. O. Reischauer & Albert Craig. EAST ASIA: THE MODERN TRANSFORMATION. 1965: Houghton Mifflin.

Chitoshi Yanaga. JAPAN SINCE PERRY. 1949: McGraw-Hill.

Hugh Borton. JAPAN'S MODERN CENTURY: FROM PERRY TO 1970. 2nd edition. 1970: Ronald.

W. G. Beasley. THE MODERN HISTORY OF JAPAN. 2nd edition. 1973: Praeger.

Kenneth Pyle. THE MAKING OF MODERN JAPAN. 1978: Heath.

Peter Duus. THE RISE OF MODERN JAPAN. 1976: Houghton Mifflin.

Mikiso Hane. JAPAN: A HISTORICAL SURVEY. 1972: Charles Scribner's Sons.

Marius B. Jansen. JAPAN AND CHINA: FROM WAR TO PEACE, 1894-1972. 1975: Rand McNally.

Ernest R. May & James C. Thomson, Jr., eds. AMERICAN-EAST ASIAN RELATIONS: A SURVEY. 1972: Harvard University Press.

Akira Iriye. ACROSS THE PACIFIC: AN INNER HISTORY OF AMERICAN-EAST ASIAN RELATIONS. 1967: Harcourt Brace & World.

_____. "Imperialism in East Asia," in Crowley, MODERN EAST ASIA: ESSAYS IN INTERPRETATION (1970: Harcourt Brace & World), 122-150.

_____. "The Legacy of Modern Japanese Diplomacy," *Journal of Social and Political Ideas in Japan* 3.2 (1965), 25-32. A survey of 1895-1945, originally published in *Chuo Koron*.

Herbert Bix. "Imagistic Historiography and the Reinterpretation of Japanese Imperialism," *Bulletin of Concerned Asian Scholars* 7.3 (1975), 51-68.

Kazuo Shibagaki. "The Logic of Japanese Imperialism," *Social Science Abstracts* 14 (Shakai Kagaku Kenkyujo, Tokyo University, 1973), 70-87.

Kimihide Mushakoji. "From Fear of Dependence to Fear of Independence--A Scenario of the Japanese International Learning Process," *Japan Annual of International Affairs* 3 (1963-1964), 68-86.

Seizaburo Sato. "Japan's World Order," in Irwin Scheiner, ed. MODERN JAPAN: AN INTERPRETIVE ANTHOLOGY (1974: Macmillan), 9-17.

_____. "The Foundations of Modern Japanese Foreign Policy," in Robert Scalapino, ed. THE FOREIGN POLICY OF MODERN JAPAN (1977: University of California Press), 367-389.

Hilary Conroy. "Lessons from Japanese Imperialism," *Monumenta Nipponica* 21.3-4 (1966), 333-345.

Hyman Kublin. "The Evolution of Japanese Colonialism," *Comparative Studies in Science and History* 2 (1959), 67-84.

Hosea B. Morse & Harley F. MacNair. FAR EASTERN INTERNATIONAL RELATIONS. 2nd edition. 1955: Houghton Mifflin.

Harley F. MacNair & Donald F. Lach. MODERN FAR EASTERN INTERNATIONAL RELATIONS. 2nd edition. 1955: Van Nostrand.

Sterling Tatsuji Takeuchi. WAR AND DIPLOMACY IN THE JAPANESE EMPIRE. 1935: University of Chicago Press. Covers 1890-1933.

Payson J. Treat. THE FAR EAST: A POLITICAL AND DIPLOMATIC HISTORY. Revised edition. 1935: Stanford University Press.

Robert A. Scalapino, ed. THE FOREIGN POLICY OF MODERN JAPAN. 1977: University of California Press.

_____. "The Foreign Policy of Modern Japan," in Roy C. Macridis, ed. FOREIGN POLICY IN WORLD POLITICS. 2nd edition (1962: Prentice-Hall), 270-313.

Michael Blaker. JAPANESE INTERNATIONAL NEGOTIATING STYLE. 1977: Columbia University Press.

BASIC CASE STUDIES FOR 1868-1945

James B. Crowley. "Japan's Military Foreign Policies," in James Morley, ed. JAPAN'S FOREIGN POLICY (1974: Columbia University Press), 3-117.

Marius B. Jansen. "Modernization and Foreign Policy in Meiji Japan," in Robert E. Ward, ed. POLITICAL DEVELOPMENT IN MODERN JAPAN (1968: Princeton University Press), 149-188.

_____. THE JAPANESE AND SUN YAT-SEN. 1954: Harvard University Press.

Hilary Conroy. THE JAPANESE SEIZURE OF KOREA, 1868-1910. 1960: University of Pennsylvania Press.

Shumpei Okamoto. THE JAPANESE OLIGARCHY AND THE RUSSO-JAPANESE WAR. 1970: Columbia University Press.

Akira Iriye. PACIFIC ESTRANGEMENT: JAPANESE AND AMERICAN EXPANSION, 1897-1911. 1972: Harvard University Press.

Ian Nish. THE ANGLO-JAPANESE ALLIANCE: THE DIPLOMACY OF TWO ISLAND EMPIRES, 1894-1907. 1966; 2nd edition, 1985: Athlone.

_____. ALLIANCE IN DECLINE: A STUDY IN ANGLO-JAPANESE RELATIONS, 1908-1923. 1972: Athlone.

Shigeki Toyama. "Politics, Economics, and the International Environment in the Meiji and Taisho Periods," *Developing Economies* 4.4 (1966), 419-446.

James W. Morley. THE JAPANESE THRUST INTO SIBERIA, 1918. 1957: Columbia University Press.

Roger Dingman. POWER IN THE PACIFIC: THE ORIGINS OF NAVAL ARMS LIMITATION, 1914-1922. 1976: University of Chicago Press.

Akira Iriye. "Japanese Imperialism and Aggression: Reconsiderations" and "Japan's Foreign Policies Between World Wars--Sources and Interpretations," in Esmonde M. Robertson, ed. THE ORIGINS OF THE SECOND WORLD WAR: HISTORICAL INTERPRETATIONS (1971: Macmillan), 243-271. Reprinted from *Journal of Asian Studies*, volumes 23 (1963) and 26 (1967).

_____. AFTER IMPERIALISM: THE SEARCH FOR A NEW ORDER IN THE FAR EAST, 1921-1931. 1965: Harvard University Press.

Takashi Saito. "Japan's Foreign Policy in the International Environment of the Nineteen-Twenties," *Developing Economies* 5.4 (1967), 685-701.

Richard Dean Burns & Edward M. Bennett, eds. DIPLOMATS IN CRISIS: UNITED STATES-CHINESE-JAPANESE RELATIONS, 1919-1941. 1974: ABC Clio.

Roger Daniels. THE POLITICS OF PREJUDICE: THE ANTI-JAPANESE MOVEMENT IN CALIFORNIA AND THE STRUGGLE FOR JAPANESE EXCLUSION. 1968: Atheneum.

Kiyoshi Oshima. "The World Economic Crisis and Japan's Foreign Economic Policy," *Developing Economies* 5.4 (1967), 628-647.

James B. Crowley. JAPAN'S QUEST FOR AUTONOMY: NATIONAL SECURITY AND FOREIGN POLICY, 1930-1938. 1968: Princeton University Press.

_____. "A New Deal for Japan and Asia: One Road to Pearl Harbor," in his MODERN EAST ASIA: ESSAYS IN INTERPRETATION (1970: Harcourt Brace & World), 235-264.

Sadako Ogata. DEFIANCE IN MANCHURIA: THE MAKING OF JAPANESE FOREIGN POLICY, 1931-1932. 1964: University of California Press.

BASIC CASE STUDIES--II

Mark Peattie. ISHIWARA KANJI AND JAPAN'S CONFRONTATION WITH THE WEST. 1975: Princeton University Press.

Christopher Thorne. THE LIMITS OF FOREIGN POLICY: THE WEST, THE LEAGUE, AND THE FAR EASTERN CRISIS OF 1931-1933. 1973: Capricorn.

Dorothy Borg. THE UNITED STATES AND THE FAR EASTERN CRISIS OF 1933-1938: FROM THE MANCHURIAN INCIDENT THROUGH THE INITIAL STAGE OF THE UNDECLARED SINO-JAPANESE WAR. 1964: Harvard University Press.

Stephen E. Pelz. RACE TO PEARL HARBOR: THE FAILURE OF THE SECOND LONDON NAVAL CONFERENCE AND THE ONSET OF WORLD WAR II. 1974: Harvard University Press.

Saburo Ienaga. THE PACIFIC WAR: WORLD WAR II AND THE JAPANESE, 1931-1945. 1978: Pantheon.

Dorothy Borg & Shumpei Okamoto, eds. PEARL HARBOR AS HISTORY: JAPANESE-AMERICAN RELATIONS, 1931-1941. 1973: Columbia University Press.

James W. Morley, ed. DETERRENT DIPLOMACY: JAPAN, GERMANY, AND THE USSR, 1935-1940. 1976: Columbia University Press.

John H. Boyle. CHINA AND JAPAN AT WAR, 1937-1945: THE POLITICS OF COLLABORATION. 1972: Stanford University Press.

Robert J. C. Butow. TOJO AND THE COMING OF THE WAR. 1961: Stanford University Press.

James W. Morley, ed. THE FATEFUL CHOICE: JAPAN'S ADVANCE INTO SOUTHEAST ASIA, 1939-1941. 1980: Columbia University Press.

Paul W. Schroeder. THE AXIS ALLIANCE AND JAPANESE-AMERICAN RELATIONS, 1941. 1958: Cornell University Press.

Nobutake Ike, transl. and ed. JAPAN'S DECISION FOR WAR: RECORDS OF THE 1941 POLICY CONFERENCES. 1967: Stanford University Press.

F. C. Jones. JAPAN'S NEW ORDER IN EAST ASIA: ITS RISE AND FALL, 1937-45. 1954: Oxford University Press.

Willard H. Elsbree. JAPAN'S ROLE IN SOUTHEAST ASIAN NATIONALIST MOVEMENTS, 1940-45. 1953: Harvard University Press.

Joyce C. Lebra. JAPANESE-TRAINED ARMIES IN SOUTHEAST ASIA: INDEPENDENCE AND VOLUNTEER FORCES IN WORLD WAR II. 1977: Columbia University Press.

_____, ed. JAPAN'S GREATER EAST ASIA CO-PROSPERITY SPHERE IN WORLD WAR II: SELECTED READINGS AND DOCUMENTS. 1975: Oxford University Press.

Alfred W. McCoy, ed. SOUTHEAST ASIA UNDER JAPANESE RULE. 1980: Yale University Southeast Asia Studies, Monograph Series 22.

David Bergamini. JAPAN'S IMPERIAL CONSPIRACY. 1971: Morrow.

Charles D. Sheldon. "Japanese Agression and the Emperor, 1931-1941, from Contemporary Diaries," *Modern Asian Studies* 10.1 (1976), 1-40.

John Toland. THE RISING SUN: THE DECLINE AND FALL OF THE JAPANESE EMPIRE, 1936-1945. 1970: Random House.

John Costello. THE PACIFIC WAR, 1941-1945. 1981: Quill.

Ronald H. Spector. EAGLE AGAINST THE SUN: THE AMERICAN WAR WITH JAPAN. 1985: Free Press.

John W. Dower. EMPIRE AND AFTERMATH: YOSHIDA SHIGERU AND THE JAPANESE EXPERIENCE, 1878-1954. 1979: Harvard East Asian Monographs.

_____. WAR WITHOUT MERCY: RACE AND POWER IN THE PACIFIC WAR. 1986: Pantheon.

Christopher Thorne. ALLIES OF A KIND: THE UNITED STATES, BRITAIN, AND THE WAR AGAINST JAPAN, 1941-1945. 1979: Oxford University Press.

_____. THE ISSUE OF WAR: STATES, SOCIETIES, AND THE FAR EASTERN CONFLICT OF 1941-1945. 1985: Hamilton.

MEIJI POLICY

Frances V. Moulder. JAPAN, CHINA AND THE MODERN WORLD ECONOMY: TOWARD A REINTERPRETATION OF EAST ASIAN DEVELOPMENT ca. 1600 TO ca. 1918. 1977: Cambridge University Press.

W. G. Beasley. SELECT DOCUMENTS ON JAPANESE FOREIGN POLICY, 1853-1868. 1955: Oxford University Press.

George B. Sansom. THE WESTERN WORLD AND JAPAN. 1950: Knopf.

Shigeki Toyama. "Politics, Economics, and the International Environment in the Meiji and Taisho Periods," *Developing Economies* 4.4 (1966), 419-446.

Marius B. Jansen. "Modernization and Foreign Policy in Meiji Japan," in Robert E. Ward, ed. POLITICAL DEVELOPMENT IN MODERN JAPAN (1968: Princeton University Press), 149-188.

_____. "The Ideological and Political Context of Meiji Expansionism" and "Personalities and Precedents," chapters 1 and 2 in his THE JAPANESE AND SUN YAT-SEN (1954: Harvard University Press), 13-58.

_____. "Japanese Imperialism: Late Meiji Perspectives," in Ramon Myers & Mark Peattie, eds. THE JAPANESE COLONIAL EMPIRE, 1895-1945 (1984: Princeton University Press), 61-79.

Marlene Mayo, ed. THE EMERGENCE OF IMPERIAL JAPAN: SELF DEFENSE OR CALCULATED AGGRESSION? 1970: Heath.

_____. "Rationality in the Meiji Restoration: The Iwakura Mission," in Bernard S. Silberman & H. D. Harootunian, eds. MODERN JAPANESE LEADERSHIP: TRANSITION AND CHANGE (1966: University of Arizona Press), 323-370.

Hazel J. Jones. LIVE MACHINES: HIRED FOREIGNERS AND MEIJI JAPAN. 1980: University of British Columbia Press.

F. C. Jones. EXTRATERRITORIALITY IN JAPAN AND THE DIPLOMATIC RELATIONS RESULTING IN ITS ABOLITION, 1853-1899. 1931: Yale University Press.

Jerry Dusenbury. "Revision of Unequal Treaties," KODANSHA ENCYCLOPEDIA OF JAPAN 8: 148-149.

Zengo Ohira. "Japan's Reception of the Law of Nations," *Annals of the Hitotsubashi Academy* 4 (1953), 55-66.

Immanuel C. Y. Hsu. CHINA'S ENTRANCE INTO THE FAMILY OF NATIONS: THE DIPLOMATIC PHASE, 1858-1880. 1960: Harvard University Press. See 121-131 on Japan's use of the Chinese translation of Wheaton.

Shinya Murase. "The Most-Favored Nation Treatment in Japan's Treaty Practice During the Period 1854- 1905," *American Journal of International Law* 70 (1976), 273-297.

James B. Crowley. "From Closed Door to Empire: the Foundation of the Meiji Military Establishment," in Silberman & Harootunian, MODERN JAPANESE LEADERSHIP (1966: University of Arizona Press), 261-285.

_____. "Japan's Military Foreign Policies," in J.W. Morley, ed. JAPAN'S FOREIGN POLICY (1974: Princeton University Press), 3-117.

E. Herbert Norman. SOLDIER AND PEASANT IN JAPAN: THE ORIGINS OF CONSCRIPTION. 1943: Institute of Pacific Relations.

Ernst L. Presseisen. BEFORE AGGRESSION: EUROPEANS PREPARE THE JAPANESE ARMY. 1965: University of Arizona Press.

Shingo Fukushima. "The Building of a National Army," *Developing Economies* 3.4 (1965), 516-539.

Hyman Kublin. "The 'Modern' Army of Early Meiji Japan," *Far Eastern Quarterly* 9.1 (1949), 20-41.

Roger Hackett. YAMAGATA ARITOMO IN THE RISE OF MODERN JAPAN, 1838-1922. 1971: Harvard University Press.

Alfred Stead, ed. JAPAN BY THE JAPANESE. 2 volumes. 1905: Heinemann. Includes an essay by Yamagata on the Army.

Shigenobu Okuma, ed. FIFTY YEARS OF THE NEW JAPAN. 2 volumes. 1909: Dutton.

Hilary Conroy. THE JAPANESE SEIZURE OF KOREA, 1868-1910. 1960: University of Pennsylvania Press.

_____. "Government vs. Patriot: The Background of Japan's Asiatic Expansion," *Pacific Historical Review* 20.1 (1951), 31-42.

Key-Hiuk Kim. THE LAST PHASE OF THE EAST ASIAN WORLD ORDER: KOREA, JAPAN, AND THE CHINESE EMPIRE, 1860-1882. 1979: University of California Press.

George A. Lensen. BALANCE OF INTRIGUE: INTERNATIONAL RIVALRY IN KOREA AND MANCHURIA, 1884-1899. 1982: University of Hawaii Press.

Peter Duus. "Economic Dimensions of Meiji Imperialism: The Case of Korea, 1895-1910," in Myers & Peattie, THE JAPANESE COLONIAL EMPIRE, 1895-1945 (1984: Princeton University Press), 128-171.

William L. Langer. THE DIPLOMACY OF IMPERIALISM, 1890-1902. 2nd edition. 1951: Knopf.

Kimitada Miwa. "Fukuzawa Yukichi's 'Departure from Asia': A Prelude to the Sino-Japanese War," in Edmund R. Skrzypczak, ed. JAPAN'S MODERN CENTURY (1968: Sophia University & Tuttle), 1-26.

E. Herbert Norman. "The Genyosha: A Study in the Origins of Japanese Imperialism," *Pacific Affairs* 17 (1944), 261-284.

Munemitsu Mutsu. KENKENROKU: A DIPLOMATIC RECORD OF THE SINO-JAPANESE WAR, 1894-1895. Gordon M. Berger, ed. and transl. 1984: Princeton University Press.

Jeffrey Dorwart. THE PIGTAIL WAR: AMERICAN INVOLVEMENT IN THE SINO-JAPANESE WAR, 1894-1895. 1975: University of Massachusetts Press.

Frank W. Ikle. "The Triple Intervention: Japan's Lesson in the Diplomacy of Imperialism," *Monumenta Nipponica* 22.1-2 (1967), 122-130.

Akira Iriye. PACIFIC ESTRANGEMENT: JAPANESE AND AMERICAN EXPANSION, 1879-1911. 1972: Harvard University Press.

Ian Nish. THE ANGLO-JAPANESE ALLIANCE: THE DIPLOMACY OF TWO ISLAND EMPIRES, 1894-1907. 2nd edition. 1985: Athlone.

Hilary Conroy. THE JAPANESE FRONTIER IN HAWAII, 1868-1898. 1953: University of California Press.

T. A. Bailey. "Japan's Protest Against the Annexation of Hawaii," *Journal of Modern History* 3.1 (1931), 46-61.

Josefa M. Saniel. JAPAN AND THE PHILIPPINES, 1868-1898. 1963: University of the Philippines Press.

E. Thadeus Flood. "The Shishi Interlude in Old Siam: An Aspect of the Meiji Impact in Old Siam," in David Wurfel, ed. MEIJI JAPAN'S CENTENNIAL: ASPECTS OF POLITICAL THOUGHT AND ACTION (1971: University of Kansas Press), 78-105.

Ian Nish. "Japan's Indecision During the Boxer Disturbances," *Journal of Asian Studies* 20.4 (1961), 449-462.

Paul A. Varg. "The Foreign Policy of Japan and the Boxer Revolt," *Pacific Historical Review* 14.3 (1946), 279-285.

Shumpei Okamoto. THE JAPANESE OLIGARCHY AND THE RUSSO-JAPANESE WAR. 1970: Columbia University Press.

Robert B. Valliant. "The Selling of Japan: Japanese Manipulation of Western Opinion, 1900-05," *Monumenta Nipponica* 29.4 (1974), 415-438.

Denis & Peggy Warner. THE TIDE AT SUNRISE: A HISTORY OF THE RUSSO-JAPANESE WAR 1904-1905. 1974: Charterhouse.

Georges Blond. ADMIRAL TOGO. Edward Hyams, transl. 1960: Macmillan.

Edwin A. Falk. TOGO AND THE RISE OF JAPANESE SEA POWER. 1936: Green.

Jean-Pierre Lehmann. THE IMAGE OF JAPAN: A CHANGING SOCIETY, 1850-1905. 1978: Allen & Unwin.

Setsuko Ono. "A Western Image of Japan: What Did the West See Through The Eyes of Loti and Hearn?" 1972: Ph.D. dissertation in Political Science, University of Geneva.

Richard Dean Burns & Edward M. Bennett, eds. DIPLOMATS IN CRISIS: UNITED STATES-CHINESE-JAPANESE RELATIONS, 1919-1941. 1974: ABC Clio.

Alvin D. Coox & Hilary Conroy, eds. CHINA AND JAPAN: A SEARCH FOR BALANCE SINCE WORLD WAR I. 1978: ABC Clio.

Gordon A. Craig & Felix Greene, eds. THE DIPLOMATS, 1919-1939. 1953: Princeton University Press.

Edward Mallett Carr. THE TWENTY YEARS' CRISIS, 1919-1939: AN INTRODUCTION TO THE STUDY OF INTERNATIONAL RELATIONS. 1939; reprinted 1964: Harper Torchbooks.

Japan & the Great War

Paul H. Clyde & Burton F. Beers. THE FAR EAST. 1976: Prentice-Hall. Chapters 21 and 22 cover World War One and its legacy in Asia.

Frederick F. Czupryna. "World War I," KODANSHA ENCYCLOPEDIA OF JAPAN 8: 270-271.

Kimitada Miwa. "Japanese Opinions on Woodrow Wilson in War and Peace," *Monumenta Nipponica* 22.3-4 (1967), 368-389.

Charles N. Spinks. "Japan's Entrance into the World War," *Pacific Historical Review* 5.4 (1936), 297-311.

V. H. Rothwell. "The British Government and Japanese Military Assistance, 1914-1918," *History* 56 (1971), 35-45.

Carnegie Endowment for International Peace, Division of Intercourse and Education. THE IMPERIAL JAPANESE MISSION, 1917: A RECORD OF THE RECEPTION THROUGHOUT THE UNITED STATES OF THE SPECIAL MISSION HEADED BY VISCOUNT ISHII, TOGETHER WITH THE EXCHANGE OF NOTES EMBODYING THE ROOT-TAKAHIRA UNDERSTANDING OF 1908 AND THE LANSING-ISHII AGREEMENT OF 1917. 1918: Carnegie Endowment for International Peace.

[For materials concerning the 21 Demands and the Paris Peace Conference, see entries under "China Relations to 1931" on page 135 below.]

The Siberian Intervention

James W. Morley. THE JAPANESE THRUST INTO SIBERIA, 1918. 1957: Columbia University Press.

Chihiro Hosoya. "Origin of the Siberian Intervention, 1917-1918," *Annals of the Hitotsubashi Academy* 9.1 (1958), 91-108.

_____. "Japanese Documents on the Siberian Intervention," *Hitotsubashi Journal of Law and Politics* 1 (1960), 30-53.

The Special Delegation of the Far Eastern Republic to the United States of America. JAPANESE INTERVENTION IN THE RUSSIAN FAR EAST. 1922: The Special Delegation of the Far Eastern Republic to the United States of America.

Henry Baerlein. THE MARCH OF THE SEVENTY THOUSAND. 1926: Parsons.

William S. Graves. AMERICA'S SIBERIAN ADVENTURE, 1918-1920. 1931: Cape & Smith.

G. Stewart. THE WHITE ARMIES OF RUSSIA: A CHRONICLE OF COUNTER-REVOLUTION AND ALLIED INTERVENTION. 1933: Macmillan.

John A. White. THE SIBERIAN INTERVENTION. 1950: Princeton University Press.

Betty M. Unterberger. AMERICA'S SIBERIAN EXPEDITION, 1918-1920. 1956: Duke University Press.

George Kennan. SOVIET-AMERICAN RELATIONS, 1917-1920: THE DECISION TO INTERVENE. 1958: Princeton University Press.

Richard R. Ullman. ANGLO-SOVIET RELATIONS 1917-1921: INTERVENTION AND THE WAR. 1961: Princeton University Press.

Christopher Lasch. "American Intervention in Siberia: A Reinterpretation," *Political Science Quarterly* 77 (1962), 205-223.

William Appleman Williams. "American Intervention in Russia: 1917-20," in David Horowitz, ed. CONTAINMENT AND REVOLUTION (1967: Beacon), 26-75.

The Washington Conference & Washington System

Takashi Saito. "Japan's Foreign Policy in the International Environment of the Nineteen-Twenties," *Developing Economies* 5.4 (1967), 685-701.

Roger Dingman. "Washington Conference" and "Washington Naval Treaty of 1922," KODANSHA ENCYCLOPEDIA OF JAPAN 8: 234-235.

_____. POWER IN THE PACIFIC: THE ORIGINS OF NAVAL ARMS LIMITATION, 1914-1922. 1976: University of Chicago Press.

Sadao Asada. "Japan's 'Special Interests' and the Washington Conference, 1921-1922," *American Historical Review* 67.1 (1961), 62-70.

William Appleman Williams. "China and Japan: A Challenge and a Choice of the Nineteen Twenties," *Pacific Historical Review* 26.3 (1957), 259-279.

Yamato Ichihashi. THE WASHINGTON CONFERENCE AND AFTER. 1928: Stanford University Press.

J. Chal Vinson. "The Annulment of the Lansing-Ishii Agreement," *Pacific Historical Review* 27.1 (1958), 57-69.

Harold & Margaret Sprout. TOWARD A NEW ORDER OF SEA POWER: AMERICAN NAVAL POLICY AND THE WORLD SCENE, 1918-1922. 1946: Princeton University Press.

Akira Iriye. AFTER IMPERIALISM: THE SEARCH FOR A NEW ORDER IN THE FAR EAST, 1921-1931. 1965: Harvard University Press.

_____. "The Failure of Economic Expansion: 1918-1931," in B. Silberman & H. Harootunian, eds. JAPAN IN CRISIS (1974: Princeton University Press), 237-269.

_____. "Japanese Imperialism and Aggression: Reconsiderations" and "Japan's Foreign Policies Between World Wars--Sources and Interpretations," in Esmonde M. Robertson, ed. THE ORIGINS OF THE SECOND WORLD WAR: HISTORICAL INTERPRETATIONS (1971: Macmillan), 243-271.

TAIWAN (FORMOSA)

Roger Daniels. THE POLITICS OF PREJUDICE: THE ANTI-JAPANESE MOVEMENT IN CALIIFORNIA AND THE STRUGGLE FOR JAPANESE EXCLUSION. 1962: University of California Press.

Ramon H. Myers & Mark R. Peattie, eds. THE JAPANESE COLONIAL EMPIRE, 1895-1945. 1984: Princeton University Press. See especially essays by Chen on police and law (213-274), Tsurumi on education (275-311), Ho on colonial development (347-398), Mizoguchi and Yamamoto on capital development (399-419), and Myers and Yamada on agricultural development (420-452).

E. Patricia Tsurumi. JAPANESE COLONIAL EDUCATION IN TAIWAN, 1895-1945. 1977: Harvard University Press.

_____. "Education and Assimilation in Taiwan under Japanese Rule, 1895-1945," *Modern Asian Studies* 13.4 (1979), 617-641.

_____. "Mental Captivity and Resistance: Lessons from Taiwanese Anti-Colonialism," *Bulletin of Concerned Asian Scholars* 12.2 (1980), 2-13.

Harry J. Lamley. "Taiwan," KODANSHA ENCYCLOPEDIA OF JAPAN 7: 306-309.

George H. Kerr. FORMOSA: LICENSED REVOLUTION AND THE HOME RULE MOVEMENT, 1895-1945. 1974: University of Hawaii Press.

Andrew J. Grajdanzev. FORMOSA TODAY. 1942: Institute of Pacific Relations.

Masakazu Iwata. OKUBO TOSHIMICHI, THE BISMARK OF JAPAN (1964: University of California Press), 184-225 on the 1874 Formosan expedition.

Leonard Gordon. "Japan's Interest in Taiwan, 1872-1895," *Orient West* 9.1 (1964), 49-59.

_____. "Japan's Abortive Colonial Venture in Taiwan, 1874," *Journal of Modern History* 37.2 (1965), 171-185.

F. Q. Quo. "British Diplomacy and the Cession of Formosa, 1894-95," *Modern Asian Studies* 2.2 (1968), 141-154.

Han-yu Chang & Ramon Myers. "Japanese Colonial Development Policy in Taiwan, 1895-1906: A Case of Bureaucratic Entrepreneurship," *Journal of Asian Studies* 22.4 (1963), 433-449.

Ramon Myers & Adrienne Ching. "Agricultural Development in Taiwan Under Japanese Colonial Rule," *Journal of Asian Studies* 23.4 (1964), 555-570.

Edward I-te Chen. "Japanese Colonialism in Korea and Formosa: A Comparison of the Systems of Political Control," *Harvard Journal of Asiatic Studies* 30 (1970), 126-158.

Yosaburo Takekoshi. JAPANESE RULE IN FORMOSA. 1907: Longmans, Green.

KOREA

"Korea and Japan," KODANSHA ENCYCLOPEDIA OF JAPAN 4: 276-287. Especially essays by Benjamin Hazard (relations to 1875), Young Ick Lew (1876-1910), and Setsuko Miyata (1910-1945).

George De Vos & Changsoo Lee. "The Colonial Experience, 1910-1945," in De Vos & Lee, KOREANS IN JAPAN: ETHNIC CONFLICT AND ACCOMODATION (1980: University of California Press), 31-57.

Ramon H. Myers & Mark R. Peattie, eds. THE JAPANESE COLONIAL EMPIRE, 1895-1945. 1984: Princeton University Press. See especially essays by Duus on Meiji economic imperatives (128-171), Tsurumi on education (275-311), Robinson on publication curbs (312-343), Ho on colonial development (347-398), Mizoguchi & Yamamoto on capital formation (399-419), and Cumings on the colonial legacy (478-496).

Hilary Conroy. THE JAPANESE SEIZURE OF KOREA, 1868-1910. 1960: University of Pennsylvania Press.

_____. "Chosen Mondai: The Korean Problem in Meiji Japan," *Proceedings of the American Philosophical Association* 100 (1956), 443-454.

George Totten et al. "Japanese Imperialism & Aggression: Reconsiderations," *Journal of Asian Studies* 22.4 (1963), 469-473. Concerning controversy provoked by Conroy's SEIZURE (above).

C. I. Eugene Kim & Han-kyo Kim. KOREA AND THE POLITICS OF IMPERIALISM, 1876-1910. 1967: University of California Press.

Fred Harvey Harrington. GOD, MAMMON AND THE JAPANESE: DR. HORACE N. ALLEN AND KOREAN-AMERICAN RELATIONS, 1884-1905. 1944: University of Wisconsin Press.

Woonsang Choi. THE FALL OF THE HERMIT KINGDOM. 1967: Oceana.

David Brudnoy. "Japan's Experiment in Korea," *Monumenta Nipponica* 25.1-2 (1970), 155-195.

Lawrence H. Battistini. "The Korean Problem in the Nineteenth Century," *Monumenta Nipponica* 8.1-2 (1952), 47-66.

Andrew C. Nahm, ed. KOREA UNDER JAPANESE COLONIAL RULE: STUDIES OF THE POLICY AND TECHNIQUES OF JAPANESE COLONIALISM. 1973: Center for Korean Studies, Western Michigan Univ.

_____. JAPANESE PENETRATION OF KOREA. 1959: Center for Korean Studies, Western Michigan University.

C. I. Eugene Kim & Doretha E. Mortimore, eds. KOREA'S RESPONSE TO JAPAN: THE COLONIAL PERIOD, 1910-1945. 1974: Center for Korean Studies, Western Michigan University.

Edward I-te Chen. "Japanese Colonialism in Korea and Formosa: A Comparison of Systems of Political Control," *Harvard Journal of Asiatic Studies* 30 (1970), 126-158.

Andrew Grajdanzev. MODERN KOREA. 1944: John Day.

Takashi Hatada. A HISTORY OF KOREA. 1969: ABC Clio.

Woo-Keun Han. THE HISTORY OF KOREA. 1971: University of Hawaii Press.

Ki-Baik Lee. A NEW HISTORY OF KOREA. 1983: Harvard University Press.

Chong-sik Lee. THE POLITICS OF KOREAN NATIONALISM. 1965: University of California Press.

G. Trumbull Ladd. IN KOREA WITH MARQUIS ITO. 1908: Charles Scribner's sons.

_____. "The Annexation of Korea: An Essay in 'Benevolent Assimilation'," *Yale Review* 1.4 (1912), 639-656.

Japan Chronicle. THE KOREAN CONSPIRACY TRIAL: FULL REPORT OF THE PROCEEDINGS IN APPEAL BY THE SPECIAL CORRESPONDENT OF THE "JAPAN CHRONICLE." 1913: Japan Chronicle.

_____. THE INDEPENDENCE MOVEMENT IN KOREA: A RECORD OF SOME OF THE EVENTS OF THE SPRING OF 1919: Japan Chronicle.

Edwin W. Pauley. REPORT ON JAPANESE ASSETS IN SOVIET-OCCUPIED KOREA TO THE PRESIDENT OF THE UNITED STATES, JUNE 1946. 1946: Government Publications Office.

Shobei Shiota. "A 'Ravaged' People: The Koreans in World War II," *Japan Interpreter* 7.1 (1971), 43-53.

CHINA RELATIONS TO 1931

Martin Collcutt. "China and Japan to 1911," KODANSHA ENCYCLOPEDIA OF JAPAN 1: 280-287.

Katsumi Usui. "China and Japan After 1912," KODANSHA ENCYCLOPEDIA OF JAPAN 1: 287-291.

Shinkichi Eto. "Japan's Policies Toward China," in J. W. Morley, ed. JAPAN'S FOREIGN POLICY (1974: Columbia University Press), 236-264.

Marius B. Jansen. "Japanese Views of China During the Meiji Period," in Albert Feuerwerker, et al. APPROACHES TO MODERN CHINESE HISTORY (1967: University of California Press), 163-189.

_____. THE JAPANESE AND SUN YAT-SEN. 1954: Harvard University Press.

_____. JAPAN AND CHINA: FROM WAR TO PEACE, 1894-1972. 1975: Rand McNally.

Akira Iriye, ed. THE CHINESE AND THE JAPANESE: ESSAYS IN POLITICAL AND CULTURAL INTERACTIONS. 1980: Princeton University Press.

_____. "The Ideology of Japanese Imperialism: Imperial Japan and China," in Grant Goodman, ed. IMPERIAL JAPAN AND ASIA: A REASSESSMENT (1967: Occasional Papers of the East Asia Institute, Columbia University), 32-45.

Immanuel C. Y. Hsu. THE RISE OF MODERN CHINA. 1970: Oxford University Press.

Hyman Kublin. "The Attitude of China During the Liu-Ch'iu Controversy, 1871-1881," _Pacific Historical Review_ 18.2 (1949), 213-231.

T. F. Tsiang. "Sino-Japanese Diplomatic Relations, 1870-1894," _Chinese Social and Political Science Review_ 14 (1933), 3-107.

Payson J. Treat. "The Cause of the Sino-Japanese War, 1894," _Pacific Historical Review_ 8.2 (1939), 149-158.

Robert T. Pollard. "Dynamics of Japanese Imperialism," _Pacific Historical Review_ 8.1 (1939), 5-35.

Akira Iriye. "Sino-Japanese War of 1894-1895," KODANSHA ENCYCLOPEDIA OF JAPAN 7: 197-198.

Munemitsu Mutsu. KENKENROKU: A DIPLOMATIC RECORD OF THE SINO-JAPANESE WAR, 1894-1895. Gordon M. Berger, transl. 1982: Princeton University Press.

Donald Keene. "The Sino-Japanese War of 1894-95 and Japanese Culture," in his LANDSCAPES AND PORTRAITS: APPRECIATIONS OF JAPANESE CULTURE (1971: Kodansha International), 259-299.

Shumpei Okamoto. IMPRESSIONS OF THE FRONT: WOODCUTS OF THE SINO-JAPANESE WAR. 1982: Philadelphia Museum of Art.

Yoshiaki Yamada & F. Warrington Eastlake. HEROIC JAPAN: A HISTORY OF THE WAR BETWEEN CHINA AND JAPAN. 1897; reprinted 1979: University Publications of America.

Jeffrey Dorwart. THE PIGTAIL WAR: AMERICAN INVOLVEMENT IN THE SINO-JAPANESE WAR, 1894-95. 1975: University of Massachusetts Press.

Giichi Ono. EXPENDITURES OF THE SINO-JAPANESE WAR. 1922: Oxford University Press.

Chester C. Tan. THE BOXER CATASTROPHE. 1955: Columbia University Press.

George Alexander Lensen. BALANCE OF INTRIGUE: INTERNATIONAL RIVALRY IN KOREA AND MANCHURIA, 1884-1899. 1982: University of Hawaii Press.

Michael M. Hunt. FRONTIER DEFENSE AND THE OPEN DOOR: MANCHURIA IN CHINESE-AMERICAN RELATIONS, 1895-1911. 1973: Yale University Press.

_____. THE MAKING OF A SPECIAL RELATIONSHIP: THE UNITED STATES AND CHINA TO 1914. 1983: Columbia University Press.

Masaru Ikei. "Japan's Response to the Chinese Revolution of 1911," *Journal of Asian Studies* 25.2 (1966), 213-227.

Ernest P. Young. THE PRESIDENCY OF YUAN SHIH-K'AI. 1976: University of Michigan Press.

_____. "Twenty-One Demands," KODANSHA ENCYCLOPEDIA OF JAPAN 8: 120-121.

Kwan-hwa Yim. "Yuan Shih-kai and the Japanese," *Journal of Asian Studies* 24.1 (1964), 63-73.

Paul S. Dull. "Count Kato Komei and the Twenty-One Demands," *Pacific Historical Review* 19.2 (1950), 151-161.

Marius B. Jansen. "Yawata, Hanyehping, and the Twenty-One Demands," *Pacific Historical Review* 23.1 (1954), 31-48.

Arthur S. Link. WILSON: THE STRUGGLE FOR NEUTRALITY 1914-1915. 1960: Princeton University Press.

Harley F. MacNair & Donald F. Lach. MODERN FAR EASTERN INTERNATIONAL RELATIONS. 2nd edition. 1955: Van Nostrand.

Thomas E. La Fargue. CHINA AND THE WORLD WAR. 1937: Stanford University Press.

Madeline Chi. CHINA DIPLOMACY 1914-1918. 1970: Harvard East Asian Monographs.

Frank C. Langdon. "Japan's Failure to Establish Friendly Relations with China in 1917-1918," *Pacific Historical Review* 26.3 (1957), 245-258.

Westel Woodbury Willoughby. CHINA AT THE CONFERENCE: A REPORT. 1922: Johns Hopkins.

Russell H. Fifield. "Japanese Policy Toward the Shantung Question at the Paris Peace Conference," *Journal of Modern History* 23.3 (1951), 265-272.

_____. WOODROW WILSON AND THE FAR EAST: THE DIPLOMACY OF THE SHANTUNG QUESTION. 1952: Crowell.

_____. "Secretary Hughes and the Shantung Question," *Pacific Historical Review* 23.4 (1954), 373-385.

F. S. Cocks. THE SECRET TREATIES AND UNDERSTANDINGS. 2nd edition. 1931: Union of Democratic Control.

Alvin D. Coox & Hilary Conroy, eds. CHINA AND JAPAN: A SEARCH FOR BALANCE SINCE WORLD WAR I. 1978: ABC Clio. Includes essays concerning the Shantung intervention, Paris peace conference, bicultural relations, anti-Japanese activities in Manchuria, the war of 1937-1945, and post-1945 Sino-Japanese relations.

Richard Dean Burns & Edward M. Bennett, eds. DIPLOMATS IN CRISIS: UNITED STATES-CHINESE-JAPANESE RELATIONS, 1919-1941. 1974: ABC Clio.

Akira Iriye. AFTER IMPERIALISM: THE SEARCH FOR A NEW ORDER IN THE FAR EAST, 1921-1931. 1965: Harvard University Press.

Nobuya Bamba. JAPANESE DIPLOMACY IN A DILEMMA: NEW LIGHT ON JAPAN'S CHINA POLICY, 1924-1929. 1973: University of British Columbia Press.

William F. Morton. TANAKA GIICHI AND JAPAN'S CHINA POLICY. 1980: St. Martin's.

Gavan McCormack. CHANG TSO-LIN IN NORTHEAST CHINA, 1911-1928: CHINA, JAPAN, AND THE MANCHURIAN IDEA. 1977: University of California Press.

John W. Young. "The Hara Cabinet and Chang Tso-lin, 1920-1," *Monumenta Nipponica* 27.2 (1972), 125-142.

Paul S. Dull. "The Assassination of Chang Tso-lin," *Far Eastern Quarterly* 11.4 (1952), 453-463.

Akira Iriye. "Chang Hsueh-liang and the Japanese," *Journal of Asian Studies* 20.1 (1960), 33-43

Paul H. Clyde. INTERNATIONAL RIVALRIES IN MANCHURIA, 1689-1922. 1928: Ohio State University Press.

Carl Walter Young. INTERNATIONAL RELATIONS OF MANCHURIA. 1929: University of Chicago Press.

Sadako N. Ogata. "Expansion and Protection of Japan's Interests in Manchuria," in her DEFIANCE IN MANCHURIA (1964: University of California Press), 3-19, covering the period prior to 1931.

Herbert P. Bix. "Japanese Imperialism and the Manchurian Economy, 1900-31," *The China Quarterly* 51 (1972), 425-443.

Ralph William Huenemann. THE DRAGON AND THE IRON HORSE: THE ECONOMICS OF RAILROADS IN CHINA, 1876-1937. 1983: Harvard University Press.

George Alexander Lensen. "Russia and Japan," KODANSHA ENCYCLOPEDIA OF JAPAN 6: 340-344.

Chihiro Hosoya. "Japan's Policies Toward Russia," in J.W. Morley, ed. JAPAN'S FOREIGN POLICY (1974: Columbia University Press), 340-406.

Donald W. Treadgold. "Russia and the Far East," in Ivo J. Lederer, ed. RUSSIAN FOREIGN POLICY: ESSAYS IN HISTORICAL PERSPECTIVE (1966: Yale University Press), 531-574.

George Alexander Lensen. THE RUSSIAN PUSH TOWARD JAPAN: RUSSO-JAPANESE RELATIONS, 1697-1875. 1959: Princeton University Press.

_____. KOREA AND MANCHURIA BETWEEN RUSSIA AND JAPAN, 1895-1904. 1966: Diplomatic Press. A reprint, with introduction, of the diary of Sir Ernest Satow.

_____. RUSSIAN EASTWARD EXPANSION. 1964: Prentice-Hall.

John A. Harrison. JAPAN'S NORTHERN FRONTIER: A PRELIMINARY STUDY IN COLONIZATION AND EXPANSION, WITH SPECIAL REFERENCE TO THE RELATIONS OF JAPAN AND RUSSIA. 1953: University of Florida Press.

D. J. Dallin. THE RISE OF RUSSIA IN ASIA. 1949: Yale University Press.

Andrew Malozemoff. RUSSIAN FAR EASTERN POLICY, 1881-1905, WITH SPECIAL EMPHASIS ON THE CAUSES OF THE RUSSO-JAPANESE WAR. 1958: University of California Press.

B. A. Romanov. RUSSIA IN MANCHURIA, 1892-1906. 1952: University of Michigan Press.

Theodore H. Von Laue. SERGEI WITTE AND THE INDUSTRIALIZATION OF RUSSIA. 1963: Columbia University Press.

A. Yarmolinsky, ed. THE MEMOIRS OF COUNT WITTE. 1921: Doubleday, Page.

Edward H. Zabriskie. AMERICAN-RUSSIAN RIVALRY IN THE FAR EAST: A STUDY IN DIPLOMACY AND POWER POLITICS, 1895-1914. 1946: University of Pennsylvania Press.

Shumpei Okamoto. "Russo-Japanese War," KODANSHA ENCYCLOPEDIA OF JAPAN 6: 345-347.

_____. THE JAPANESE OLIGARCHY AND THE RUSSO-JAPANESE WAR. 1970: Columbia University Press.

Denis & Peggy Warner. THE TIDE AT SUNRISE: A HISTORY OF THE RUSSO-JAPANESE WAR, 1904-1905. 1974: Charterhouse.

D. Walder. THE SHORT VICTORIOUS WAR: THE RUSSO-JAPANESE CONFLICT, 1904-1905. 1974: Harper & Row.

Frederic William Unger. THE AUTHENTIC HISTORY OF THE WAR BETWEEN RUSSIA AND JAPAN. 1905: World Bible House.

Richard Hough. THE FLEET THAT HAD TO DIE. 1960: Ballentine.

Tadayoshi Sakurai. HUMAN BULLETS: A SOLDIER'S STORY OF PORT ARTHUR. 1907: Houghton Mifflin.

Kanichi Asakawa. THE RUSSO-JAPANESE CONFLICT: ITS CAUSES AND ISSUES. 1904: Houghton Mifflin.

John A. White. THE DIPLOMACY OF THE RUSSO-JAPANESE WAR. 1964: Princeton University Press.

Eugene P. Trani. THE TREATY OF PORTSMOUTH: AN ADVENTURE IN AMERICAN DIPLOMACY. 1969: University of Kentucky Press.

Michael Futrell. "Colonel Akashi and Japanese Contacts with Russian Revolutionaries in 1904-5," *St. Anthony's Papers* (1967), 7-22.

Hyman Kublin. "The Japanese Socialists and the Russo-Japanese War," *Journal of Modern History* 22.4 (1950), 322-339.

Ernest Batson Price. THE RUSSO-JAPANESE TREATIES OF 1907-1916 CONCERNING MANCHURIA AND MONGOLIA. 1933: Johns Hopkins.

Peter S. H. Tang. RUSSIAN AND SOVIET POLICY IN MANCHURIA AND OUTER MONGOLIA, 1911-1931. 1959: Duke University Press.

James. W. Morley. THE JAPANESE THRUST INTO SIBERIA, 1918. 1957: Columbia University Press.

Adam B. Ulam. EXPANSION AND COEXISTENCE: THE HISTORY OF SOVIET FOREIGN POLICY, 1917-67. 1968: Praeger.

David J. Dallin. SOVIET RUSSIA AND THE FAR EAST. 1948: Yale University Press.

B. Nicolaevsky. "Russia, Japan, and the Pan-Asiatic Movement to 1925," *Far Eastern Quarterly* 8.3 (1949), 259-295.

Xenia Joukoff Eudin & Robert C. North. SOVIET RUSSIA AND THE EAST, 1920-1927. 1957: Stanford University Press.

George Alexander Lensen. JAPANESE RECOGNITION OF THE U.S.S.R.: SOVIET-JAPANESE RELATIONS, 1921-1930. 1970: Monumenta Nipponica Monographs.

_____. THE DAMNED INHERITANCE: THE SOVIET UNION AND THE MANCHURIAN CRISIS, 1924-1935. 1974: Diplomatic Press.

Ikuhiko Hata. REALITY AND ILLUSION: THE HIDDEN CRISIS BETWEEN JAPAN AND THE USSR, 1932-1934. 1967: Occasional Papers of the East Asia Institute, Columbia University.

James W. Morley, ed. DETERRENT DIPLOMACY: JAPAN, GERMANY, AND THE USSR, 1935-1940. 1976: Columbia University Press. Includes Tokushiro Ohata on "The Anti-Comintern Pact, 1935-1939" (1-111) and Ikuhiko Hata on "The Japanese-Soviet Confrontation, 1935-1939" (113-178).

Max Beloff. THE FOREIGN POLICY OF SOVIET RUSSIA, 1929-1941. 2 volumes. 1953: Oxford University Press.

Harriet L. Moore. SOVIET FAR EASTERN DIPLOMACY, 1931-1945. 1945: Princeton University Press.

Victor A. Yakhontoff. RUSSIA AND THE SOVIET UNION IN THE FAR EAST. 1932: Allen & Unwin.

G. Safarov. THE FAR EAST ABLAZE. 1933: Worker's Library.

Larry W. Moses. "Soviet-Japanese Confrontation in Outer Mongolia: The Battle of Nomonhan-Khalkin Gol," *Journal of Asian History* 1.1 (1967), 64-85.

Katsu H. Young. "The Nomonhan Incident: Imperial Japan and the Soviet Union," *Monumenta Nipponica* 22.1-2 (1967), 82-102.

Alvin D. Coox. THE ANATOMY OF A SMALL WAR: THE SOVIET-JAPANESE STRUGGLE FOR CHANGKUFENG/ KHANSAN, 1938. 1977: Greenwood.

_____. NOMONHAN: JAPAN AGAINST RUSSIA, 1939. 2 volumes. 1985: Stanford University Press.

hn J. Stephan. THE RUSSIAN FASCISTS: TRAGEDY AND FARCE IN EXILE, 1925-1945. 1978: Harper & Row.

conid L. Kutakov. JAPANESE FOREIGN POLICY ON THE EVE OF THE PACIFIC WAR: A SOVIET VIEW. 1972: Diplomatic Press.

eorge Alexander Lensen. THE STRANGE NEUTRALITY: SOVIET-JAPANESE RELATIONS DURING THE SECOND WORLD WAR, 1941-1945. 1972: Diplomatic Press.

iane Shaver Clemens. YALTA. 1970: Oxford University Press.

aymond L. Garthoff. "The Soviet Manchurian Campaigns, August 1945," *Military Affairs* 34 (1970), 312-335.

. S. Department of Defense. THE ENTRY OF THE SOVIET UNION INTO THE WAR AGAINST JAPAN: MILITARY PLANS, 1941-1945. 1955: Government Publications Office.

GREAT BRITAIN

Ian Nish. "Japan's Policies Toward Britain," in J. W. Morley, ed. JAPAN'S FOREIGN POLICY (1974: Columbia University Press), 184-235.

_____. "United Kingdom and Japan," KODANSHA ENCYCLOPEDIA OF JAPAN 8: 150-153.

_____. "Anglo-Japanese Alliance," KODANSHA ENCYCLOPEDIA OF JAPAN 1: 56-57.

William G. Beasley. GREAT BRITAIN AND THE OPENING OF JAPAN, 1834-1858. 1951: Luzac.

Grace Fox. BRITAIN AND JAPAN, 1858-1883. 1969: Clarendon.

Ian Nish. THE ANGLO-JAPANESE ALLIANCE: THE DIPLOMACY OF TWO ISLAND EMPIRES, 1894-1907. 1966; 2nd edition, 1985: Athlone.

_____. ALLIANCE IN DECLINE: A STUDY IN ANGLO-JAPANESE RELATIONS, 1908-23. 1972: Athlone.

_____. "Japan and the Ending of the Anglo-Japanese Alliance," in K. Bourne & D. C. Watt, eds. STUDIES IN INTERNATIONAL HISTORY (1967: Longman's), 369-384.

_____, ed. ANGLO-JAPANESE ALIENATION, 1919-1952. 1982: Cambridge University Press.

John C. Perry. "Great Britain and the Emergence of Japan as a Naval Power," *Monumenta Nipponica* 21.3-4 (1966), 305-321.

Peter Lowe. GREAT BRITAIN AND JAPAN, 1911-1915. 1969: Macmillan.

Malcom D. Kennedy. THE ESTRANGEMENT OF GREAT BRITAIN AND JAPAN, 1917-35. 1969: University of California Press.

William Roger Louis. BRITISH STRATEGY IN THE FAR EAST, 1919-1939. 1971: Clarendon.

Irving S. Friedman. BRITISH RELATIONS WITH CHINA, 1931-1939. 1940: Institute of Pacific Relations.

Ann Trotter. BRITAIN AND EAST ASIA, 1933-1937. 1975: Cambridge University Press.

Stephen Lyon Endicott. DIPLOMACY AND ENTERPRISE: BRITISH CHINA POLICY, 1933-1937. 1975: University of British Columbia Press.

Bradford A. Lee. BRITAIN AND THE SINO-JAPANESE WAR, 1937-1939: A STUDY IN THE DILEMMAS OF BRITISH DECLINE. 1973: Stanford University Press.

Nicolas R. Clifford. RETREAT FROM CHINA: BRITISH POLICY IN THE FAR EAST, 1937-1941. 1967: University of Washington Press.

John W. Dower. EMPIRE AND AFTERMATH: YOSHIDA SHIGERU AND THE JAPANESE EXPERIENCE, 1878-1954 (1979: Harvard East Asian Monographs), 123-212.

Peter Lowe. GREAT BRITAIN AND THE ORIGINS OF THE PACIFIC WAR. 1977: Clarendon.

Christopher Thorne. ALLIES OF A KIND: THE UNITED STATES, BRITAIN, AND THE WAR AGAINST JAPAN, 1941-1945. 1978: Oxford University Press.

William Roger Louis. IMPERIALISM AT BAY, 1941-1945: THE UNITED STATES AND THE DECOLONIALIZATION OF THE BRITISH EMPIRE. 1977: Clarendon.

S. Woodburn Kirby, et al. THE WAR AGAINST JAPAN. 4 volumes. 1959: Her Majesty's Stationery Office.

GREAT BRITAIN--II

E. L. Woodward & Rohan Butler, eds. DOCUMENTS ON BRITISH FOREIGN POLICY, 1919-1939. 9 volumes. 1949-1955: Her Majesty's Stationery Office.

Sir Ernest Satow. A DIPLOMAT IN JAPAN. 1921: Seeley Service.

Major General F. S. G. Piggott. BROKEN THREAD: AN AUTOBIOGRAPHY. 1950: Gale & Polden. Piggott served as military attache in Japan before the outbreak of war.

Robert Craigie. BEHIND THE JAPANESE MASK. 1946: Hutchinson. Craigie was His Majesty's Ambassador to Japan from 1937 to 1942.

141

U. S. RELATIONS TO 1931

General Texts

Ernest R. May & James C. Thomson Jr., eds. AMERICAN-EAST ASIAN RELATIONS: A SURVEY. 1972: Harvard University Press. A collection of 17 essays organized by strict chronology and covering the period 1794 to the 1960s.

Akira Iriye. "United States and Japan," KODANSHA ENCYCLOPEDIA OF JAPAN 8: 154-160.

_____. "Japan's Policies Toward the United States," in J.W. Morley, ed. JAPAN'S FOREIGN POLICY (1974: Columbia University Press), 407-459.

_____. ACROSS THE PACIFIC--AN INNER HISTORY OF AMERICAN-EAST ASIAN RELATIONS. 1967: Harcourt Brace & World.

_____, ed. MUTUAL IMAGES: ESSAYS IN AMERICAN-JAPANESE RELATIONS. 1975: Harvard University Press.

_____. "Western Perceptions and Asian Realities," in Joe C. Dixon, ed. THE AMERICAN MILITARY AND THE FAR EAST (a 1980 U.S. Air Force symposium: Office of Air Force History), 9-19.

Shunsuke Kamei. "Japanese See America: A Century of Firsthand Impressions," *Japan Interpreter* 11.1 (1976), 6-35.

William L. Neumann. AMERICA ENCOUNTERS JAPAN: FROM PERRY TO MACARTHUR. 1963: Johns Hopkins.

Charles E. Neu. THE TROUBLED ENCOUNTER: THE UNITED STATES AND JAPAN. 1975: Wiley.

Edwin O. Reischauer. THE UNITED STATES AND JAPAN. 3rd edition. 1965: Harvard University Press.

George Kennan. AMERICAN DIPLOMACY, 1900-1950. 1951: University of Chicago Press.

James C. Thomson Jr., Peter W. Stanley & John C. Perry. SENTIMENTAL IMPERIALISTS: THE AMERICAN EXPERIENCE IN EAST ASIA. 1981: Harper & Row.

Robert A. Hart. THE ECCENTRIC TRADITION: AMERICAN DIPLOMACY IN THE FAR EAST. 1976: Charles Scribner's Sons.

Young Hum Kim. AMERICAN FRONTIER ACTIVITIES IN ASIA: U.S.-ASIAN RELATIONS IN THE TWENTIETH CENTURY. 1981: Nelson-Hall.

A. Whitney Griswold. THE FAR EASTERN POLICY OF THE UNITED STATES. 1938: Yale University Press.

Eleanor Tupper & George E. McReynolds. JAPAN IN AMERICAN PUBLIC OPINION. 1937: Macmillan.

Case Studies

Hikomatsu Kamikawa. JAPANESE-AMERICAN RELATIONS IN THE MEIJI-TAISHO ERA. 1958: Obunsha.

Tyler Dennett. AMERICANS IN EASTERN ASIA: A CRITICAL STUDY OF UNITED STATES POLICY IN THE FAR EAST IN THE NINETEENTH CENTURY. 1922: Macmillan.

Robert S. Schwantes. "America and Japan," in May & Thomson, AMERICAN-EAST ASIAN RELATIONS (1972: Harvard University Press), 97-128. Focus on 19th century.

kira Iriye. PACIFIC ESTRANGEMENT: JAPANESE AND AMERICAN EXPANSION, 1897-1911. 1972: Harvard University Press.

aymond A. Esthus. THEODORE ROOSEVELT AND JAPAN. 1966: University of Washington Press.

harles E. Neu. AN UNCERTAIN FRIENDSHIP: THEODORE ROOSEVELT AND JAPAN, 1906-1909. 1967: Harvard University Press.

oward K. Beale. THEODORE ROOSEVELT AND THE RISE OF AMERICA TO WORLD POWER. 1956: Johns Hopkins.

. A. Bailey. THEODORE ROOSEVELT AND THE JAPANESE-AMERICAN CRISIS. 1934: Stanford University Press.

_____. "The Root-Takahira Agreement of 1908," *Pacific Historical Review* 9 (1940), 19-35.

harles Vevier. THE UNITED STATES AND CHINA, 1906-1913. 1955: University of British Columbia Press.

oy Watson Curry. WOODROW WILSON AND FAR EASTERN POLICY, 1913-1921. 1957: Bookman Associates.

'ien-yi Li. WOODROW WILSON'S CHINA POLICY, 1913-1917. 1969: Octagon.

dward H. Buehrig. WOODROW WILSON AND THE BALANCE OF POWER. 1955: Indiana University Press.

rthur S. Link. WILSON: THE STRUGGLE FOR NEUTRALITY, 1914-1915. 1960: Princeton University Press.

rno Mayer. POLITICS AND DIPLOMACY OF PEACEMAKING: CONTAINMENT AND COUNTERREVOLUTION AT VERSAILLES, 1918-1919. 1967: Knopf.

urton F. Beers. "Robert Lansing's Proposed Bargain with Japan," *Pacific Historical Review* 26.4 (1957), 391-400.

_____. VAIN ENDEAVOR: ROBERT LANSING'S ATTEMPT TO END THE AMERICAN-JAPANESE RIVALRY. 1962: Duke University Press.

ussell H. Fifield. WOODROW WILSON AND THE FAR EAST: THE DIPLOMACY OF THE SHANTUNG QUESTION. 1952: Crowell.

Villiam Reynolds Braisted. THE UNITED STATES NAVY IN THE PACIFIC, 1897-1909. 1958: University of Texas Press.

_____. THE UNITED STATES NAVY IN THE PACIFIC, 1909-1922. 1971: University of California Press.

). J. Clinard. JAPAN'S INFLUENCE ON AMERICAN NAVAL POWER, 1897-1917. 1947: Princeton University Press.

Iarold & Margaret Sprout. THE RISE OF AMERICAN NAVAL POWER, 1776-1918. 1946: Princeton University Press.

_____. TOWARD A NEW ORDER OF SEA POWER: AMERICAN NAVAL POLICY AND THE WORLD SCENE, 1918-1922. 1946: Princeton University Press.

. Chalmers Vinson. THE PARCHMENT PEACE: THE UNITED STATES SENATE AND THE WASHINGTON CONFERENCE, 1921-1922. 1955: University of Georgia Press.

Thomas H. Buckley. THE UNITED STATES AND THE WASHINGTON CONFERENCE, 1921-1922. 1970: University of Tennessee Press.

U. S. RELATIONS TO 1931--III

Herbert Yardley. THE AMERICAN BLACK CHAMBER. 1931: Blue Ribbon Books.

Roger Dingman. "American Policy and Strategy in East Asia, 1898-1950: The Creation of a Commitment," in Joe C. Dixon, ed. THE AMERICAN MILITARY AND THE FAR EAST (1980: a U.S. Air Force Symposium: Office of Air Force History), 20-45.

_____. "1917-1922," in May & Thomson, AMERICAN-EAST ASIAN RELATIONS (1972: Harvard University Press), 190-218.

_____. POWER IN THE PACIFIC: THE ORIGINS OF NAVAL ARMS LIMITATION, 1914-1922. 1976: University of Chicago Press.

Gerald Wheeler. PRELUDE TO PEARL HARBOR: THE UNITED STATES NAVY AND THE FAR EAST, 1921-1931. 1963: University of Missouri Press.

_____. "Isolated Japan: Anglo-American Diplomatic Cooperation, 1927-1936," *Pacific Historical Review* 30.2 (1961), 165-178.

Akira Iriye. "1922-1931," in May & Thomson, AMERICAN-EAST ASIAN RELATIONS (1972: Harvard University Press), 221-242.

William A. Williams. "China and Japan: A Challenge and a Choice of the 1920s," *Pacific Historical Review* 26.3 (1957), 259-279.

Roger Daniels. THE POLITICS OF PREJUDICE: THE ANTI-JAPANESE MOVEMENT IN CALIFORNIA AND THE STRUGGLE FOR JAPANESE EXCLUSION. 1968: University of California Press.

Erich Pauer. "Germany and Japan," KODANSHA ENCYCLOPEDIA OF JAPAN 3: 26-28.

Frank W. Ikle. "Japan's Policies Toward Germany," in J. W. Morley, ed. JAPAN'S FOREIGN POLICY (1974: Columbia University Press), 265-339.

Minge C. Bee. "The Origins of German Far Eastern Policy," *Chinese Social and Political Science Review* 21 (1937), 65-97.

Kurt Bloch. GERMAN INTERESTS AND POLICIES IN THE FAR EAST. 1939: Institute of Pacific Relations.

John P. Fox. GERMANY AND THE FAR EASTERN CRISIS, 1931-1938: A STUDY IN DIPLOMACY AND IDEOLOGY. 1982: Oxford University Press.

John Huizenga. "Yosuke Matsuoka and the Japanese-German Alliance," in Gordon A. Craig & Felix Gilbert, eds. THE DIPLOMATS, 1919-1939 (1953: Princeton University Press), 615-648.

J. W. Morley, ed. DETERRENT DIPLOMACY: JAPAN, GERMANY AND THE U.S.S.R., 1935-1940. 1976: Columbia University Press. Includes Tokushiro Ohata, "The Anti-Comintern Pact, 1935-1939" (1-111) and Chihiro Hosoya, "The Tripartite Pact, 1939-1940" (179-257).

Frank W. Ikle. GERMAN-JAPANESE RELATIONS, 1936-1940: A STUDY OF TOTALITARIAN DIPLOMACY. 1956: Bookman Associates.

Carl Boyd. THE EXTRAORDINARY ENVOY: GENERAL HIROSHI OSHIMA AND DIPLOMACY IN THE THIRD REICH, 1934-1939. 1980: University Press of America.

James T. C. Liu. "German Mediation in the Sino-Japanese War, 1937-38," *Far Eastern Quarterly* 8.2 (1949), 157-171.

Ernst L. Presseisen. GERMANY AND JAPAN: A STUDY IN TOTALITARIAN DIPLOMACY, 1933-1941. 1958: Martinus Nijhoff.

Johanna Menzel Meskill. HITLER AND JAPAN: THE HOLLOW ALLIANCE. 1966: Atherton.

Paul W. Schroeder. THE AXIS ALLIANCE AND JAPANESE-AMERICAN RELATIONS, 1941. 1958: Cornell University Press.

Milan Hauner. INDIA IN AXIS STRATEGY: GERMANY, JAPAN, AND INDIAN NATIONALISTS IN THE SECOND WORLD WAR. 1981: Klett-Cotta.

L. L. Trefousse. "Germany and Pearl Harbor," *Far Eastern Quarterly* 11.1 (1951), 35-50.

THE MANCHURIAN INCIDENT & AFTERMATH

[See also the numerous official publications concerning Manchuria and Manchukuo cited in the "Primary Materials" bibliography below, especially pages 185-190.]

The Manchurian Incident

Mark R. Peattie. "Manchurian Incident," KODANSHA ENCYCLOPEDIA OF JAPAN 5: 97-99.

Takehiko Yoshihashi. "Manchukuo," KODANSHA ENCYCLOPEDIA OF JAPAN 5: 96-97.

James W. Morley, ed. JAPAN ERUPTS: THE LONDON NAVAL CONFERENCE AND THE MANCHURIAN INCIDENT, 1928-1932. 1984: Columbia University Press.

Sadako N. Ogata. DEFIANCE IN MANCHURIA: THE MAKING OF JAPANESE FOREIGN POLICY, 1931-1932. 1964: University of California Press.

Takehiko Yoshihashi. CONSPIRACY AT MUKDEN: THE RISE OF THE JAPANESE MILITARY. 1963: Yale University Press.

Sara R. Smith. THE MANCHURIAN CRISIS, 1931-1932. 1948: Columbia University Press.

Christopher Thorne. THE LIMITS OF FOREIGN POLICY: THE WEST, THE LEAGUE, AND THE FAR EASTERN CRISIS OF 1931-1933. 1973: Capricorn.

Robert H. Ferrell. AMERICAN DIPLOMACY IN THE GREAT DEPRESSION: HOOVER-STIMSON FOREIGN POLICY, 1929-1933. 1957: Yale University Press.

Justus D. Doenecke. THE DIPLOMACY OF FRUSTRATION: THE MANCHURIAN CRISIS OF 1931-1933 AS REVEALED IN THE PAPERS OF STANLEY K. HORNBECK. 1981: Hoover Institution Press.

Armin Rappaport. HENRY L. STIMSON AND JAPAN, 1931-1933. 1963: University of Chicago Press.

Richard N. Current. SECRETARY STIMSON, A STUDY IN STATECRAFT. 1954: Rutgers University Press.

Elting E. Morison. TURMOIL AND TRADITION: A STUDY OF THE LIFE AND TIMES OF HENRY L. STIMSON. 1960: Houghton Mifflin.

Henry L. Stimson. THE FAR EASTERN CRISIS: RECOLLECTIONS AND OBSERVATIONS. 1936: Harper.

George Alexander Lensen. "Japan and Manchuria: Ambassador Forbes's Appraisal of American Policy Toward Japan in 1931-32," *Monumenta Nipponica* 23.1-2 (1968), 66-89.

Owen Lattimore. MANCHURIA: CRADLE OF CONFLICT. Revised edition. 1935: Macmillan.

John R. Stewart. MANCHURIA SINCE 1931. 1936: Institute of Pacific Relations.

F. C. Jones. MANCHURIA SINCE 1931. 1949: Royal Institute of International Affairs.

Irving I. Kramer. "Japan in Manchuria." Four articles in *Contemporary Japan* : volume 22 (1953), 584-611; 23 (1954), 75-100; 25 (1958), 224-237 and 299-417.

Chong-sik Lee. REVOLUTIONARY STRUGGLE IN MANCHURIA: CHINESE COMMUNISM AND SOVIET INTEREST, 1922-1945. 1983: University of California Press.

____. COUNTERINSURGENCY IN MANCHURIA: THE JAPANESE EXPERIENCE. 1967: RAND Corporation Memorandum RM-5012-ARPA.

sin Gioro Pu-Yi. FROM EMPEROR TO CITIZEN. 2 volumes. 1964-1965: Peking Foreign Language Press.

B. Schumpeter, ed. THE INDUSTRIALIZATION OF JAPAN AND MANCHUKUO, 1930-1940. 1940: Macmillan.

asic Treaty Issues

hn van Antwerp MacMurray. TREATIES AND AGREEMENTS WITH AND CONCERNING CHINA, 1894-1919. 2 volumes. 1921: Oxford University Press.

rnegie Endowment for International Peace, Division of International Law. MANCHURIA: TREATIES AND AGREEMENTS. 1921: Carnegie Endowment for International Peace.

u-hsi Hsu. CHINA AND HER POLITICAL ENTITY: A STUDY OF CHINA'S FOREIGN RELATIONS WITH REFERENCE TO KOREA, MANCHURIA, AND MONGOLIA. 1926: Oxford University Press.

. W. Willoughby. FOREIGN RIGHTS AND INTERESTS IN CHINA. 2 volumes, revised edition. 1927: Johns Hopkins.

rl Walter Young. THE INTERNATIONAL RELATIONS OF MANCHURIA: A DIGEST AND ANALYSIS OF TREATIES, AGREEMENTS, AND NEGOTIATIONS CONCERNING THE THREE EASTERN PROVINCES OF CHINA. 1929: University of Chicago Press.

____. JAPAN'S JURISDICTION AND INTERNATIONAL LEGAL POSITION IN MANCHURIA. 3 volumes. 1931: Johns Hopkins.

1. THE INTERNATIONAL LEGAL STATUS OF THE KWANTUNG LEASED TERRITORY.
2. JAPAN'S SPECIAL POSITION IN MANCHURIA: ITS ASSERTION, LEGAL INTERPRETATION AND PRESENT MEANING.
3. JAPANESE JURISDICTION IN THE SOUTH MANCHURIAN RAILWAY AREAS.

homas A. Bisson. BASIC TREATY ISSUES IN MANCHURIA BETWEEN JAPAN AND CHINA. 1931: Foreign Policy Association.

an-tao Wu. JAPAN'S ACTS OF TREATY VIOLATION AND ENCROACHMENT UPON THE SOVEREIGN RIGHTS OF CHINA IN THE NORTHEASTERN PROVINCES. 1932: The Northeastern Affairs Research Institute.

lo Shen. JAPAN IN MANCHURIA: AN ANALYTICAL STUDY OF TREATIES AND DOCUMENTS. 1960: University of the Philippines Press.

/. W. Willoughby. THE SINO-JAPANESE CONTROVERSY AND THE LEAGUE OF NATIONS. 1935: Johns Hopkins.

oyal Institute of International Affairs. SURVEY OF INTERNATIONAL AFFAIRS. See especially the volumes for 1931 and 1937: Royal Institute of International Affairs.

147

THE ROAD TO WAR, 1931-1941

[In addition to the references cited below, see also the excellent textbook treatment in Marius Jansen, JAPAN AND CHINA (1975: Rand McNally), 354-408; Hugh Borton, JAPAN'S MODERN CENTURY (1970: Ronald), 367-428; Edwin Reischauer, John K. Fairbank & Albert Craig, EAST ASIA: THE MODERN TRANSFORMATION (1965: Houghton Mifflin), 579-612; and Mikiso Hane, JAPAN (1972: Charles Scribner's Sons), 452-526.]

Pre (and Post) 1937

Dorothy Borg & Shumpei Okamoto, eds. PEARL HARBOR AS HISTORY: JAPANESE-AMERICAN RELATIONS, 1931-1941. 1973: Columbia University Press.

Saburo Ienaga. THE PACIFIC WAR: WORLD WAR II AND THE JAPANESE, 1931-1945. 1978: Pantheon.

James B. Crowley. JAPAN'S QUEST FOR AUTONOMY: NATIONAL SECURITY AND FOREIGN POLICY, 1930-3 1966: Princeton University Press.

_____. "Japan's Foreign Military Policies," in James W. Morley, ed. JAPAN'S FOREIGN POLICY (1974: Columbia University Press), 54-103 for 1931 and after.

Yale C. Maxon. CONTROL OF JAPANESE FOREIGN POLICY: A STUDY OF CIVIL-MILITARY RIVALRY, 1930-1945. 1957: University of California Press.

James W. Morley, ed. JAPAN'S ROAD TO THE PACIFIC WAR series (adapted from the Japanese series *Taiheiyo Senso e no Michi*). Columbia University Press:

1. JAPAN ERUPTS: THE LONDON NAVAL CONFERENCE AND THE MANCHURIAN INCIDENT, 1928-1932. 1984.
2. THE CHINA QUAGMIRE: JAPAN'S EXPANSION ON THE ASIAN CONTINENT, 1933-1941. 1983.
3. DETERRENT DIPLOMACY: JAPAN, GERMANY, AND THE U.S.S.R., 1935-1940. 1976.
4. THE FATEFUL CHOICE: JAPAN'S ADVANCE INTO SOUTHEAST ASIA, 1939-1941. 1980.

Gordon M. Berger. PARTIES OUT OF POWER IN JAPAN, 1931-1941. 1976: Princeton University Press.

Richard Storry. "The Road to War: 1931-1945," in Arthur E. Tiedmann, ed. AN INTRODUCTION TO JAPANESE CIVILIZATION (1974: Heath), 247-276.

Waldo H. Heinrichs, Jr. "1931-1937," in Ernest May & James Thomson, eds. AMERICAN-EAST ASIAN RELATIONS (1972: Harvard University Press), 243-259.

Gerald E. Wheeler. "The Road to War: The United States and Japan, 1931-1941." *Forum Series* pamphlet, 1963.

Akira Iriye. "Japanese Imperialism and Aggression: Reconsiderations" and "Japan's Foreign Policies Between World Wars--Sources and Interpretations," in Esmonde M. Robertson, ed. THE ORIGINS OF THE SECOND WORLD WAR: HISTORICAL INTERPRETATIONS (1971: Macmillan), 243-271.

_____. "The Failure of Military Expansionism," in James W. Morley, ed. DILEMMAS OF GROWTH IN PREWAR JAPAN (1971: Princeton University Press), 107-138.

_____. "The Historical Background," in his THE COLD WAR IN ASIA: A HISTORICAL INTRODUCTION (1974: Prentice-Hall), 8-46.

Dorothy Borg. THE UNITED STATES AND THE FAR EASTERN CRISIS OF 1933-1938: FROM THE MANCHURIAN INCIDENT THROUGH THE INITIAL STAGES OF THE UNDECLARED SINO-JAPANESE WAR. 1964: Harvard University Press.

illiam L. Newmann. "Ambiguity and Ambivalence in Ideas of National Security in Asia," in Alexander DeConde, ed. ISOLATION AND SECURITY (1957: Duke University Press), 133-158.

muel E. Morison. THE RISING SUN IN THE PACIFIC, 1931-APRIL 1942. Volume 3 of Morison's HISTORY OF THE UNITED STATES NAVAL OPERATIONS IN WORLD WAR II. 1947; revised edition, 1953: Little, Brown.

ephen E. Pelz. RACE TO PEARL HARBOR: THE FAILURE OF THE SECOND LONDON NAVAL CONFERENCE AND THE ONSET OF WORLD WAR II. 1974: Harvard University Press.

umao Harada. THE SAIONJI-HARADA MEMOIRS, 1931-40: COMPLETE TRANSLATION INTO ENGLISH. Available in 3 mircrofilm reels from University Publications of America.

oichi Kido. THE DIARY OF MARQUIS KIDO, 1931-45: SELECTED TRANSLATIONS INTO ENGLISH. 1984: University Publications of America.

igeru Honjo. EMPEROR HIROHITO AND HIS CHIEF AIDE-DE-CAMP: THE HONJO DIARY, 1933-36. Mikiso Hane, transl. 1983: University of Tokyo Press.

ark R. Peattie. ISHIWARA KANJI AND JAPAN'S CONFRONTATION WITH THE WEST. 1975: Princeton University Press.

iroyuki Agawa. THE RELUCTANT ADMIRAL: YAMAMOTO AND THE IMPERIAL NAVY. 1979: Kodansha International.

aburo Shiroyama. WAR CRIMINAL: THE LIFE AND DEATH OF HIROTA KOKI. 1974: Kodansha International.

an Kurzman. KISHI AND JAPAN: THE SEARCH FOR THE SUN. 1960: Ivan Obolensky.

ichard Dean Burns & Edward M. Bennett, eds. DIPLOMATS IN CRISIS: UNITED STATES-CHINESE-JAPANESE RELATIONS, 1919-1941. 1974: ABC Clio.

aldo H. Heinrichs, Jr. AMERICAN AMBASSADOR: JOSEPH C. GREW AND THE DEVELOPMENT OF THE UNITED STATES DIPLOMATIC TRADITION. 1966: Little, Brown.

seph C. Grew. TEN YEARS IN JAPAN: A CONTEMPORARY RECORD DRAWN FROM THE DIARIES AND PRIVATE AND OFFICIAL PAPERS OF JOSEPH C. GREW, UNITED STATES AMBASSADOR TO JAPAN, 1932-1942. 1944: Simon & Schuster.

____. TURBULENT ERA: A DIPLOMATIC RECORD OF FORTY YEARS, 1904-1945. 2 volumes. 1952: Houghton Mifflin.

ussell D. Buhite. NELSON T. JOHNSON AND AMERICAN POLICY TOWARD CHINA, 1925-1941. 1968: Michigan State University Press.

arren I. Cohen. THE CHINESE CONNECTION: ROGER S. GREENE, THOMAS W. LAMONT, GEORGE E. SOKOLSKY AND AMERICAN-EAST ASIAN RELATIONS. 1978: Columbia University Press.

vine H. Anderson, Jr. STANDARD VACUUM OIL COMPANY AND UNITED STATES EAST ASIAN POLICY, 1933-1941. 1975: Princeton University Press.

andra C. Taylor. ADVOCATE OF UNDERSTANDING: SIDNEY GULICK AND THE SEARCH FOR PEACE WITH JAPAN. 1985: Kent State University Press.

aniel B. Ramsdell. "Asia Askew: U.S. Best-Sellers on Asia, 1931-1980," *Bulletin of Concerned Asian Scholars* 15.4 (1983), 2-25.

THE ROAD TO WAR, 1931-1941--III

1937-1941

Louis Morton. "War Plan ORANGE: Evolution of a Strategy," *World Politics* 11 (1959), 221-250.

_____. "Japan's Decision for War," in K. R. Greenfield, ed. COMMAND DECISIONS (1959: Harcourt Brace), 63-87.

Chihiro Hosoya. "The Military and the Foreign Policy of Prewar Japan," *Hitotsubashi Journal of Law and Politics* 7 (1974), 1-7.

_____. "Japan's Decision for War in 1941," *Hitotsubashi Journal of Law and Politics* 5 (1967), 10-19.

_____. "Miscalculations in Deterrent Policy: Japanese-U.S. Relations, 1938-1941," *Hitotsubashi Journal of Law and Politics* 6 (1968), 29-47.

_____. "Twenty-Five Years After Pearl Harbor: A New Look at Japan's Decision for War," in Grant K. Goodman, ed. IMPERIAL JAPAN AND ASIA (1967: Occasional Papers of the East Asia Institute, Columbia University), 52-63.

H. P. Willmott. EMPIRES IN THE BALANCE: JAPANESE AND ALLIED STRATEGIES TO APRIL 1942. 1982: Naval Institute.

Robert J. C. Butow. TOJO AND THE COMING OF THE WAR. 1961: Princeton University Press.

_____. "The Hull-Nomura Conversations: A Fundamental Misconception," *American Historical Review* 65.4 (1960), 822-836.

_____. "Backdoor Diplomacy in the Pacific: The Proposal for a Konoye-Roosevelt Meeting, 1941," *Journal of American History* 59.1 (1972), 48-72.

_____. THE JOHN DOE ASSOCIATES: BACKDOOR DIPLOMACY FOR PEACE, 1941. 1974: Stanford University Press.

Herbert Feis. THE ROAD TO PEARL HARBOR: THE COMING OF THE WAR BETWEEN THE UNITED STATES AND JAPAN. 1950: Princeton University Press.

David J. Lu. FROM THE MARCO POLO BRIDGE TO PEARL HARBOR: JAPAN'S ENTRY INTO WORLD WAR II. 1961: Public Affairs.

John Toland. THE RISING SUN: THE DECLINE AND FALL OF THE JAPANESE EMPIRE, 1936-1945. 1970: Random House.

David Bergamini. JAPAN'S IMPERIAL CONSPIRACY. 1971: Morrow.

Charles D. Sheldon. "Japanese Aggression and the Emperor, 1931-1941, from Contemporary Diaries," *Modern Asian Studies* 10.1 (1976), 1-40.

_____. "Scapegoat or Instigator of Japanese Aggression? Inoue Kiyoshi's Case Against the Emperor," *Modern Asian Studies* 12.1 (1978), 1-35.

William L. Langer & S. E. Gleason. THE WORLD CRISIS AND AMERICAN FOREIGN POLICY. 1952-1953: Harper.

> Volume 1: THE CHALLENGE TO ISOLATION, 1937-1940. 1952.
> Volume 2: THE UNDECLARED WAR, 1940-1941. 1953.

HE ROAD TO WAR, 1931-1941--IV

mes H. Herzog. CLOSING THE OPEN DOOR: AMERICAN-JAPANESE DIPLOMATIC NEGOTIATIONS, 1936-1941. 1973: Naval Institute.

nathan Utley. GOING TO WAR WITH JAPAN, 1937-1941. 1985: University of Tennessee Press.

nald J. Friedman. THE ROAD FROM ISOLATION: THE CAMPAIGN OF THE AMERICAN COMMITTEE FOR NON-PARTICIPATION IN JAPANESE AGGRESSION, 1938-1941. 1968: Harvard East Asian Monographs.

manuel Hsu. "Kurusu's Mission to the United States and the Abortive Modus Vivendi," *Journal of Modern History* 24.3 (1952), 301-307.

chard N. Current. "How Stimson Meant to 'Maneuver' the Japanese," *Mississippi Valley Historical Review* 60 (1953), 67-74.

dislas Farago. THE BROKEN SEAL: THE STORY OF 'OPERATION MAGIC' AND THE PEARL HARBOR DISASTER. 1967: Random House.

ul W. Schroeder. THE AXIS ALLIANCE AND JAPANESE-AMERICAN RELATIONS, 1941. 1958: Cornell University Press.

obutake Ike, transl. JAPAN'S DECISION FOR WAR: RECORDS OF THE 1941 POLICY CONFERENCES. 1967: Stanford University Press.

. S. Department of State. PEACE AND WAR: UNITED STATES FOREIGN POLICY, 1931-1941. 1943: Government Printing Office. See especially the narrative summation on 1-151.

_____. FOREIGN RELATIONS OF THE UNITED STATES: JAPAN, 1931-1941. 2 volumes. 1943: Government Printing Office. See especially the "Account of Informal Conversations Between the Government of the United States and the Government of Japan, 1941" in volume 2, 325-386.

. S. Department of the Army (Historical Section, G-2, GHQ, FEC), "Politico-Military Evolution Toward War," in REPORTS OF GENERAL MACARTHUR (1966: Government Printing Office), volume 2, part 1: 30-43.

. S. Congress, Joint Committee on the Pearl Harbor Attack. REPORT (1946). See especially 1: 1-49 and 289-444 on the diplomatic background prior to Pearl Harbor.

. S. Department of Defense. THE "MAGIC" BACKGROUND OF PEARL HARBOR. 5 volumes. 1978: Department of Defense.

he Pearl Harbor Controversy

hn Costello. "Pearl Harbor--Warning or Decision?", in his THE PACIFIC WAR, 1941-1945 (1982: Quill), 617-659.

artin V. Melosi. THE SHADOW OF PEARL HARBOR: POLITICAL CONTROVERSY OVER THE SURPRISE ATTACK, 1941-1946. 1977: Texas A & M University Press.

_____. "National Security Misused: The Aftermath of Pearl Harbor," *Prologue* 9.2 (1977), 75-90.

ouis Morton. "1937-1941," in May & Thomson, AMERICAN-EAST ASIAN RELATIONS (1972: Harvard University Press), 260-290.

hn McKechney, S. J. "The Pearl Harbor Controversy: A Debate Among Historians," *Monumenta Nipponica* 18.1-4 (1963), 45-88.

THE ROAD TO WAR, 1931-1941--V

Robert H. Ferrell. "Pearl Harbor and the Revisionists," *The Historian* 17 (1955), reprinted in Esmonde M. Robertson, ed. THE ORIGINS OF THE SECOND WORLD WAR (1971: Macmillan), 272-292.

Joseph Grew. "Pearl Harbor: From the Perspective of Ten Years," chapter 34 in his TURBULENT ERA, volume 2 (1952: Houghton Mifflin), 1244-1375.

George M. Waller, ed. PEARL HARBOR: ROOSEVELT AND THE COMING OF THE WAR. 3rd edition. 1976: Heath.

Thomas Breslin. "Mystifying the Past: Establishment Historians and the Origins of the Pacific War," *Bulletin of Concerned Asian Scholars* 8.4 (1976), 18-36.

Robert Dallek. FRANKLIN ROOSEVELT AND AMERICAN FOREIGN POLICY, 1932-1945. 1979: Oxford University Press.

Roberta Wohlstetter. PEARL HARBOR: WARNING AND DECISION. 1962: Stanford University Press.

Richard Collier. THE ROAD TO PEARL HARBOR: 1941. 1981: Atheneum.

Gordon W. Prange with Donald M. Goldstein & Katherine V. Dillon. PEARL HARBOR: THE VERDICT OF HISTORY. 1985: McGraw-Hill.

Gordon W. Prange. AT DAWN WE SLEPT: THE UNTOLD STORY OF PEARL HARBOR. 1981: Penguin.

Edwin T. Layton, with Roger Pineau & John Costello. "AND I WAS THERE": PEARL HARBOR AND MIDWAY-- BREAKING THE SECRETS. 1985: Morrow.

John Toland. INFAMY: PEARL HARBOR AND ITS AFTERMATH. 1982: Doubleday.

David Kahn. "Did FDR Invite the Pearl Harbor Attack?", *New York Review of Books* (May 27, 1982), 36-40. Review of Prange and Toland.

John Costello. "Remember Pearl Harbor," *U. S. Naval Academy Proceedings* (1983), 53-62. Review of Prange and Toland.

Ronald H. Spector. "Someone Had Blundered, but Who?", *New York Times Book Review*, December 5, 1985, 9-10. Review of Prange's PEARL HARBOR and Layton's "AND I WAS THERE."

James R. Leutze. BARGAINING FOR SUPREMACY: ANGLO-AMERICAN NAVAL COLLABORATION, 1937-194 1977: University of North Carolina Press.

Arthur Marder. OLD FRIENDS, NEW ENEMIES: THE ROYAL NAVY AND THE IMPERIAL JAPANESE NAVY-- STRATEGIC ILLUSIONS, 1936-1941. 1981: Oxford University Press.

Jeffrey M. Dorwart. CONFLICT OF DUTY: THE U. S. NAVY'S INTELLIGENCE DILEMMA, 1919-1945. 1983 : Naval Institute.

Harry E. Barnes, ed. PERPETUAL WAR FOR PERPETUAL PEACE: A CRITICAL EXAMINATION OF THE FOREIG POLICY OF FRANKLIN DELANO ROOSEVELT AND ITS AFTERMATH. 1953: Caxton.

_____. PEARL HARBOR AFTER A QUARTER OF A CENTURY. 1972: Arno.

William Newmann. "How American Policy Toward Japan Contributed to War in the Pacific," in Harry E. Barnes, ed. PERPETUAL WAR FOR PERPETUAL PEACE (1953: Caxton), 231-268.

ɔam Chomsky. "The Revolutionary Pacifism of A. J. Muste: On the Backgrounds of the Pacific War," in his AMERICAN POWER AND THE NEW MANDARINS (1969: Pantheon), 159-220.

uce M. Russett. NO CLEAR AND PRESENT DANGER: A SKEPTICAL VIEW OF THE UNITED STATES ENTRY INTO WORLD WAR II. 1972: Harper & Row.

he Japanese & the Jews

ıvid Kranzler. JAPANESE, NAZIS AND JEWS: THE JEWISH REFUGEE COMMUNITY OF SHANGHAI, 1938-1945. 1975: Paragon.

____. "Japanese Policy Toward the Jews, 1938-1941," *Japan Interpreter* 11.4 (1977), 493-527.

ɪarvin Tokayer & May Swartz. THE FUGU PLAN: THE UNTOLD STORY OF THE JAPANESE AND THE JEWS DURING WORLD WAR II. 1979: Paddington.

ɛrman Dicker. WANDERERS AND SETTLERS IN THE FAR EAST: A CENTURY OF JEWISH LIFE IN CHINA AND JAPAN. 1962: Twayne.

"JAPAN'S CASE"

Masamichi Royama. FOREIGN POLICY OF JAPAN, 1914-1939. 1941: Japan Council, Institute of Pacific Relations ("Far Eastern Conflict" Series 7).

Kiyoshi K. Kawakami. AMERICAN-JAPANESE RELATIONS: AN INSIDE VIEW OF JAPAN'S POLICIES AND PURPOSES. 1912: Felming H. Revell.

_____. JAPAN IN WORLD POLITICS. 1917: Macmillan.

_____. JAPAN AND WORLD PEACE. 1919: Macmillan.

_____. WHAT JAPAN THINKS. 1921: Macmillan.

_____. JAPAN SPEAKS ON THE SINO-JAPANESE CRISIS. 1932: Macmillan.

_____. MANCHUKUO: CHILD OF CONFLICT. 1933: Macmillan.

_____. JAPAN IN CHINA: HER MOTIVES AND AIMS. 1938: Macmillan.

Yusuke Tsurumi. PRESENT-DAY JAPAN. 1926: Columbia University Press.

_____. "Japan in the Modern World," *Foreign Affairs* 9.2 (1931), 254-265.

Yosuke Matsuoka. "Japan's Interests in Manchuria," *Asiatic Review* 27 (1931), 510-519.

League of Nations. DOCUMENT A: THE PRESENT CONDITION OF CHINA, WITH REFERENCE TO CIRCUMSTANCES AFFECTING INTERNATIONAL RELATIONS AND GOOD UNDERSTANDING BETWEEN NATIONS UPON WHICH PEACE DEPENDS. 1932: League of Nations.

_____. DOCUMENT B: RELATIONS OF JAPAN WITH MANCHURIA AND MONGOLIA. 1932: League of Nations.

_____. V. K. Wellington Koo. MEMORANDA PRESENTED TO THE LYTTON COMMISSION. 2 volumes. 1932-33: League of Nations.

_____. The Lytton Commission. REPORT OF THE COMMISSION OF INQUIRY. 1932: League of Nations.

Japanese Association in China, comp. PRESENTING JAPAN'S SIDE OF THE CASE. 1931: Japanese Association in China.

Chih Meng. CHINA SPEAKS: ON THE CONFLICT BETWEEN CHINA AND JAPAN. 1932: Kennikat.

Yasaka Takagi. "World Peace Machinery and the Asia Monroe Doctrine," *Pacific Affairs* 5 (1932), 941-953.

George H. Blakeslee. "The Japanese Monroe Doctrine," *Foreign Affairs* 11.4 (1933), 671-681.

Kikujiro Ishii. "The Permanent Basis of Japanese Foreign Policy," *Foreign Affairs* 11.2 (1933), 220-229.

_____. DIPLOMATIC COMMENTARIES. William R. Langdon, transl. and ed. 1936: Johns Hopkins.

W. Watkin Davies. "Japan and Western Example," *The Fortnightly* (June 1935), 718-727.

Hiroshi Saito. JAPAN'S POLICIES AND PURPOSES: SELECTIONS FROM RECENT ADDRESSES AND WRITINGS. 1935: Jones.

George Bronson Rhea. THE CASE FOR MANCHUKUO. 1935: Appleton-Century.

W. Willoughby. THE SINO-JAPANESE CONTROVERSY AND THE LEAGUE OF NATIONS. 1935: Johns Hopkins.

nji G. Kasai. THE UNITED STATES AND JAPAN IN THE PACIFIC: AMERICAN NAVAL MANEUVERS AND JAPAN'S PACIFIC POLICY. 1935; reprinted 1970: Arno.

ota Ishimaru. JAPAN MUST FIGHT BRITAIN. G. V. Rayment, transl. 1936: Telegraph.

injiro Fujihara. THE SPIRIT OF JAPANESE INDUSTRY. 1936: Hokuseido.

erbert Max Bratter. "The Cases for Japan and China," Asia 37 (November 1937).

oreign Affairs Association of Japan. WHY JAPAN HAD TO FIGHT IN SHANGHAI. 1937: Foreign Affairs Association of Japan.

_____. THE SINO-JAPANESE CONFLICT AND FINANCIAL RESOURCES: A SYMPOSIUM. 1937: Foreign Affairs Association of Japan.

_____. THE SINO-JAPANESE CONFLICT: A SHORT SURVEY. 1937: Foreign Affairs Association of Japan.

iyoshi Miki. "The China Affair and Japanese Thought," Contemporary Japan 6 (1938), 601-610.

atsuo Kawai. THE GOAL OF JAPANESE EXPANSION. 1938: Hokuseido.

oyal Institute of International Affairs. SURVEY OF INTERNATIONAL AFFAIRS. Annual volumes include primary documents from various governments: Oxford University Press.

oyal Institute of International Affairs, Information Department. CHINA AND JAPAN. 3rd edition. 1941: Oxford University Press.

harles R. Shepherd. THE CASE AGAINST JAPAN. 1939: Jarrolds.

V. W. Willoughby. JAPAN'S CASE EXAMINED. 1940: Johns Hopkins.

eiji G. Hishida. JAPAN AMONG THE GREAT POWERS: A SURVEY OF HER INTERNATIONAL RELATIONS. 1940: Longmans, Green.

iyoshi Miki & Karoku Hosokawa. INTRODUCTORY STUDIES ON THE SINO-JAPANESE CONFLICT. 1941: Japan Council, Institute of Pacific Relations.

ir Frederick Whyte. JAPAN'S PURPOSE IN ASIA. 1941: Royal Institute of International Affairs.

reater East Asia War Inquiry Commission. THE AMERICAN-BRITISH CHALLENGE DIRECTED AGAINST JAPAN. 1943: Mainichi Shimbunsha. Japanese war-crimes charges against the Anglo-Americans.

IDEOLOGIES OF EMPIRE

[See also pages 94-100 on "Nationalism & the Emperor System" and "'Fascism,' Militarism & the Showa Crisis." Also the "Japan at War" citations below on pages 163-164.]

Byron K. Marshall. CAPITALISM AND NATIONALISM IN PREWAR JAPAN: THE IDEOLOGY OF THE BUSINESS ELITE, 1868-1941. 1967: Stanford University Press.

Marlene Mayo, ed. THE EMERGENCE OF IMPERIAL JAPAN: SELF-DEFENSE OR CALCULATED AGGRESSION? 1970: Heath. See especially the essays by Yoshitake Oka, Sannosuke Matsumoto, and Shoichi Fujii.

George Sansom. THE WESTERN WORLD AND JAPAN. 1950: Knopf. Especially Chapter 14.

Kimitada Miwa. "Fukuzawa Yukichi's 'Departure from Asia': A Prelude to the Sino-Japanese War," in Edmund Skryzpczak, ed. JAPAN'S MODERN CENTURY (1968: Monumenta Nipponica), 1-26.

Albert M. Craig. "Fukuzawa Yukichi: The Philosophical Foundations of Meiji Nationalism," in Robert Ward, ed. POLITICAL DEVELOPMENT IN MODERN JAPAN (1968: Princeton University Press), 99-148.

Marius B. Jansen. "Oi Kentaro's Radicalism and Chauvinism," *Far Eastern Quarterly* 11.3 (1952), 305-316.

_____. THE JAPANESE AND SUN YAT-SEN. 1954: Harvard University Press.

E. Herbert Norman. "The Genyosha: A Study in the Origins of Japanese Imperialism," *Pacific Affairs* 17.3 (1944), 261-284

Kazuo Shibagaki. "The Logic of Japanese Imperialism," *Social Science Abstracts* 14 (Shakai Kagaku Kenkyujo, Tokyo University, 1973), 70-87.

Masanori Nakamura. "The Emperor System of the 1900s,"*Bulletin of Concerned Asian Scholars* 16.2 (1984), 2-11.

Donald Keene. "The Sino-Japanese War of 1894-95 and Japanese Culture," in his LANDSCAPES AND PORTRAITS: APPRECIATIONS OF JAPANESE CULTURE (1971: Kodansha International), 259-299.

Mark R. Peattie. "Japanese Attitudes Toward Colonialism, 1895-1945," in Ramon Myers & Mark Peattie, eds. THE JAPANESE COLONIAL EMPIRE (1984: Princeton University Press), 80-127.

Shinkichi Eto. "Asianism and Duality of Japanese Colonialism, 1879-1945," in L. Blusse, H. L. Wesseling & G. D. Winius, eds. HISTORY AND UNDERDEVELOPMENT (1980: Centre for the History of European Expansion, Leiden), 114-126.

Inazo Nitobe. BUSHIDO: THE SOUL OF JAPAN. 1905: Putnam.

O. Tanin & E. Yohan. MILITARISM AND FASCISM IN JAPAN. 1934: Lawrence & Wishart. Translated from the Russian, with an introduction by Karl Radek.

_____. WHEN JAPAN GOES TO WAR. 1936: Lawrence & Wishart.

Masao Maruyama. THOUGHT AND BEHAVIOR IN MODERN JAPANESE POLITICS. 1963: Oxford Univ. Press.

Richard Storry. THE DOUBLE PATRIOTS: A STUDY OF JAPANESE NATIONALISM. 1957: Houghton Mifflin.

Grant Goodman, ed. IMPERIAL JAPAN AND ASIA. 1967: Occasional Papers of the East Asia Institute, Columbia University. Includes Akira Iriye's "The Ideology of Japanese Imperialism" (32-45) and George Wilson's "Reflections on Japanese Imperialist Ideology" (46-51).

Hilary Conroy. "Japanese Nationalism and Expansionism," *American Historical Review* 60 (1955), 818-829.

T. R. H. Havens. "Nationalism," KODANSHA ENCYCLOPEDIA OF JAPAN 5: 342-343.

George M. Wilson. "Ultranationalism," KODANSHA ENCYCLOPEDIA OF JAPAN 8: 145-146.

Gordon Berger. "The Three-dimensional Empire: Japanese Attitudes and the New Order in Asia, 1937-1945," *Japan Interpreter* 12.3-4 (1979), 355-383.

_____. "New Order Movement (Shin Taisei Undo)," KODANSHA ENCYCLOPEDIA OF JAPAN 5: 365-366.

James B. Crowley. "A New Deal for Japan and Asia: One Road to Pearl Harbor," in his MODERN EAST ASIA (1970: Harcourt Brace & World), 235-264.

_____. "A New Asian Order: Some Notes on Prewar Japanese Nationalism," in B. Silberman & H. Harootunian, eds. JAPAN IN CRISIS (1974: Princeton University Press), 270-298.

_____. "Intellectuals as Visionaries of the New Asian Order," in James W. Morley, ed. DILEMMAS OF GROWTH IN PREWAR JAPAN (1972: Princeton University Press), 319-373.

Louis M. Allen. "Fujiwara and Suzuki: Patterns of Asian Liberation," in William H. Newell, ed. JAPAN IN ASIA (1981: Singapore University Press), 83-103.

Miles Fletcher. "Intellectuals and Fascism in Early Showa Japan," *Journal of Asian Studies* 39.1 (1979), 39-63.

_____. THE SEARCH FOR A NEW ORDER: INTELLECTUALS AND FASCISM IN PREWAR JAPAN. 1982: University of North Carolina Press.

Mark R. Peattie. ISHIWARA KANJI AND JAPAN'S CONFRONTATION WITH THE WEST. 1975: Princeton University Press.

Katsumi Usui. "Pursuing an Illusion: The New Order in East Asia," *Japan Interpreter* 6.3 (1970), 326-337.

Toru Yano. "Southern Expansion Doctrine," KODANSHA ENCYCLOPEDIA OF JAPAN 7: 236-237.

Jaya Deva. JAPAN'S KAMPF. 1942: Left Book Club.

Otto D. Tolischus, ed. THROUGH JAPANESE EYES. 1945: Reynal & Hitchcock.

Chalmers A. Johnson. AN INSTANCE OF TREASON: OZAKI HOZUMI AND THE SORGE SPY RING. 1964: Stanford University Press.

F. W. Deakin & G. R. Storry. THE CASE OF RICHARD SORGE. 1966: Chatto & Windus.

Gordon Prange, with Donald Goldstein & Katherine Dillon. TARGET TOKYO: THE STORY OF THE SORGE SPY RING. 1984: McGraw-Hill.

Japanese Ministry of Education. KOKUTAI NO HONGI: CARDINAL PRINCIPLES OF THE NATIONAL ENTITY OF JAPAN. Translated by John O. Gauntlett and edited by Robert K. Hall. 1949: Harvard University Press. The basic expression of government orthodoxy, first issued in 1937.

_____. THE WAY OF THE SUBJECT (*Shinmin no Michi*), 1941; in Otto Tolischus, TOKYO RECORD (1943: Reynal & Hitchcock), 405-427.

John Paul Reed. KOKUTAI: A STUDY OF CERTAIN SACRED AND SECULAR ASPECTS OF JAPANESE NATIONALISM. 1940: University of Chicago Press.

Robert K. Hall. SHUSHIN: THE ETHICS OF A DEFEATED NATION. 1949: Columbia University Press.

D. C. Holtom. THE NATIONAL FAITH OF JAPAN: A STUDY IN MODERN SHINTO. 1938: Dutton.

_____. MODERN JAPAN AND SHINTO NATIONALISM. 1943; revised edition, 1947: Univ. of Chicago Press.

ECONOMICS OF EMPIRE

[See also the general "Economic Development" section on pages 78-81, as well as the citations to primary materials within pages 179-198 below.]

Overviews

Takafusa Nakamura. ECONOMIC GROWTH IN PREWAR JAPAN. 1982: University of Tokyo Press.

William Lockwood. THE ECONOMIC DEVELOPMENT OF JAPAN: GROWTH AND STRUCTURAL CHANGE, 1868-1938. 1954: Princeton University Press.

Frances V. Moulder. JAPAN, CHINA AND THE MODERN WORLD ECONOMY: TOWARD A REINTERPRETATION OF EAST ASIAN DEVELOPMENT, ca. 1600 TO ca. 1918. 1977: Cambridge University Press.

Byron K. Marshall. CAPITALISM AND NATIONALISM IN PREWAR JAPAN: THE IDEOLOGY OF THE BUSINESS ELITE, 1868-1941. 1967: Stanford University Press.

John Halliday. A POLITICAL HISTORY OF JAPANESE CAPITALISM. 1975: Pantheon.

Shigeki Toyama. "Politics, Economics, and the International Environment in the Meiji and Taisho Periods," *Developing Economies* 4 (1966), 419-426.

Shoichi Fujii. "Capitalism, International Politics, and the Emperor System," in Marlene Mayo, ed. THE EMERGENCE OF IMPERIAL JAPAN (1970: Heath), 75-82.

Kenneth E. Boulding & Alan H. Gleason. "War As an Investment: The Strange Case of Japan," *Peace Research Society (International) Papers* 3 (1965), reprinted in Kenneth E. Boulding & Tapan Mukerjee, eds. ECONOMIC IMPERIALISM: A BOOK OF READINGS (1972: University of Michigan Press), 240-261.

Yoshio Ando. "The Formation of Heavy Industry--One of the Processes of Industrialization in the Meiji Period," *Developing Economies* 3 (1965), 450-470.

Kozo Yamamura. "Success Illgotten? The Role of Meiji Militarism in Japan's Technical Progress," *Journal of Economic History* 37.1 (1977), 113-135.

Hugh Borton. "The Economic Basis of the New Empire, 1890-1915," chapter 14 in his JAPAN'S MODERN CENTURY (1970: Ronald).

_____. "War and the Rise of Industrialization in Japan," in Jesse D. Clarkson & Thomas C. Cochran, eds. WAR AS A SOCIAL INSTITUTION (1941: Columbia University Press), 224-234.

Hilary Conroy. "A Rebuttal to Economic Determinism," in Marlene Mayo, ed. THE EMERGENCE OF IMPERIAL JAPAN (1970: Heath), 83-87.

Arthur E. Tiedemann. "Japan's Economic Foreign Policies, 1868-1893," in J. W. Morley, ed. JAPAN'S FOREIGN POLICY, 1868-1941 (1974: Columbia University Press), 118-152.

William D. Wray. MITSUBISHI AND THE N.Y.K., 1870-1914: BUSINESS STRATEGY IN THE JAPANESE SHIPPING INDUSTRY. 1984: Harvard East Asian Monographs.

John G. Roberts. MITSUI: THREE CENTURIES OF JAPANESE BUSINESS. 1973: Weatherhill.

G. Best. "Financing a Foreign War: Jacob Schiff and Japan, 1904-1905," *American Jewish Historical Quarterly* 62 (1972), 313-324.

Ushisaburo Kobayashi. WAR AND ARMAMENT LOANS OF JAPAN. 1922: Oxford University Press.

_____. WAR AND ARMAMENT TAXES OF JAPAN. 1922: Oxford University Press.

Seiichi Ono. WAR AND ARMAMENT EXPENDITURES OF JAPAN. 1922: Oxford University Press.

The Formal Empire

Ramon H. Myers & Mark R. Peattie, eds. THE JAPANESE COLONIAL EMPIRE, 1895-1945. 1984: Princeton
  University Press. See especially Peter Duus on "Economic Dimensions of Meiji Imperialism: The Case of
  Korea, 1895-1910" (128-171), and essays by Samuel Pao-San Ho, Toshiyuki Mizoguchi & Yuzo
  Yamamoto, and Ramon Myers & Saburo Yamada pertaining to "The Economic Dynamics of Empire,"
  especially involving Korea and Taiwan (347-452).

James I. Nakamura. "Incentives, Productivity Gaps, and Agricultural Growth Rates in Prewar Japan, Taiwan and
  Korea," in B. Silberman & H. Harootunian, eds. JAPAN IN CRISIS (1974: Princeton University Press),
  329-373.

Akira Iriye. "The Failure of Economic Expansion, 1918-1931," in Silberman & Harootunian, JAPAN IN CRISIS
  (1974: Princeton University Press), 237-269.

Arthur E. Tiedemann. "Big Business and Politics in Prewar Japan," in J. W. Morley, ed. DILEMMAS OF
  GROWTH IN PREWAR JAPAN (1971: Princeton University Press), 267-316.

Kiyoshi Oshima. "The World Economic Crisis and Japan's Foreign Economic Policy," *Developing Economies*
  5.4 (1967), 628-647.

Tsutomu Ouchi. "Agricultural Depression and Japanese Villages," *Developing Economies* 4.4 (1967), 597-627.

Kozo Yamamura. "Then Came the Great Depression: Japan's Interwar Years," in Herman van der Wee, ed. THE
  GREAT DEPRESSION REVISITED (1972: Martinus Nijhoff), 182-211.

_____. "The Japanese Economy, 1911-1930: Concentration, Conflicts, and Crises," in Silberman &
  Harootunian, JAPAN IN CRISIS (1974: Princeton University Press), 299-328.

Shigeto Tsuru. "Japan's Economy Under the Strain of the China Incident," in his ESSAYS ON JAPANESE
  ECONOMY (1958: Institute of Pacific Relations), 154-236.

Yukio Cho. "From the Showa Economic Crisis to Military Economy--with Special Reference to the Inoue and
  Takahashi Financial Policies," *Developing Economies* 5.4 (1967), 568-596.

_____. "Exposing the Incompetence of the Bourgeoisie: The Financial Panic of 1927," *Japan Interpreter* 8.4
  (1974), 492-501.

_____. "Keeping Step With the Military: The Beginning of the Automobile Age," *Japan Interpreter* 7.2
  (1972), 168-178.

Mitsuharu Ito. "Munitions Unlimited: The Controlled Economy," *Japan Interpreter* 7.3-4 (1972), 353-363.

Makoto Takahashi. "The Development of Wartime Economic Controls," *Developing Economies* 5.4 (1967),
  648-665.

H. T. Oshima. "Japan's Economic Structure," *Pacific Affairs* 15 (1942), 262-279.

Richard Rice. "Economic Mobilization in Wartime Japan: Business, Bureaucracy, and Military in Conflict,"
  Journal of Asian Studies 38.4 (1979), 689-706.

Ernest Notar. "Japan's Wartime Labor Policy: A Search for Method," *Journal of Asian Studies* 44.2 (1985),
  311-328.

ECONOMICS OF EMPIRE--III

Jerome B. Cohen. JAPAN'S ECONOMY IN WAR AND RECONSTRUCTION. 1949: University of Minnesota Press.

T. A. Bisson. JAPAN'S WAR ECONOMY. 1945: Institute of Pacific Relations.

_____. ZAIBATSU DISSOLUTION IN JAPAN. 1954: University of California Press.

Eleanor M. Hadley. ANTI-TRUST IN JAPAN. 1970: Princeton University Press.

Mitsubishi Economic Research Institute. MITSUI-MITSUBISHI-SUMITOMO: PRESENT STATUS OF THE FORMER ZAIBATSU ENTERPRISES. 1955: Mitsubishi Economic Research Institute.

Kozo Yamamura. "Zaibatsu, Prewar and Zaibatsu, Postwar," *Journal of Asian Studies* 23.4 (1964), 539-554.

Edwin W. Pauley. REPORT ON JAPANESE REPARATIONS TO THE PRESIDENT OF THE UNITED STATES, NOVEMBER 1945 TO APRIL 1946. Department of State Publication 3174, Far Eastern Series 25. The Pauley Report. See also separate Pauley reports on JAPANESE ASSETS IN MANCHURIA and JAPANESE ASSETS IN SOVIET-OCCUPIED KOREA.

U. S. Department of State. REPORT OF THE MISSION ON JAPANESE COMBINES, PART I, ANALYTICAL AND TECHNICAL DATA. Department of State Publication 2628, Far Eastern Series 14, 1946. The Edwards Report.

Frederick Thayer Merrill. JAPAN AND THE OPIUM MENACE. 1942: Institute of Pacific Relations.

Chalmers Johnson. MITI AND THE JAPANESE MIRACLE: THE GROWTH OF INDUSTRIAL POLICY, 1925-1975. 1982: Stanford University Press.

China & the Pacific

Stephen C. Thomas. FOREIGN INTERVENTION AND CHINA'S INDUSTRIAL DEVELOPMENT, 1870-1911. 1984: Westview.

Ping-shu Kao. FOREIGN LOANS TO CHINA. 1946: Sino-International Economic Research Center.

Charles F. Remer. FOREIGN INVESTMENTS IN CHINA. 1933: Macmillan.

_____. A STUDY OF CHINESE BOYCOTTS. 1935: Johns Hopkins.

Ralph W. Huenemann. THE DRAGON AND THE IRON HORSE: ECONOMICS OF RAILROADS IN CHINA, 1876-1937. 1983: Harvard University Press.

Kia-ngau Chang. CHINA'S STRUGGLE FOR RAILROAD DEVELOPMENT. 1943: John Day.

Norton S. Ginsburg. "Manchurian Railway Development," *Far Eastern Quarterly* 8.4 (1949), 398-411.

H. L. Kingman. EFFECTS OF CHINESE NATIONALISM UPON MANCHURIAN RAILWAY DEVELOPMENTS, 1925-1931. 1932: University of California Press.

John Young. "South Manchurian Railway," KODANSHA ENCYCLOPEDIA OF JAPAN 7: 237-238.

Herbert Bix. "Japanese Imperialism and the Manchurian Economy, 1900-31," *China Quarterly* 52 (1972), 425-443.

ECONOMICS OF EMPIRE--IV

ungtu C. Sun. THE ECONOMIC DEVELOPMENT OF MANCHURIA IN THE FIRST HALF OF THE TWENTIETH CENTURY. 1968: Harvard East Asian Monographs.

B. Schumpeter, ed. THE INDUSTRIALIZATION OF JAPAN AND MANCHUKUO, 1930-1940. 1940: Macmillan.

. I. Ladejinsky. "Manchurian Agriculture Under Japanese Control," *Foreign Agriculture* 5 (1941), 309-340.

. C. Allen. JAPAN, THE HUNGRY GUEST. 1938: Allen & Unwin.

____. JAPANESE INDUSTRY: ITS RECENT DEVELOPMENT AND PRESENT CONDITION. 1940: Institute of Pacific Relations.

____ & A. C. Donnithorne. WESTERN ENTERPRISE IN FAR EASTERN ECONOMIC DEVELOPMENT: CHINA AND JAPAN. 1954: Allen & Unwin.

. D. Cowan, ed. THE ECONOMIC DEVELOPMENT OF CHINA AND JAPAN: STUDIES IN ECONOMIC HISTORY AND POLITICAL ECONOMY. 1964: Praeger.

rancis E. Hyde. FAR EASTERN TRADE, 1860-1914. 1973: Harper & Row.

ohn E. Orchard. JAPAN'S ECONOMIC POSITION: THE PROGRESS OF INDUSTRIALIZATION. 1930: McGraw-Hill.

. F. Penrose. FOOD SUPPLY AND RAW MATERIALS IN JAPAN. 1930: University of Chicago Press.

arold G. Moulton. JAPAN, AN ECONOMIC AND FINANCIAL APPRAISAL. 1931: Brookings Institution.

lbert E. Hindmarsh. THE BASIS OF JAPAN'S FOREIGN POLICY. 1936: Harvard University Press.

. Tanin & E. Yohan. WHEN JAPAN GOES TO WAR. 1936: Lawrence & Wishart.

reda Utley. JAPAN'S FEET OF CLAY. 1937: Norton.

. E. Hubbard. EASTERN INDUSTRIALIZATION AND ITS EFFECTS ON THE WEST, WITH SPECIAL REFERENCE TO GREAT BRITIAN AND JAPAN. 2nd edition. 1938: Royal Institute of International Affairs.

William L. Holland & Kate Mitchell, eds. PROBLEMS OF THE PACIFIC, 1936. PROCEEDINGS OF THE SIXTH CONFERENCE OF THE INSTITUTE OF PACIFIC RELATIONS (AUGUST 15-29, 1936). 1937: University of Chicago Press.

____. PROBLEMS OF THE PACIFIC, 1939. PROCEEDINGS OF THE STUDY MEETING OF THE INSTITUTE OF PACIFIC RELATIONS (NOVEMBER 18-DECEMBER 2, 1939). 1940: Institute of Pacific Relations.

oyal Institute of International Affairs. CHINA AND JAPAN. See the economic sections in the 1939 and 1941 editions of this publication (102-130 and 127-151 respectively).

ate L. Mitchell. JAPAN'S INDUSTRIAL STRENGTH: AN INQUIRY INTO THE INDUSTRIALIZATION OF THE WESTERN PACIFIC. 1942: Knopf.

. Sternberg. "Japan's Economic Imperialism," *Social Research* 13 (1945), 328-349.

161

ECONOMICS OF EMPIRE--V

Cooperation, Depression, Embargo

Dorothy Borg & Shumpei Okamoto, eds. PEARL HARBOR AS HISTORY: JAPANESE-AMERICAN RELATIONS, 1931-1941. 1973: Columbia University Press. On the Japanese side, see essays by Katsuro Yamamura on the Finance Ministry; Yukio Cho on U.S. capital export to Manchuria; and Hideichiro Nakamura on the Japan Economic Frederation. On the U.S. side, see Lloyd Gardner on the Commerce and Treasury Departments and Mira Wilkins on U.S. business.

Lloyd Gardner. ECONOMIC ASPECTS OF NEW DEAL DIPLOMACY. 1964: University of Wisconsin Press.

Michael J. Hogan. INFORMAL ENTENTE: THE PRIVATE STRUCTURE OF COOPERATION IN ANGLO-AMERICA ECONOMIC DIPLOMACY, 1918-1928. 1977: University of Missouri Press.

Joan Hoff Wilson. AMERICAN BUSINESS & FOREIGN POLICY 1920-1933. 1971: University of Kentucky Press.

Charles P. Kindleberger. THE WORLD IN DEPRESSION 1929-1939. 1973: University of California Press.

Osamu Ishii. COTTON TEXTILE DIPLOMACY: JAPAN, GREAT BRITAIN, AND THE UNITED STATES, 1930-1936. 1981: Arno.

Irvine H. Anderson. STANDARD-VACUUM OIL COMPANY AND THE UNITED STATES EAST ASIAN POLICY, 1933-1941. 1975: Princeton University Press.

Jonathan Utley. "Upstairs, Downstairs at Foggy Bottom: Oil Exports and Japan, 1940-1941," *Prologue: The Journal of the National Archives* 8.1 (1976), 17-28.

U. S. Department of State. "Economic Measures by the United States Affecting Trade with Japan," in FOREIGN RELATIONS OF THE UNITED STATES: JAPAN, 1931-1941. Pages 201-273 in volume 2 cover 1937 to 1941.

Donald J. Friedman. THE ROAD FROM ISOLATION: THE CAMPAIGN OF THE AMERICAN COMMITTEE FOR NON-PARTICIPATION IN JAPANESE AGGRESSION, 1938-1941. 1968: Harvard East Asian Monographs.

American Committee for Non-Participation in Japanese Aggression. AMERICA'S SHARE IN JAPAN'S WAR GUILT. 1938: American Committee for Non-Participation in Japanese Agression.

Philip J. Jaffe. "Economic Provincialism and American Far Eastern Policy," *Science and Society* 5.4 (1941), 289-309.

Greater East Asia War Inquiry Commission. THE AMERICAN-BRITISH CHALLENGE DIRECTED AGAINST JAPAN 1943: Mainichi Shimbunsha.

JAPAN AT WAR: GENERAL STUDIES

Waldo Heinrichs. "World War II," KODANSHA ENCYCLOPEDIA OF JAPAN 8: 271-277.

John W. Dower. "Rethinking World War Two in Asia," *Reviews in American History* 12.2 (1984), 155-169.

____. WAR WITHOUT MERCY: RACE AND POWER IN THE PACIFIC WAR. 1986: Pantheon.

Saburo Ienaga. THE PACIFIC WAR: WORLD WAR II AND THE JAPANESE, 1931-1945. 1978: Pantheon.

John Toland. THE RISING SUN: THE DECLINE AND FALL OF THE JAPANESE EMPIRE. 1970: Random House.

John Costello. THE PACIFIC WAR, 1941-1945. 1981: Quill.

Ronald H. Spector. EAGLE AGAINST THE SUN: THE AMERICAN WAR WITH JAPAN. 1985: Free Press.

Akira Iriye. POWER AND CULTURE: THE JAPANESE-AMERICAN WAR, 1941-1945. 1981: Harvard Univ. Press.

Christopher Thorne. ALLIES OF A KIND: THE UNITED STATES, BRITAIN, AND THE WAR AGAINST JAPAN, 1941-1945. 1979: Oxford University Press.

____. THE ISSUE OF WAR: STATES, SOCIETIES, AND THE FAR EASTERN CONFLICT, 1941-1945. 1985: Oxford University Press.

David Bergamini. JAPAN'S IMPERIAL CONSPIRACY. 1971: Morrow.

Basil Collier. THE WAR IN THE FAR EAST, 1941-1945: A MILITARY HISTORY. 1969: Morrow.

Charles Bateson. THE WAR WITH JAPAN: A CONCISE HISTORY. 1968: Ure Smith.

Christopher J. Argyle. JAPAN AT WAR, 1937-1946. 1976: Barker.

Arthur Marder. OLD FRIENDS, NEW ENEMIES: THE ROYAL NAVY AND THE IMPERIAL JAPANESE NAVY-- STRATEGIC ILLUSIONS, 1936-1941. 1981: Oxford University Press.

John Sbrega. THE WAR AGAINST JAPAN. 1985: Garland.

Stanley Falk. "Japanese Strategy in World War II," *Military Review* 42 (1962), 70-81.

____. "Organization and Military Power: The Japanese High Command in World War II," *Political Science Quarterly* 76 (1961), 503-518.

Hans-Adolf Jacobsen & Arthur L. Smith, Jr., eds. WORLD WAR II: POLICY AND STRATEGY. 1979: ABC Clio.

H. P. Willmott. EMPIRES IN THE BALANCE: JAPANESE AND ALLIED PACIFIC STRATEGIES TO APRIL 1942. 1982: Naval Institute.

____. THE BARRIER AND THE JAVELIN: JAPANESE AND ALLIED PACIFIC STRATEGIES, FEBRUARY TO JUNE 1942. 1983: Naval Institute.

____. "A6M Zero," in CLASSIC AIRCRAFT OF WORLD WAR II (1982: Bison Books), 201-264.

J. R. M. Butler. THE WAR AGAINST JAPAN. United Kingdom Military Series. 1957: Her Majesty's Stat. Office.

John J. Stephan. HAWAII UNDER THE RISING SUN: JAPAN'S PLANS FOR CONQUEST AFTER PEARL HARBOR. 1983: University of Hawaii Press.

Ronald Lewin. THE AMERICAN MAGIC: CODES, CIPHERS, AND THE DEFEAT OF JAPAN. 1982: Farrar Straus & Giroux.

Edward van der Rhoer. DEADLY MAGIC. 1978: Charles Scribner's Sons.

JAPAN AT WAR: GENERAL STUDIES--II

David Kahn, ed. MAGIC DIPLOMATIC SUMMARY. 8 volumes. 1980: Garland.

Alvin Coox. JAPAN: THE FINAL AGONY. 1970: Ballentine.

Louis Allen. THE END OF THE WAR IN ASIA. 1979: Hart-Davis MacGibbon.

Robert J. C. Butow. JAPAN'S DECISION TO SURRENDER. 1954: Stanford University Press.

Lester Brooks. BEHIND JAPAN'S SURRENDER: THE SECRET STRUGGLE THAT ENDED AN EMPIRE. 1968: McGraw-Hill.

Ellis M. Zacharias. SECRET MISSIONS: THE STORY OF AN INTELLIGENCE OFFICER. 1946: Putnam.

Sidney Forrester Mashbir. I WAS AN AMERICAN SPY. 1953: Vantage.

Pacific War Research Society. JAPAN'S LONGEST DAY. 1965: Kodansha International.

Otis Cary, ed. WAR-WASTED ASIA: LETTERS, 1945-46. 1975: Kodansha International.

U.S. Army. REPORTS OF GENERAL MACARTHUR. Four volumes prepared by MacArthur's staff in Tokyo in 1950, but not published until 1966.
   I.   THE CAMPAIGNS OF MACARTHUR IN THE PACIFIC
   I.   Supplement. MACARTHUR IN JAPAN: THE OCCUPATION: THE MILITARY PHASE
   II.   Part 1. JAPANESE OPERATIONS IN THE SOUTHWEST PACIFIC AREA
   II.   Part 2. JAPANESE OPERATIONS IN THE SOUTHWEST PACIFIC AREA.

U. S. Army, Office of the Chief of Military History. WAR IN ASIA AND THE PACIFIC, 1937-1949. 1980: Garland. A reprint edition of monographs prepared after the war primarily within the Japanese Demobilization Agency, coordinated and translated by G-2 Section of GHQ, Far Eastern Command. The project produced 184 monographs on Japanese operations and 18 studies of Manchuria. The 15 published volumes are as follows:
   1. INTRODUCTION AND GUIDE
   2. POLITICAL BACKGROUND OF THE WAR
   3. COMMAND, ADMINISTRATION, AND SPECIAL OPERATIONS
   4. THE NAVAL ARMAMENT PROGRAM AND NAVAL OPERATIONS (PART I)
   5. THE NAVAL ARMAMENT PROGRAM AND NAVAL OPERATIONS (PART II)
   6. THE SOUTHERN AREA (PART I)
   7. THE SOUTHERN AREA (PART II)
   8. CHINA, MANCHURIA, AND KOREA (PART I)
   9. CHINA, MANCHURIA, AND KOREA (PART II)
   10. JAPAN AND THE SOVIET UNION (PART I)
   11. JAPAN AND THE SOVIET UNION (PART II)
   12. DEFENSE OF THE HOMELAND AND END OF THE WAR
   13. THE SINO-JAPANESE AND CHINESE CIVIL WARS (PART I)
   14. THE SINO-JAPANESE AND CHINESE CIVIL WARS (PART II)
   15. THE SINO-JAPANESE AND CHINESE CIVIL WARS (PART III)

United States Strategic Bombing Survey. PACIFIC WAR, 108 volumes. 1945-1947. See especially:
   1. SUMMARY REPORT (PACIFIC WAR)
   2. JAPAN'S STRUGGLE TO END THE WAR
   3. THE EFFECTS OF ATOMIC BOMBS ON HIROSHIMA AND NAGASAKI
   14. THE EFFECTS OF STRATEGIC BOMBING ON JAPANESE MORALE
   42. THE JAPANESE WARTIME STANDARD OF LIVING AND UTILIZATION OF MANPOWER
   53. THE EFFECTS OF STRATEGIC BOMBING ON JAPAN'S WAR ECONOMY
   55. EFFECTS OF AIR ATTACK ON JAPANESE URBAN ECONOMY (SUMMARY REPORT)
   72. INTERROGATIONS OF JAPANESE OFFICIALS (Volumes 1 and 2)
   73. CAMPAIGNS OF THE PACIFIC WAR
   96. A REPORT ON PHYSICAL DAMAGE IN JAPAN (SUMMARY REPORT)
   97. JAPANESE MILITARY AND NAVAL INTELLIGENCE

hn H. Boyle. "Sino-Japanese War of 1937-1945," KODANSHA ENCYCLOPEDIA OF JAPAN 7: 199-202.

____. CHINA AND JAPAN AT WAR, 1937-1945: THE POLITICS OF COLLABORATION. 1972: Stanford University Press.

____. "An Incident Becomes a War: Konoe's *Aite ni Sezu* Declaration," *Japan Interpreter* 6.3 (1970), 309-325.

____. "The Road to Sino-Japanese Collaboration: The Background to the Defection of Wang Ching-wei," *Monumenta Nipponica* 25.3-4 (1970), 267-301.

ank Dorn. THE SINO-JAPANESE WAR, 1937-1941: FROM THE MARCO POLO BRIDGE TO PEARL HARBOR. 1974: Macmillan.

ichael Lindsay. THE UNKNOWN WAR: NORTH CHINA, 1937-1945. 1975: Bergstrom & Boyle.

ick Wilson. WHEN TIGERS FIGHT: THE STORY OF THE SINO-JAPANESE WAR, 1937-1945. 1982: Viking.

ncoln Li. THE JAPANESE ARMY IN NORTH CHINA, JULY 1937-DECEMBER 1941: PROBLEMS OF POLITICAL AND ECONOMIC CONTROL. 1975: Oxford University Press.

halmers A. Johnson. PEASANT NATIONALISM AND COMMUNIST POWER: THE EMERGENCE OF REVOLUTIONARY CHINA, 1937-1945. 1962: Stanford University Press.

erald E. Bunker. THE PEACE CONSPIRACY: WANG CHING-WEI AND THE CHINA WAR, 1937-1941. 1972: Harvard University Press.

eorge Taylor. JAPANESE SPONSORED REGIME IN NORTH CHINA. 1939: Institute of Pacific Relations.

imitada Miwa. "The Chinese Communists' Role in the Spread of the Marco Polo Bridge Incident into a Full-Scale War," *Monumenta Nipponica* 18.1-4 (1963), 313-328.

____. "The Wang Ching-Wei Regime and Japanese Efforts to Terminate the China Conflict," in Joseph Roggendorf, ed. STUDIES IN JAPANESE CULTURE: TRADITION AND EXPERIMENT (1963: Monumenta Nipponica Monographs), 123-142.

oy M. Stanley. PRELUDE TO PEARL HARBOR: WAR IN CHINA, 1937-1941. JAPAN'S REHEARSAL FOR WORLD WAR II. 1983: Charles Scribner's Sons.

loyd Eastman. SEEDS OF DESTRUCTION: NATIONALIST CHINA IN WAR AND REVOLUTION, 1937-1949. 1984: Stanford University Press.

. F. Liu. A MILITARY HISTORY OF MODERN CHINA, 1924-1949. 1956: Princeton University Press.

rthur N. Young. CHINA AND THE HELPING HAND, 1937-1945. 1963: Harvard University Press.

illiam H. Chamberlin. JAPAN OVER ASIA. Revised edition. 1937: Little, Brown.

. A. Bisson. JAPAN IN CHINA. 1938: Macmillan.

arold J. Timperly, ed. THE JAPANESE TERROR IN CHINA. 1938: New York Books for Libraries.

hong-sik Lee. REVOLUTIONARY STRUGGLE IN MANCHURIA: CHINESE COMMUNISM AND SOVIET INTEREST, 1922-1945. 1983: UNIVERSITY OF CALIFORNIA PRESS.

____. COUNTERINSURGENCY IN MANCHURIA: THE JAPANESE EXPERIENCE. 1967: RAND Corporation Memorandum RM-5012-ARPA.

THE SINO-JAPANESE WAR OF 1937-1945--II

Kiyoshi Miki & Karoku Hosokawa. INTRODUCTORY STUDIES ON THE SINO-JAPANESE CONFLICT. 1941: Institute of Pacific Relations.

Royal Institute of International Affairs. CHINA AND JAPAN. 3rd edition. 1941: Oxford University Press.

CHINA HANDBOOK, 1937-1945. 1947: Macmillan.

Frederick T. Merrill. JAPAN AND THE OPIUM MENACE. 1942: Institute of Pacific Relations & Foreign Policy Association.

Michael Schaller. THE U. S. CRUSADE IN CHINA, 1938-1945. 1979: Columbia University Press.

SOUTHEAST ASIA & THE CO-PROSPERITY SPHERE

John H. Boyle. "Greater East Asia Co-Prosperity Sphere," KODANSHA ENCYCLOPEDIA OF JAPAN 3: 60-62.

Harry J. Benda. "The Japanese Interregnum in Southeast Asia," in Grant K. Goodman, ed. IMPERIAL JAPAN AND ASIA (1967: Occasional Papers of the East Asia Institute, Columbia University), 65-79.

Katsumi Usui. "Pursuing an Illusion: The New Order in East Asia," Japan Interpreter 6.3 (1970), 326-337.

Grant K. Goodman. "Japan and Southeast Asia in the Pacific War: A Case of Cultural Ambiguity," in The Japan P. E. N. Club, ed. STUDIES ON JAPANESE CULTURE (1973: The Japan P. E. N. Club), 2: 235-241.

Joel V. Berreman. "The Japanization of Far Eastern Occupied Areas," Pacific Affairs 17 (1944), 168-180.

F. C. Jones. JAPAN'S NEW ORDER IN EAST ASIA: ITS RISE AND FALL, 1937-1945. 1954: Oxford University Press.

Joyce C. Lebra, ed. JAPAN'S GREATER EAST ASIA CO-PROSPERITY SPHERE IN WORLD WAR II: SELECTED READINGS & DOCUMENTS. 1975: Oxford University Press.

_____. JAPANESE-TRAINED ARMIES IN SOUTHEAST ASIA: INDEPENDENCE AND VOLUNTEER FORCES IN WORLD WAR II. 1977: Columbia University Press.

_____. JUNGLE ALLIANCE: JAPAN AND THE INDIAN NATIONAL ARMY IN WORLD WAR II. 1971: Asia Pacific.

Willard H. Elsbree. JAPAN'S ROLE IN SOUTHEAST ASIAN NATIONALIST MOVEMENTS, 1940-1945. 1953: Harvard University Press.

Alfred W. McCoy, ed. SOUTHEAST ASIA UNDER JAPANESE RULE. 1980: Yale University Southeast Asia Studies, Monograph Series 22. Ten essays covering aspects of the war in Indonesia, Sumatra, Malaya, Vietnam, Burma, the Philippines, Papua New Guinea, and Siam.

William H. Newell, ed. JAPAN IN ASIA. 1981: Singapore University Press. Seven essays on the World War Two period.

Josef Silverstein, ed. SOUTHEAST ASIA IN WORLD WAR II: FOUR ESSAYS. 1966: Yale University Press.

James W. Morley, ed. THE FATEFUL CHOICE: JAPAN'S ADVANCE INTO SOUTHEAST ASIA, 1939-1941. 1980: Columbia University Press.

Eric Robertson. THE JAPANESE FILE: PRE-WAR JAPANESE PENETRATION IN SOUTHEAST ASIA. 1980: Heinemann.

Iwaichi Fujiwara. F KIKAN: JAPANESE ARMY INTELLIGENCE OPERATIONS IN SOUTHEAST ASIA DURING WORLD WAR II. Yoji Akashi, transl. 1983: Heinemann.

Benedict R. O'G. Anderson. "Japan: 'The Light of Asia'," in Josef Silverstein, ed. SOUTH-EAST ASIA IN WORLD WAR II: FOUR ESSAYS. 1966: Yale University Press.

Robert S. Ward. ASIA FOR THE ASIATICS. THE TECHNIQUES OF JAPANESE OCCUPATION. 1945: University of Chicago Press.

Anthony Reid. "The Japanese Occupation and Rival Indonesian Elites: Northern Sumatra in 1942," Journal of Asian Studies 35.1 (1975), 49-61.

Harry J. Benda, James K. Irikura & Koichi Kishi, eds. JAPANESE MILITARY ADMINISTRATION IN INDONESIA: SELECTED DOCUMENTS. 1965: Yale University Southeast Asia Studies, Translation Series 6.

SOUTHEAST ASIA & THE CO-PROSPERITY SPHERE--II

M. Z. Aziz. JAPAN'S COLONIALISM AND INDONESIA. 1955: Martinus Nijhoff.

Harry J. Benda. THE CRESCENT AND THE RISING SUN: INDONESIAN ISLAM UNDER THE JAPANESE OCCUPATION, 1942-1945. 1958: Institute of Pacific Relations.

Benedict R. O'G. Anderson. SOME ASPECTS OF INDONESIAN POLITICS UNDER THE JAPANESE OCCUPATION: 1944-1945. 1961: Cornell University Press.

Barbara Gifford Shimer & Guy Hobbs, transl. THE KENPEITAI IN JAVA AND SUMATRA (Selections from *Nihon Kenpei Seishi*). 1986: Cornell Modern Indonesia Project, Translation Series 65.

Ba Maw. BREAKTHROUGH IN BURMA: MEMOIRS OF A REVOLUTION, 1939-1946. 1968: Yale University Press.

Frank N. Trager. BURMA, JAPANESE MILITARY ADMINISTRATION. SELECTED DOCUMENTS, 1941-1945. 1973: University of Pennsylvania Press.

Maurice Collis. LAST AND FIRST IN BURMA (1941-1948). 1956: Faber & Faber.

Won Z. Yoon. JAPAN'S SCHEME FOR THE LIBERATION OF BURMA: THE ROLE OF THE MINAMI KIKAN AND THE "THIRTY COMRADES." 1973: Center for International Studies, Ohio University.

Thamsook Numnonda. THAILAND AND THE JAPANESE PRESENCE, 1941-45. 1977: Institute of Southeast Asian Studies (Singapore).

John McAlister. VIET NAM: THE ORIGINS OF REVOLUTION. 1969: Knopf.

H. J. Lethbridge. "Hong Kong Under Japanese Occupation," in I. C. Jarvie, ed. HONG KONG: A SOCIETY IN CHANGE (1969: Praeger and Routledge & Kegan Paul), chapter 5.

Louis Allen. THE END OF THE WAR IN ASIA. 1976: Hart-Davis MacGibbon.

Grant Goodman. "Philippines and Japan," KODANSHA ENCYCLOPEDIA OF JAPAN 6: 183-184.

Teodoro Agoncillo. THE FATEFUL YEARS: JAPAN'S ADVENTURE IN THE PHILIPPINES, 1941-1945. 2 volumes. 1965: Garcia.

Hernando Abaya. BETRAYAL IN THE PHILIPPINES. 1946: A. A. Wyn.

A. V. H. Hartendorp. THE JAPANESE OCCUPATION OF THE PHILIPPINES. 2 volumes. 1967: Bookmark.

D. J. Steinberg. PHILIPPINE COLLABORATION IN WORLD WAR II. 1967: University of Michigan Press.

Elmer Lear. THE JAPANESE OCCUPATION OF THE PHILIPPINES: LEYTE, 1941-1945. 1961: Cornell South East Asian Studies, Data Paper 42.

_____. "Collaboration in Leyte: The Philippines Under Japanese Occupation," *Far Eastern Quarterly* 11.2 (1952), 183-206.

Inofre D. Corpuz. THE PHILIPPINES. 1965: Prentice-Hall.

Carlos P. Romulo. I SEE THE PHILIPPINES RISE. 1946: Doubleday.

n-Ami Shillony. POLITICS AND CULTURE IN WARTIME JAPAN. 1981: Oxford University Press.

____. "Japanese Intellectuals During the Pacific War," Proceedings of the British Association for Japanese Studies 2 (1977), 90-99.

ɔmas R. H. Havens. VALLEY OF DARKNESS: THE JAPANESE PEOPLE AND WORLD WAR TWO. 1978: Norton.

____. "Japanese Society During World War II," KODANSHA ENCYCLOPEDIA OF JAPAN 8: 277-278.

zuko Tsurumi. SOCIAL CHANGE AND THE INDIVIDUAL: JAPAN BEFORE AND AFTER DEFEAT IN WORLD WAR II. 1970: Princeton University Press. See especially the chapters on ideological conversion in the 1930s (29-79), the Army and the emperor system (80-98), "socialization for death" in the schools and military (99-137), and "the voice of the dead" (138-179).

ɪn W. Dower. EMPIRE AND AFTERMATH: YOSHIDA SHIGERU AND THE JAPANESE EXPERIENCE, 1878-1954. 1979: Harvard East Asian Monographs. Chapters 7 and 8 deal with conservative criticism of the war and the fear of revolution in wartime Japan.

____. WAR WITHOUT MERCY: RACE AND POWER IN THE PACIFIC WAR. 1986: Pantheon.

nald Keene. "Japanese Literature and Politics in the 1930s," Journal of Japanese Studies 2.2 (1976), 225-248.

____. "Japanese Writers and the Greater East Asia War," Journal of Asian Studies 23.2 (1964), 209-225.

____. "The Barren Years: Japanese War Literature," Monumenta Nipponica 33.1 (1978), 67-112.

____. "War Literature," in his DAWN TO THE WEST: JAPANESE LITERATURE OF THE MODERN ERA (1984: Holt, Rinehart & Winston), 906-961.

ɔriko Mizuta Lippit. "War Literature," KODANSHA ENCYCLOPEDIA OF JAPAN 8: 225-228.

ɪeph L. Anderson & Donald Ritchie. THE JAPANESE FILM: ART AND INDUSTRY. Expanded edition. 1982: Princeton University Press. Chapters 7 and 8 cover the period 1939-1945.

ɪne-Life Books. JAPAN AT WAR. 1980: Time-Life.

L. Mayer, ed. THE JAPANESE WAR MACHINE. 1976: Chartwell.

ɪsanobu Tsuji. SINGAPORE, THE JAPANESE VERSION. 1962: St. Martin's.

ɪvin D. Coox & Saburo Hayashi. KOGUN: THE JAPANESE ARMY IN THE PACIFIC WAR. 1959: Marine Corps Association.

ɪsaki Hanama. LONG THE IMPERIAL WAY. 1950: Houghton Mifflin.

ɪo Horikoshi. EAGLES OF MITSUBISHI: THE STORY OF THE ZERO FIGHTER. 1981: University of Washington Press.

D. Meo. JAPAN'S RADIO WAR ON AUSTRALIA, 1941-1945. 1968: Melbourne University Press.

ɪnis & Peggy Warner. THE SACRED WARRIORS: JAPAN'S SUICIDE LEGIONS. 1982: Avon.

chard O'Neill. SUICIDE SQUADS. 1981: Ballantine.

THE WAR IN JAPANESE EYES--II

Rikihei Inoguchi & Takashi Nakajima. THE DIVINE WIND: JAPAN'S KAMIKAZE FORCE IN WORLD WAR II. 1958: U.S. Naval Academy.

Ryuji Nagatsuka. I WAS A KAMIKAZE. 1973: Macmillan.

Hagaromo Society of Kamikaze Divine Thunderbolt Corps Survivors, comp. BORN TO DIE: THE CHERRY BLOSSOM SQUADRONS. Andrew Adams, ed. 1973: Ohara.

Mitsuru Yoshida. REQUIEM FOR BATTLESHIP 'YAMATO'. Richard H. Minear, transl. 1985: University of Washington Press.

Shohei Ooka. FIRES ON THE PLAIN. Ivan Morris, transl. 1957: Knopf. A translation of *Nobi*, the most famous Japanese recreation of a soldier's dehumanizing experiences.

Hiroshi Noma. ZONE OF EMPTINESS. Bernard Frechtman, transl. 1956: World.

Tetsuro Ogawa. TERRACED HELL: A JAPANESE MEMOIR OF DEFEAT AND DEATH IN NORTHERN LUZON, PHILIPPINES. 1972: Tuttle.

Michio Takeyama. HARP OF BURMA. Howard Hibbett, transl. 1966: Tuttle.

Jiro Osaragi. HOMECOMING. Brewster Horowitz, transl. 1955: Knopf.

Masuo Kato. THE LOST WAR: A JAPANESE REPORTER'S INSIDE STORY. 1946: Knopf.

Toshikazu Kase. JOURNEY TO THE MISSOURI. 1950: Yale University Press.

Yoshio Kodama. I WAS DEFEATED. Robert Booth & Taro Fukuda, transl. 1951: Taro Fukuda.

Shigenori Togo. THE CAUSE OF JAPAN. 1956: Simon & Schuster.

Mamoru Shigemitsu. JAPAN AND HER DESTINY: MY STRUGGLE FOR PEACE. 1958: Dutton.

Gwen Terasaki. BRIDGE TO THE SUN. 1957: University of North Carolina Press.

"The War and Japan: Revisionist Views." Special issue of *Japan Echo* 11 (1984). Articles by Japanese writers.

THE ATOMIC BOMBS

Martin J. Sherwin. A WORLD DESTROYED: THE ATOMIC BOMB AND THE GRAND ALLIANCE. 1975: Knopf.

Barton J. Bernstein, ed. THE ATOMIC BOMB: THE CRITICAL ISSUES. 1976: Little, Brown.

_____. "The Perils and Politics of Surrender: Ending the War with Japan and Avoiding the Third Atomic Bomb," *Pacific Historical Review* 46.1 (1977), 1-27.

Edwin Fogelman, ed. HIROSHIMA: THE DECISION TO USE THE A-BOMB. 1964: Charles Scribner's Sons.

James West Davidson & Mark Hamilton Lytle. "The Decision to Drop the Bomb," in their AFTER THE FACT: THE ART OF HISTORICAL DETECTION (1982: Knopf), 2: 320-355.

Gar Alperovitz. ATOMIC DIPLOMACY: HIROSHIMA AND POTSDAM. 1965; 1985: Vintage. See especially the 1985 edition, with an updated introduction by the author.

_____. "The Use of the Atomic Bomb," in his COLD WAR ESSAYS (1970: Doubleday-Anchor), 51-73. A critique of the orthodox American position on the use of the atomic bombs by Feis (1966) below.

P. M. S. Blackett. FEAR, WAR, AND THE BOMB. 1949: Whittlesey. The first major criticism of the use of the bomb, by an eminent British nuclear physicist and policy adviser.

Louis Morton. "The Decision to Use the Atomic Bomb," in K. R. Greenfield, ed. COMMAND DECISIONS (1959: Harcourt Brace), 388-410.

Herbert Feis. THE ATOMIC BOMB AND THE END OF WORLD WAR II. 1966: Princeton University Press. A revision of the author's 1961 monograph entitiled JAPAN SUBDUED: THE ATOMIC BOMB AND THE END OF THE WAR IN THE PACIFIC.

Otis Cary. "Atomic Bomb Targeting--Myths and Realities," *Japan Quarterly* 26.4 (1979), 506-514. On the deletion of Kyoto from U.S. atomic-bomb targets.

John Hersey. HIROSHIMA. 1946: Bantam.

Pacific War Research Society. THE DAY MAN LOST: HIROSHIMA, 6 AUGUST 1945. 1983: Kodansha International.

Dan Kurzman. DAY OF THE BOMB: COUNTDOWN TO HIROSHIMA. 1985: McGraw-Hill.

Committee for the Compilation of Materials on Damage Caused by the Atomic Bombs in Hiroshima and Nagasaki. HIROSHIMA AND NAGASAKI: THE PHYSICAL, MEDICAL, AND SOCIAL EFFECTS OF THE ATOMIC BOMBINGS. Translated by Eisei Ishikawa & David L. Swain from the 1979 Iwanami Shoten publication *Hiroshima Nagasaki no Genbaku Saigai*. 1981: Basic Books.

Robert J. Lifton. DEATH IN LIFE: SURVIVORS OF HIROSHIMA. 1967: Random House.

Michael J. Yavenditti. "The American People and the Use of Atomic Bombs on Japan: the 1940s," *The Historian* 36 (1974), 224-247.

Paul Boyer. BY THE BOMB'S EARLY LIGHT: AMERICAN THOUGHT AND CULTURE AT THE DAWN OF THE ATOMIC AGE. 1985: Pantheon.

Masuji Ibuse. BLACK RAIN. A translation of *Kuroi Ame* , by John Bester. 3rd edition. 1981: Kodansha International.

Kenzaburo Oe, ed. THE CRAZY IRIS AND OTHER STORIES OF THE ATOMIC AFTERMATH. 1985: Grove.

THE ATOMIC BOMBS--II

Michihiko Hachiya. HIROSHIMA DIARY: THE JOURNAL OF A JAPANESE PHYSICIAN, AUGUST 6-SEPTEMBER 30, 1945. 1955: University of North Carolina Press.

Arata Osada, comp. CHILDREN OF HIROSHIMA. 1959; 1982: Harper.

Takashi Nagai. WE OF NAGASAKI. 1951: Duell, Sloan & Pearce.

_____. THE BELLS OF NAGASAKI. William Johnston, S. J., transl. 1984: Kodansha International.

Tatsuichiro Akizuki. NAGASAKI 1945. 1982: Charles Rivers.

Miyao Ohara. THE SONGS OF HIROSHIMA. 1971: Taihei Shuppansha.

David G. Goodman, transl. AFTER APOCALYPSE: FOUR JAPANESE PLAYS OF HIROSHIMA AND NAGASAKI. 1986: Columbia University Press.

John W. Dower & John Junkerman, eds. THE HIROSHIMA MURALS: THE ART OF IRI MARUKI AND TOSHI MARUKI. 1985: Kodansha International.

Japan Broadcasting Corporation (NHK), ed. UNFORGETTABLE FIRE: PICTURES DRAWN BY ATOMIC BOMB SURVIVORS. 1977: Pantheon.

Keiji Nakazawa. BAREFOOT GEN. 2 volumes. 1979: Project Gen. English versions of the famous comic-strip style Japanese serial *Hadashi no Gen* , depicting the life of a young survivor of Hiroshima and based on the artist's own experiences.

Sadao Asada. "Japanese Perceptions of the A-Bomb Decision," in Joe C. Dixon, ed. THE AMERICAN MILITARY AND THE FAR EAST (1980: an American Air Force symposium; Office of Air Force History), 199-219.

John W. Dower. "Science, Society, and the Japanese Atomic-Bomb Project During World War Two," *Bulletin of Concerned Asian Scholars* 10.2 (1978), 41-54.

I.M.T.F.E. & OTHER WAR CRIMES TRIALS

R. John Pritchard & Sonia Zaide Pritchard, eds. THE TOKYO WAR CRIMES TRIAL: THE COMPLETE TRANSCRIPTS OF THE PROCEEDINGS OF THE INTERNATIONAL MILITARY TRIBUNAL FOR THE FAR EAST IN TWENTY-TWO VOLUMES. 1981: Garland. The most accessible version of the I.M.T.F.E. proceedings; includes an index. The Proceedings are also available on microfilm from the Library of Congress (37 reels).

Paul S. Dull & Michael Umemura. THE TOKYO TRIALS: A FUNCTIONAL INDEX TO THE PROCEEDINGS OF THE IMTFE. 1957: University of Michigan Press.

U. S. War Department. JUDGMENT OF THE INTERNATIONAL MILITARY TRIBUNAL FOR THE FAR EAST. 7 parts in 2 volumes. 1948: Government Printing Office.

Radhabinod Pal. THE INTERNATIONAL MILITARY TRIBUNAL FOR THE FAR EAST: DISSENTIENT JUDGMENT. 1953: Sanyal.

B. V. A. Roling & C. F. Ruter, eds. THE TOKYO JUDGMENT: THE INTERNATIONAL MILITARY TRIBUNAL FOR THE FAR EAST (I.M.T.F.E.), 26 APRIL 1946 - 12 NOVEMBER 1948. 3 volumes. 1977: APA University Press. A convenient source for the Judgment (volume 1), and full text of Justice Pal's dissent (volume 2).

Solis Horowitz. "The Tokyo Trial," *International Conciliation* 465 (1950: Carnegie Endowment for International Peace), 473-584. A brief summary of the trial by a member of the prosecution.

Kenzo Takayanagi. THE TOKIO TRIALS AND INTERNATIONAL LAW; ANSWER TO THE PROSECUTION'S ARGUMENTS ON INTERNATIONAL LAW DELIVERED AT THE INTERNATIONAL MILITARY TRIBUNAL FOR THE FAR EAST ON 3 AND 4 MARCH 1978. 1948: Yuhikaku.

Baron M. P. A. Hankey. POLITICS, TRIALS AND ERRORS. 1950: Regnery.

Richard Minear. VICTOR'S JUSTICE: THE TOKYO WAR CRIMES TRIAL. 1971: Princeton University Press.

Chihiro Hosoya, Nisuke Ando, Yasuaki Onuma & Richard Minear, eds. THE TOKYO WAR CRIMES TRIAL: AN INTERNATIONAL SYMPOSIUM. 1986: Kodansha International.

Saburo Shiroyama. WAR CRIMINAL: THE LIFE AND DEATH OF HIROTA KOKI. John Bester, transl. 1974: Kodansha International.

Philip R. Piccigallo. THE JAPANESE ON TRIAL: ALLIED WAR CRIMES OPERATIONS IN THE EAST, 1945-1951. 1979: University of Texas Press.

A. Frank Reel. THE CASE OF GENERAL YAMASHITA. 1949: University of Chicago Press.

Arthur Swinson. FOUR SAMURAI: A QUARTET OF JAPANESE ARMY COMMANDERS IN THE SECOND WORLD WAR. 1968: Hutchinson.

Richard R. Lael. THE YAMASHITA PRECEDENT: WAR CRIMES AND COMMAND RESPONSIBLITY. 1982: Scholarly Resources.

Lawrence Taylor. A TRIAL OF GENERALS: HOMMA, YAMASHITA, MACARTHUR. 1981: Icarus.

Kurt Steiner. "War Crimes and Command Responsibility: From the Bataan Death March to the MyLai Massacre," *Pacific Affairs* 58.2 (1986), 293-298. A review of Lael and Taylor.

John Frederick Hanson. "The Trial of Lieutenant General Masaharu Homma." 1977: Mississippi State University Ph.D. dissertation.

Edward F. Langley Russell, Lord of Liverpool. THE KNIGHTS OF BUSHIDO: THE SHOCKING HISTORY OF JAPANESE WAR ATROCITIES. 1958: Dutton.

MATERIALS ON THE TRIAL OF FORMER SERVICEMEN OF THE JAPANESE ARMY CHARGED WITH MANUFACTURING AND EMPLOYING BACTERIOLOGICAL WEAPONS. 1950: Moscow, Foreign Languages Publishing House. Proceedings of the December 25-30, 1949 Khabarovsk trial of 12 former Japanese military men.

John W. Powell. "Japan's Germ Warfare: The U.S. Cover-up of a War Crime," *Bulletin of Concerned Asian Scholars* 12.2 (1980), 2-17.

_____. "Japan's Biological Weapons, 1930-1945: A Hidden Chapter in History," *Bulletin of the Atomic Scientists* 37.8 (October 1981), 43-53.

Richard Falk. "The Shimoda Case: A Legal Appraisal of the Atomic Attacks Upon Hiroshima and Nagasaki," *American Journal of International Law* 59 (1965), 759-793.

Japan and the Crisis in Asia, 1931-1945: 'Primary' Materials in English

JAPAN AND THE CRISIS IN ASIA, 1931-1945:

'PRIMARY' MATERIALS IN ENGLISH

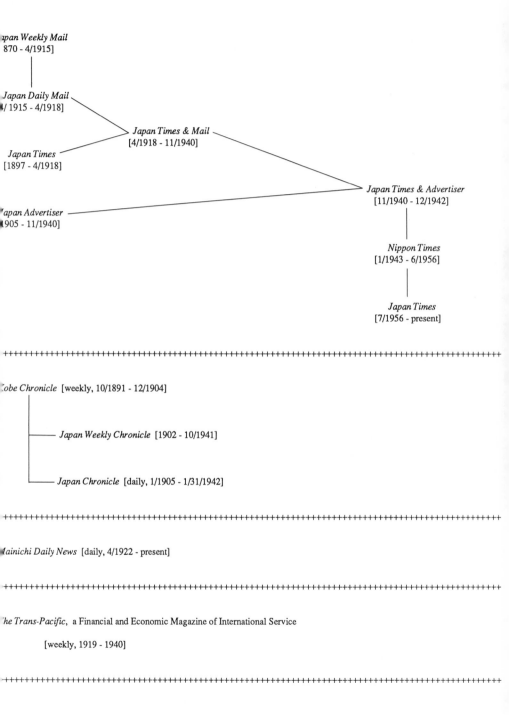

Japan Weekly Mail
870 - 4/1915]

Japan Daily Mail
/ 1915 - 4/1918]

Japan Times & Mail
[4/1918 - 11/1940]

Japan Times
[1897 - 4/1918]

Japan Times & Advertiser
[11/1940 - 12/1942]

apan Advertiser
905 - 11/1940]

Nippon Times
[1/1943 - 6/1956]

Japan Times
[7/1956 - present]

obe Chronicle [weekly, 10/1891 - 12/1904]

Japan Weekly Chronicle [1902 - 10/1941]

Japan Chronicle [daily, 1/1905 - 1/31/1942]

ainichi Daily News [daily, 4/1922 - present]

he Trans-Pacific, a Financial and Economic Magazine of International Service

[weekly, 1919 - 1940]

ENGLISH-LANGUAGE PRESS IN JAPAN--II

Japan Times Weekly [- 3/1918]

Japan Times Weekly & Trans-Pacific [1918 - 1941]

Japan Times & Mail, Weekly Edition [4/1918 - 1942]

Nippon Times Weekly [1943 - 6/1956]

China Weekly Review [*Millard's*], 1917 - 1953

    Title varies as follows:

    6/1917 - 5/1921   *Millard's Review of the Far East*

    6/1921 - 7/1922   *The Weekly Review of the Far East*

    7/1922 - 6/1923   *The Weekly Review*

    6/1923 - 8/1950   *The China Weekly Review*
                                    [suspended 12/13/1941 - 10/13/1945]

    9/1950 - 1953   *China Monthly Review*

++

North China Herald [1850 - 3/1867]

                               — *North China Herald & Market Report*
                                 [4/1867 - 1869]

                                              — *North China Herald & Supreme Court & Consular Gazette*
                                                [1871-1941; weekly out of Shanghai]

++

North China Daily News [7/1864 - 3/1951]   daily; Shanghai

China Critic [5/1928 - 1946]   weekly; Shanghai

China Press [1925 -12/1941; 10/1945 - 3/1949]   daily; Shanghai

PERIODICALS PUBLISHED PRIOR TO 1945

Amerasia [1937 - 1947]. An essentially leftwing analysis.

American Chamber of Commerce of Shanghai, *Bulletin* [monthly]

Asia [1898 - 12/1946]

>A lavishly illustrated monthly, published by the American Asiatic Association. Title varies:
>
>| | |
>|---|---|
>| 1898 - 1/1917 | *Journal of the American Asiatic Association* |
>| 3/1917 - 10/1942 | *Asia* |
>| 11/1942 - 12/1946 | *Asia and the Americas* |

British Chamber of Commerce of Shanghai, *Journal* [monthly]

China At War [4/1938 - 12/1945]

>A monthly propaganda journal published by the China Information Committee, Chungking.

China Today: A Monthly Magazine of Information and Opinion on the Far East [1934 - 1942]

>Published by the leftwing American Friends of the Chinese People, and eventually merged with *Amerasia*.

Chinese Social and Political Science Review [1916 -]

>Index to volumes 1-20 (1916 - 1937).

Communist International [1919 - 1940]

>London.
>5/1919 - 1924 = nos. 1-30.
>1924 - 12/1940 = New Series, vols. 1-17.

Contemporary Japan [1932 - present]

>Foreign Affairs Association of Japan. A valuable semi-official Japanese publication which includes chronologies and documents. Index to vols. 1-10 (6/1932 - 12/1941).

Contemporary Manchuria [4/1937 - 1/1941]

>A bimonthly magazine published by the South Manchurian Railway Company.

Contemporary Opinions on Current Topics; Translated from Japanese Magazines, Books, and Government Bulletins, Pamphlets and Reports from Various Sources [1936 - 1941]

>Tokyo Information Bureau; Shigeyoshi Okamura, ed. Partially available on Library of Congress microfilm, 2 reels.

PERIODICALS PUBLISHED PRIOR TO 1945--II

Empire Review [1901 - 1951]

    A British periodical. Monthly to 1942; quarterly thereafter. Title varies:

1901 - 1914	*The Empire Review*
1914 - 1922	*The Empire Review and Journal of British Trade*
1923 - 1944	*The Empire Review*
1944 - 1951	*The Commonwealth and Empire Review*

Far Eastern Review (*Engineering - Finance - Commerce*) [1904 - 1941]

    Shanghai commercial interests.

Far Eastern Survey [3/1932 - 2/1961]

    Weekly publication of the American Council of the Institute of Pacific Relations. Issued as "I.P.R. Memoranda" until volume 4.

Foreign Affairs [1922 - present]

    Monthly publication of the elite Council on Foreign Relations, N.Y.

Foreign Policy Bulletin [3/1920 - 6/1961]

    Foreign Policy Association, N.Y. A vehicle for more progressive and leftwing analysis.

Foreign Policy Reports [1925 - 1951]

    Foreign Policy Association, N.Y. Some variation in title.

The Fortnightly [1865 - 12/1954]

    London.

Illustrated London News [1842 - 1975]

International Affairs [1922 - present]

    Royal Institute of International Affairs, London. The R.I.I.A.'s voluminous publications in general are a valuable first-hand source for the pre-1945 period.

Oriental Economist, A Monthly Journal of Practical Finance and Economics for Japan and Eastern Asia [5/1934 - present]

    English edition of *Toyo Keizai Shimpo* , edited before the war by Tanzan Ishibashi.

PERIODICALS PUBLISHED PRIOR TO 1945--III

Pacific Affairs [1928 - present]

Institute of Pacific Relations.

The Round Table, A Quarterly Review of the Politics of the British Commonwealth [1910 - present]

Index for vols. 1-25 (1910 - 1935).

Tokyo Gazette, A Monthly Report of Current Politics, Official Statements and Statistics [1937 - 1941]

Japanese Government, Cabinet Information Bureau.

Japan Year Book [1905 - 1931]

Japan Times Year Book, 1933

Japan-Manchukuo Year Book [1934, 1938, 1939, 1940]

Contemporary Manchuria [1937, 1938, 1939, 1940]

Japan Year Book [1938/39, 1943/44, 1944/45, 1949/52]

    Foreign Affairs Association of Japan.

South Seas Handbook [1942/43, 1943/44, 1944/45]

    Foreign Affairs Association of Japan; complements *Japan Year Book.*

Japan Advertiser Annual Review: Finance, Industry, and Commerce [1931 - 1940]

Financial and Economic Annual of Japan [1901 - 1940]

    Department of Finance, Japan.

YEARBOOKS, ETC. -- CHINA, ASIA & THE WEST

China Year Book [1912 - 1939]

> North China Daily News & Herald.
> H. G. W. Woodhead, ed.

Chinese Year Book [1935 -]

> Council on International Affairs, Shanghai.

China Handbook [1937 - 1945]

> Ministry of Information, China.

Annual Report of the National Economic Council, China

Armaments Year-book: General and Statistical Information [1924 - 1939]

> League of Nations, 15 volumes.

Problems of the Pacific [1928 -]

> Biennial by Institute of Pacific Relations.

Survey of International Affairs [1920 - 1963]

> Royal Institute of International Affairs.
> Annual to 1938.
> Multi-volume problem focus for 1939 - 1946.
> Biennial or annual for 1947 - 1963.
> Index for 1920 - 1938.

The United States in World Affairs: An Account of American Foreign Relations [1931 - 1970]

> Council on Foreign Relations, N.Y.
> From 1971, incorporated in *American Foreign Relations: A Documentary Record.*

GENERAL COLLECTIONS OF OFFICIAL DOCUMENTS

Documents on International Affairs [1928 - 1963]

> Royal Institute of International Affairs.
> Annual volumes for 1928 - 1938.
> Two volumes cover 1939 - 1946.
> One volume for 1947/48, 1948/49.
> Annual volumes for 1950 - 1963.
> Companion to *Survey of International Affairs*, with consolidated index for 1920 - 1938.

Documents on American Foreign Relations [1938 - present]

> World Peace Foundation, 1938/39 - 1951.
> Council on Foreign Relations, 1951 - present.
> Beginning with volume for 1971, retitled *American Foreign Relations: A Documentary Record*.
> Essentially companion to *The United States in World Affairs* (CFR, 1931 - 1970).

Documents on British Foreign Policy, 1919 - 1939. Third Series

> E. L. Woodward and Rohan Butler, eds.
> 9 volumes. See volumes 8 and 9 on the Far East.

Documents on German Foreign Policy, 1918 - 1945, from the Archives of the German Foreign Ministry

> U.S. Department of State.
> Issued in 16 volumes (1949 - 1957).

Documents on Japanese Foreign Policy]

> Included regularly as end matter in Foreign Affairs Association of Japan's journal *Contemporary Japan* (from 1932).

LEAGUE OF NATIONS MATERIALS ON THE SINO-JAPANESE CONFLICT OF 1931 - 1933

Basic index to League materials

> *Guide to League of Nations Publications: A Bibliographic Survey of the Work of the League, 1920 - 1947.* Hans Aufricht, ed. (1951: Columbia University Press).

Minutes of the Council

> *Official Journal* [especially for December 1931 and March and December 1932].

China's basic position

> *Memoranda Presented to the Lytton Commission* by V. K. Wellington Koo, assessor. 1932. 3 volumes.

Japan's basic position

> *Document A--The Present Condition of China: With Reference to Circumstances Affecting International Relations and the Good Understanding between Nations upon which Peace Depends* [revised edition, July 1932].

> *Document B--Relations of Japan with Manchuria and Mongolia* [revised edition, July 1932].

> *The Manchurian Question: Japan's Case in the Sino-Japanese Dispute as Presented Before the League of Nations* [1932].

Report of the Lytton Commission

> *Report of the Commission of Inquiry* [1932].

JAPANESE MATERIALS IN ENGLISH

Bank of Japan, Statistics Department

Hundred-Year Statistics of the Japanese Economy [Iko Hompo Shuyo Keizai Tokei, 1966: Nihon Ginko].

Cabinet Information Bureau

Tokyo Gazette: A Monthly Report of Current Politics, Official Statements and Statistics [1937 - 1941].

Greater East Asia War Inquiry Commission

The American-British Challenge Directed Against Nippon [1943: Mainichi Shimbunsha].

Ministry of Education

Shushin-sho [Japanese ethics textbooks] in Robert King Hall, SHUSHIN: THE ETHICS OF A DEFEATED NATION (1949: Teachers College, Columbia University), 73-234.

KOKUTAI NO HONGI: CARDINAL PRINCIPLES OF THE NATIONAL ENTITY OF JAPAN [1937]. John Owen Gauntlett, transl., Robert King Hall, ed. 1949: Harvard University Press.

Shinmin no Michi [The Way of the Subject, March 1941] Translation in Otto Tolischus, TOKYO RECORD
(1943: Reynal & Hitchcock), 405-427.

South Manchurian Railway Company

Report on Progress in Manchuria, 1907 - 1928 [plus sequel and companion publications: 1930, 1932, 1934, 1936].

Minutes of the top-level Liaison and Imperial Conferences, 1941

Nobutake Ike, transl. and ed. JAPAN'S DECISION FOR WAR: RECORDS OF THE 1941 POLICY CONFERENCES. 1967: Stanford University Press. Based on volume 8 of *Taiheiyo Senso e no Michi*.

Documents pertaining to the Greater East Asia Co-Prosperity Sphere

Joyce C. Lebra, ed. JAPAN'S GREATER EAST ASIA CO-PROSPERITY SPHERE IN WORLD WAR II: SELECTED READINGS AND DOCUMENTS. 1975: Oxford University Press.

Harry J. Benda, James K. Irikura & Koichi Kishi, eds. JAPANESE MILITARY ADMINISTRATION IN INDONESIA: SELECTED DOCUMENTS. 1965: Yale University Southeast Asia Studies, Translation Series 6; based on Shigetada Nishijima & Koichi Kishi, eds. *Indonesia ni okeru Nihon Gunsei no Kenkyu.*

Japanese Military Administration [the Philippines]. THE OFFICIAL JOURNAL OF THE JAPANESE MILITARY ADMINISTRATION [published regularly in English in Manila from 1942].

Frank N. Trager, ed. BURMA: JAPANESE MILITARY ADMINISTRATION: SELECTED DOCUMENTS, 1941-1945. 1971: University of Pennsylvania Press.

189

OFFICIAL U. S. PUBLICATIONS

Roosevelt, Franklin D.

THE PUBLIC PAPERS AND ADDRESSES OF FRANKLIN D. ROOSEVELT. 13 volumes. 1950: Random House.

U. S. Air Force

THE ARMY AIR FORCES IN WORLD WAR II. Volumes 1, 4, and 5 deal with Japan.

U. S. Congress

HEARINGS OF THE JOINT COMMITTEE ON THE INVESTIGATION OF THE PEARL HARBOR ATTACK. 3ᶜ parts. 1946.

REPORT OF THE JOINT COMMITTEE ON THE INVESTIGATION OF THE PEARL HARBOR ATTACK. 1 volume. 1946.

U. S. Department of the Army

JAPANESE MONOGRAPH SERIES. 185 studies dealing with the war in the Pacific and originally prepared primarily by former Japanese military officers. Available on Library of Congress microfilm in 14 reels. 47 of the most important monographs are available in a 15-volume reprint edition by Garland Publishing Inc.: WAR IN ASIA AND THE PACIFIC, 1937-1945 (1980). See page 164 above.

JAPANESE STUDIES ON MANCHURIA. 13 studies originally prepared by former Japanese military officers. Available on Library of Congress microfilm.

REPORTS OF GENERAL MACARTHUR. 2 volumes in 4 books. Originally prepared by MacArthur's General Staff in 1950, but not published until 1966.
  I. *The Campaigns of MacArthur in the Pacific.*
  I, Supplement. *MacArthur in Japan: The Occupation: Military Phase.*
  II, Parts 1 and 2. *Japanese Operations in the Southwest Pacific Area.*

THE UNITED STATES ARMY IN WORLD WAR II. This series, including various related publications, is published under the auspices of the Office of the Chief of Military History, and included over 70 volumes as of 1980.

U. S. Department of Defense

THE ENTRY OF THE SOVIET UNION INTO THE WAR AGAINST JAPAN: MILITARY PLANS, 1941-1945. 1955.

U. S. Department of State

For consular reports and related materials pertaining to U.S. relations with Japan and China and available on microfilm from the U.S. government, consult *Catalog of National Archives Microfilm Publications*. See also
pages 192-194 below for privately issued collections of official documents.

FOREIGN RELATIONS OF THE UNITED STATES. "Far East" volumes in this basic State Department series are:

1931	vol.	3	1937	vol.	3 & 4
1932		3 & 4	1938		3 & 4
1933		3	1939		3 & 4
1934		3	1940		4
1935		3	1941		4 & 5
1936		4			

FOREIGN RELATIONS OF THE UNITED STATES: JAPAN, 1931-1941. 2 volumes, published in 1943 while the war (and debate over Pearl Harbor) was going on.

PEACE AND WAR: UNITED STATES FOREIGN POLICY, 1931-1941. Published in 1943 and focusing on pre-Pearl Harbor relations with Japan and Germany.

REPORT ON JAPANESE REPARATIONS TO THE PRESIDENT OF THE UNITED STATES, NOVEMBER 194 TO April 1946. DOS Publication 3174, Far Eastern Series 25. [The Pauley Report. See also the complementary report by Edwin W. Pauley entitled REPORT ON JAPANESE ASSETS IN MANCHURIA TO THE PRESIDENT OF THE UNITED STATES, JULY 1946.]

UNITED STATES RELATIONS WITH CHINA, WITH SPECIAL REFERENCE TO THE PERIOD 1944-1949. 1949. DOS Publication 3573, Far Eastern Series 30. The famous "China White Paper" of August 1949.

U. S. Strategic Bombing Survey

PACIFIC WAR [1945 - 1947]. Consists of 108 reports. For the most useful general reports, see page 164 above.

U. S. ARCHIVAL MATERIALS AVAILABLE IN MICROFILM FROM COMMERCIAL SOURCES

The extensive declassification of formerly confidential U.S. government documents since the 1960s has facilitated the extensive copying of both civilian and military archival materials. The following large collections, covering post-1945 as well as pre-1945 activities, are offered by University Publications of America (usually accompanied by an index):

* *Confidential U. S. Diplomatic Post Records: Japan*

    Part 1. Japan, 1914-1918. 11 reels.
    Part 2. Japan, 1919-1929. 50 reels.
    Part 3. Japan, 1930-1941. 80 reels.

* *The MAGIC Documents: Summaries and Transcripts of the Top-Secret Diplomatic Communications of Japan, 1938-1945.* 14 reels.

* *Confidential U. S. State Department Central Files*

    Japan: Internal Affairs, 1945-1949. 42 reels.
    Japan: Internal Affairs, 1950-1954. 62 reels.

* *U.S. Military Intelligence Reports: Japan, 1918-1941.* 31 reels.

* *U.S. Military Intelligence Reports: China, 1911-1941.* 15 reels.

* *Records of the Joint Chiefs of Staff*

    Pacific Theater, 1942-1945. 14 reels.
    The Far East, 1946-1953. 14 reels.

* *OSS / State Department Intelligence and Research Reports*

    Japan and Its Occupied Territories during World War II. 16 reels.
    Postwar Japan, Korea and Southeast Asia. 6 reels.
    Japan, Korea, Southeast Asia, and the Far East Generally: 1950-1961 Supplement. 7 reels.

* *CIA Research Reports*

    China, 1946-1976. 6 reels.
    Japan, Korea, and the Security of Asia, 1946-1976. 5 reels.
    Vietnam and Southeast Asia, 1946-1976. 7 reels.

* *The Special Studies Series* (reports by various "think tanks")

    China, 1970-1980. 8 reels.
    Japan, Korea, and the Security of Asia, 1970-1980. 4 reels.
    Vietnam and Southeast Asia, 1960-1980. 13 reels.
    Asia, 1980-1982 Supplement. 5 reels.
    Asia, 1982-1985 Supplement. 12 reels.

In addition to the preceding University Publications of America collections, the following archives are avaiable on microfilm from Scholarly Resources, Inc., under the collective title *Official Records of the U.S. Department of State Relating to Japan* (Record Group 59):

19th-CENTURY RECORDS

Diplomatic Instructions of the Department of State Regarding Japan, 1855-1906. 5 reels.

Despatches from U. S. Ministers to Japan, 1855-1906. 82 reels.

Records of the U. S. Legation in Japan, 1855-1912. 94 reels.

Despatches from U. S. Consuls in Japan, 1856-1906. 41 reels.

Notes from the Japanese Legation in the United States to the Department of State, 1858-1906. 9 reels.

Notes to the Legation of Japan in the United States from the Department of State, 1860-1906. 2 reels.

20th-CENTURY RECORDS

Records Relating to Political Relations Between the United States and Japan, 1910-1929. 9 reels.

Records Relating to Political Relations Between Japan and Other States, 1910-1929. 1 reel.

Records Relating to the Internal Affairs of Japan:

        1910-1929. 43 reels.
        1930-1939. 33 reels.
        1940-1944. 20 reels.
        1945-1949. 39 reels.
        1950-1954. Forthcoming.

Records Relating to Political Relations Between China and Japan, 1930-1944. 96 reels.

BRITISH ARCHIVAL MATERIALS AVAILABLE FROM COMMERCIAL SOURCES

University Publications of America. *British Documents on Foreign Affairs: Reports and Papers from the Foreign Office Confidential Print*. Offered as a counterpart to the U.S. State Department's *Foreign Relations of the United States* series, these volumes are scheduled for publication between 1985 and 1988:

> *Part I. From the Mid-Nineteenth Century to the First World War: Asia*. 30 volumes.
> *Part II. From the First to the Second World War: Asia*. 50 volumes.

Scholarly Resources, Inc. *The Japan Correspondence of the British Foreign Office, 1856-1945* (Files 46 and 371). Available in the following microfilm collections:

1856-1867.	48 reels.
1868-1875.	61 reels.
1876-1882.	59 reels.
1883-1893.	65 reels.
1894-1904.	78 reels.
1905.	57 reels.
1906-1929.	Forthcomng.
1930-1936.	38 reels.
1937-1941.	48 reels.
1942-1945.	28 reels.
Registers, 1856-1905.	6 reels.

Microfilming Corporation of America. *The London Times Intelligence File: The Far East (1906-1969)*. 27 microfilm reels (5 of which pertain to Japan alone).

M. T. F. E. & OTHER WAR CRIMES TRIALS

See pages 173-174 above. The Proceedings of the Tokyo war crimes trails, long inaccessible or inconvenient to use, are now available in a 27-volume reprint edition (including a 5-volume index and guide):

R. John Pritchard & Sonia Zaide Pritchard, eds. THE TOKYO WAR CRIMES TRIAL (Garland Publishing, Inc.).

Both the Judgment and dissenting opinions, including the famous lengthy dissent of Justice Pal, have been conveniently reprinted in 3 volumes in:

B. V. A. Roling & C. F. Ruter, eds. THE TOKYO JUDGMENT: THE INTERNATIONAL MILITARY TRIBUNAL FOR THE FAR EAST (I.M.T.F.E.), 29 APRIL 1946-12 NOVEMBER 1948 (1977: APA-University Press, Amsterdam BV).

A 535-page English transcript of the December 1949 Soviet trial of Japanese accused of engaging in biological-warfare research involving prisoners of war in Manchuria (the notorious "Unit 731") is:

MATERIALS ON THE TRIAL OF FORMER SERVICEMEN OF THE JAPANESE ARMY CHARGED WITH MANUFACTURING AND EMPLOYING BACTERIOLOGICAL WEAPONS (1950: Foreign Language Publishing House, Moscow).

ACCOUNTS BY PARTICIPANTS

Joseph W. Ballantine. "Mukden to Pearl Harbor: The Foreign Policies of Japan," *Foreign Affairs* 27 (July 1949), 651-664.

Ba Maw. BREAKTHROUGH IN BURMA: MEMOIRS OF A REVOLUTION, 1939-1946. 1968: Yale University Press.

Alexander Cadogan. THE DIARIES OF SIR ALEXANDER CADOGAN, 1938-1945. David Dilks, ed. 1971: Cassell.

Winston Churchill. THE SECOND WORLD WAR (1948-1954). Multivolume. 1948-1954: Houghton Mifflin.

Sir Robert Craigie. BEHIND THE JAPANESE MASK. 1945: Hutchinson.

John P. Davies. DRAGON BY THE TAIL. 1972: Norton.

Herbert von Dirkson. MOSCOW, TOKYO, LONDON. 1951: Hutchinson.

Anthony Eden. THE MEMOIRS OF ANTHONY EDEN, EARL OF AVON. Volume 1: FACING THE DICTATORS, 1932-1938. 1962: Cassell.

Robert L. Eichelberger. OUR JUNGLE ROAD TO TOKYO. 1950: Viking.

John K. Emmerson. THE JAPANESE THREAD: A LIFE IN THE U.S. FOREIGN SERVICE. 1978: Holt, Rinehart & Winston.

Joseph Grew. REPORT FROM TOKYO. 1942: Simon & Schuster.

_____. TEN YEARS IN JAPAN. 1944: Simon & Schuster.

_____. TURBULENT ERA: A DIPLOMATIC RECORD OF FORTY YEARS, 1904-1945. 2 volumes. 1952: Houghton Mifflin.

Kumao Harada. See SAIONJI-HARADA MEMOIRS below.

Herbert Hoover. MEMOIRS. 3 volumes. 1951: Macmillan. Volume 2 covers 1920-1932.

Jiro Horikoshi. EAGLES OF MITSUBISHI: THE STORY OF THE ZERO FIGHTER. 1980: University of Washington Press.

Stanley K. Hornbeck. THE U.S. AND THE FAR EAST: CERTAIN FUNDAMENTALS OF POLICY. 1942: World Peace Foundation.

Cordell Hull. THE MEMOIRS OF CORDELL HULL. 2 volumes. 1948: Macmillan.

Harold L. Ickes. THE SECRET DIARY OF HAROLD L. ICKES. 3 volumes. 1953-1954: Simon & Schuster.

Kikujiro Ishii. DIPLOMATIC COMMENTARIES. William R. Langdon, transl. 1936: Johns Hopkins.

Toshikazu Kase. JOURNEY TO THE "MISSOURI." 1952: Yale University Press.

Masuo Kato. THE LOST WAR: A JAPANESE REPORTER'S INSIDE STORY. 1946: Knopf.

Koichi Kido. THE DIARY OF MARQUIS KIDO, 1931-45: SELECTED TRANSLATIONS INTO ENGLISH. 1984: University Publications of America. Reprinted from translations prepared for the IMTFE or Tokyo war crimes trials.

Sir Hughe Knatchbull-Hugessen. DIPLOMAT IN PEACE AND WAR. 1949: John Murray.

CCOUNTS BY PARTICIPANTS--II

)shio Kodama. I WAS DEFEATED. Robert Booth & Taro Fukuda, transl. 1951: Taro Fukuda.

imimaro Konoye. "Memoirs of Prince Konoye," Exhibit No. 173 in U.S. Congress, HEARINGS OF THE JOINT COMMITTEE ON THE INVESTIGATION OF THE PEARL HARBOR ATTACK, part 20, 3958-4029.

"The Memoirs of Prince Fumimaro Konoye, with Appended Papers," translated and reproduced by 5250th Technical
Intelligence Co., 10 June 1946. Record Group 331. Washington National Records Center.

See also Library of Congress microfilm WT6 from the IMTFE.

iomas W. Lamont. ACROSS WORLD FRONTIERS. 1951: Harcourt Brace.

r Frederick Leith-Ross. MONEY TALKS: FIFTY YEARS OF INTERNATIONAL FINANCE. 1968: Hutchinson.

iney Forrester Mashbir. I WAS AN AMERICAN SPY. 1953: Vantage.

ederick Moore. WITH JAPAN'S LEADERS: AN INTIMATE RECORD OF FOURTEEN YEARS AS COUNSELLOR TO THE JAPANESE GOVERNMENT, ENDING DECEMBER 7, 1941. 1942: Charles Scribner's Sons.

enry Morgenthau, Jr. FROM THE MORGENTHAU DIARIES. Volume 2: YEARS OF URGENCY, 1938-1941. John Morton Blum, ed. (1965: Houghton Mifflin), 344-393.

. G. Nichols, ed. WASHINGTON DESPATCHES, 1941-1945: WEEKLY POLITICAL REPORTS FROM THE BRITISH EMBASSY. 1981: University of Chicago Press.

S. G. Piggot. BROKEN THREAD, AN AUTOBIOGRAPHY. 1950: Gale & Polden.

r John Pratt. WAR AND POLITICS IN CHINA. 1943: Cape.

_____. CHINA AND BRITAIN. 1944: Hastings House.

isin Gioro Pu-Yi. FROM EMPEROR TO CITIZEN. 2 volumes. 1964-1965: Foreign Language Press, Peking. Autobiography of the last Ch'ing emperor, who was "restored" to the throne by the Japanese in Manchukuo.

ranklin D. Roosevelt. F. D. R.--HIS PERSONAL LETTERS, 1928-1945. Elliott Roosevelt, ed. 2 volumes. 1950: Duell Sloan & Pearce.

HE SAIONJI-HARADA MEMOIRS, 1931-1940: COMPLETE TRANSLATION INTO ENGLISH. 1978 (3 microfilm reels issued by University Publications). The famous record kept by Harada Kumao for Prince Saionji Kimmochi. Also available as Library of Congress microfilms SP49-51 from IMTFE.

iroshi Saito. JAPAN'S POLICIES AND PURPOSES: SELECTIONS FROM RECENT ADDRESSES AND WRITINGS. 1935: Marshall Jones. Ambassador to U.S., 1934-35.

'amoru Shigemitsu. JAPAN AND HER DESTINY: MY STRUGGLE FOR PEACE. 1958: Dutton.

'ohan Singh. SOLDIER'S CONTRIBUTION TO INDIAN INDEPENDENCE: THE EPIC OF THE INDIAN NATIONAL ARMY. 1974: Army Educational Stores, New Delhi.

'illiam Slim. DEFEAT INTO VICTORY. 1960: Cassell.

enry L. Stimson. THE FAR EASTERN CRISIS: RECOLLECTIONS AND OBSERVATIONS. 1936: Harper.

_____ & McGeorge Bundy. ON ACTIVE SERVICE IN PEACE AND WAR. 1948: Harper.

ACCOUNTS BY PARTICIPANTS--III

Gwen Terasaki. BRIDGE TO THE SUN. 1957: University of North Carolina Press.

Shigenori Togo. THE CAUSE OF JAPAN. 1956: Simon & Schuster.

Otto Tolischus. TOKYO RECORD. 1943: Reynal & Hitchcock. Reconstruced "diary" covering January 1941 to August 1942, by the former *New York Times* correspondent in Japan.

Harry S. Truman. YEAR OF DECISIONS, 1945. 1955: Doubleday.

Masanobu Tsuji. SINGAPORE: THE JAPANESE VERSION. 1960: St. Martin's.

_____. UNDERGROUND ESCAPE. Robert Booth & Taro Fukuda, transl. 1952: Taro Fukuda.

Lord Vansittart. THE MIST PROCESSION. 1958: Hutchinson.

Amleto Vespa. SECRET AGENT OF JAPAN. 1938: Little, Brown.

Hugh R. Wilson. DIPLOMAT BETWEEN WARS. 1941: Longmans, Green.

Arthur N. Young. CHINA AND THE HELPING HAND. 1963: Harvard University Press. U.S. financial adviser to China.

Ellis M. Zacharias. SECRET MISSIONS: THE STORY OF AN INTELLIGENCE OFFICER. 1946: Putnam.

Occupied Japan & the Cold War in Asia

OCCUPIED JAPAN & THE COLD WAR IN ASIA

GENERAL SOURCES

John W. Dower. "Occupied Japan as History and Occupation History as Politics," *Journal of Asian Studies* 34.2 (1975), 485-504.

Carol Gluck. "Entangling Illusions--Japanese and American Views of the Occupation," in Warren I. Cohen, ed. NEW FRONTIERS IN AMERICAN-EAST ASIAN RELATIONS: ESSAYS PRESENTED TO DOROTHY BORG (1983: Columbia University Press), 169-236.

Robert E. Ward & Frank Joseph Shulman. THE ALLIED OCCUPATION OF JAPAN, 1945-1952: AN ANNOTATED BIBLIOGRAPHY OF WESTERN-LANGUAGE MATERIALS. 1974: American Library Association.

Frank Joseph Shulman, comp. DOCTORAL DISSERTATIONS ON THE ALLIED OCCUPATION OF JAPAN, 1945-1952. 1978, with periodic supplements. Prepared for the MacArthur Memorial Symposium.

Royal Institute of International Affairs. SURVEY OF INTERNATIONAL AFFAIRS.

1. THE FAR EAST, 1942-1946. (Hugh Borton on Japan, 307-428).
2. 1947-1948 (F. C. Jones on Japan, 328-346).
3. 1949-1950 ("   , 443-466).
4. 1951 ("   , 378-433).
5. 1952 ("   , 355-393).
6. See also companion volumes in RIIA. DOCUMENTS ON INTERNATIONAL AFFAIRS.

Supreme Commander for the Allied Powers. POLITICAL REORIENTATION OF JAPAN, SEPTEMBER 1945 TO SEPTEMBER 1948. 2 volumes. 1949: Government Printing Office. The official history of the reformist phase of the Occupation. Volume 2 is a valuable collection of basic documents.

Peter Frost. "Occupation," KODANSHA ENCYCLOPEDIA OF JAPAN 6: 51-55.

Hugh Patrick. "The Phoenix Risen from the Ashes: Postwar Japan," in James Crowley, ed. EAST ASIA: ESSAYS IN INTERPRETATION (1970: Harcourt Brace & World), 298-335.

Ikuhiko Hata. "Japan Under the Occupation," *Japan Interpreter* 10.3-4 (1976), 361-380.

_____. "The Occupation of Japan, 1945-1952," in Joe C. Dixon, ed. THE AMERICAN MILITARY AND THE FAR EAST (1981: Office of Air Force History), 92-108.

John W. Dower. EMPIRE AND AFTERMATH: YOSHIDA SHIGERU AND THE JAPANESE EXPERIENCE, 1878-1954. 1979: Harvard East Asian Monographs. See especially pages 273-492.

Michael Schaller. THE AMERICAN OCCUPATION OF JAPAN: THE ORIGINS OF THE COLD WAR IN ASIA. 1985: Oxford University Press.

Kazuo Kawai. JAPAN'S AMERICAN INTERLUDE. 1960: University of Chicago Press.

Edwin M. Martin. THE ALLIED OCCUPATION OF JAPAN. 1948: Stanford University Press.

Robert Fearey. THE OCCUPATION OF JAPAN: SECOND PHASE, 1948-1950. 1950: Macmillan.

Baron E. J. Lewe van Aduard. JAPAN: FROM SURRENDER TO PEACE. 1964: Praeger.

Hugh Borton. JAPAN'S MODERN CENTURY: FROM PERRY TO 1970 (1970: Ronald), chapter 20.

Edwin O. Reischauer. THE UNITED STATES AND JAPAN. 3rd edition. 1965: Viking.

Masataka Kosaka. A HISTORY OF POSTWAR JAPAN. Originally published as 100-MILLION JAPANESE. 1982: Harper & Row.

GENERAL SOURCES--II

Harry Emerson Wildes. TYPHOON IN TOKYO: THE OCCUPATION AND ITS AFTERMATH. 1954: Macmillan.

John D. Montgomery. FORCED TO BE FREE: THE ARTIFICIAL REVOLUTION IN GERMANY AND JAPAN. 1957: University of Chicago Press.

Harold S. Quigley & John E. Turner. THE NEW JAPAN: GOVERNMENT AND POLITICS. 1956: University of Minnesota Press.

P. Linebarger, C. Djang & A. Burks. FAR EASTERN GOVERNMENTS AND POLITICS: CHINA AND JAPAN (1954: Van Nostrand), chapters 20, 21.

Herbert Passin. THE LEGACY OF THE OCCUPATION--JAPAN. 1968: East Asia Institute, Columbia University.

Grant Goodman, comp. THE AMERICAN OCCUPATION OF JAPAN: A RETROSPECTIVE VIEW. 1968: Center for East Asian Studies, Kansas University.

Robert Ward. "Reflections on the Allied Occupation and Planned Political Change in Japan," in his POLITICAL DEVELOPMENT IN MODERN JAPAN (1973: Princeton University Press), 477-536.

Ray Moore. "Reflections on the Occupation of Japan," *Journal of Asian Studies* 38.4 (1979), 721-734.

_____. "The Occupation of Japan as History: Some Recent Research," *Monumenta Nipponica* 36.3 (1981), 317-328.

Harry Wray & Hilary Conroy, eds. JAPAN EXAMINED: PERSPECTIVES ON MODERN JAPANESE HISTORY (1983: University of Hawaii Press), 331-363. Essays on "The Allied Occupation: How Significant Was It?" by Edwin Reischauer, John Dower, Rinjiro Sodei, and Eiji Takemae.

Howard Schonberger. "The Japan Lobby in American Diplomacy, 1947-1952," *Pacific Historical Review* 46 (1977), 327-359.

_____. "U. S. Policy in Post-war Japan: The Retreat from Liberalism," *Science and Society* 46 (1982), 39-59.

Asahi Shimbun, ed. THE PACIFIC RIVALS: A JAPANESE VIEW OF JAPANESE-AMERICAN RELATIONS (1972: Weatherhill & Asahi), 109-209.

D. Clayton James. THE YEARS OF MACARTHUR: TRIUMPH AND DISASTER, 1945-1964. 1985: Houghton Mifflin. The third and final volume of the major biography of MacArthur.

John Curtis Perry. BENEATH THE EAGLE'S WINGS: AMERICANS IN OCCUPIED JAPAN. 1980: Dodd, Mead.

Robert Wolfe, ed. AMERICANS AS PROCONSULS: UNITED STATES MILITARY GOVERNMENT IN GERMANY JAPAN, 1944-1952. 1984: Southern Illinois University Press. Includes articles by Marlene Mayo on presurrender planning and also censorship; Ralph Braibanti on the "MacArthur Shogunate"; Eleanor Hadley on economic deconcentration and the reverse course; and Hans Baerwald on the purge.

MACARTHUR MEMORIAL SYMPOSIA. The major ongoing coordinated inquiry concerning Occupied Japan has been conferences sponsored by the MacArthur Memorial in Norfolk, Virginia (with later joint sponsorship by Old Dominion University). Conference papers and discussions--by both scholars and former participants--are published, recently under the editorship of Thomas Burkham. Conferences through 1984 have been focused as follows on specific aspects of the Occupation:

1. THE OCCUPATION OF JAPAN AND ITS LEGACY TO THE POSTWAR WORLD. 1975.
2. THE OCCUPATION OF JAPAN: IMPACT OF LEGAL REFORM. 1977.
3. THE OCCUPATION OF JAPAN: ECONOMIC POLICY AND REFORM. 1978.
4. THE OCCUPATION OF JAPAN: EDUCATION AND SOCIAL REFORM. 1980.
5. THE OCCUPATION OF JAPAN: THE INTERNATIONAL CONTEXT. 1982.
6. THE OCCUPATION OF JAPAN: ARTS AND CULTURE. 1984.

CONTEMPORARY ACCOUNTS (1944-1952)

W. Macmahon Ball. JAPAN: ENEMY OR ALLY? 1949: Cassell.

Thomas A. Bisson. PROSPECTS FOR DEMOCRACY IN JAPAN. 1949: Macmillan.

Hugh Borton, ed. JAPAN. 1950: Cornell University Press.

Russell Brines. MACARTHUR'S JAPAN. 1948: J. B. Lippincott.

Brookings Institution. MAJOR PROBLEMS OF UNITED STATES FOREIGN POLICY, 1948-49. 1949: Brookings Insitution.

Noel Busch. FALLEN SUN: A REPORT ON JAPAN. 1948: Appleton-Century.

William Costello. DEMOCRACY VS. FEUDALISM IN POSTWAR JAPAN. 1948: Hagaki Shoten.

Miriam S. Farley. ASPECTS OF JAPAN'S LABOR PROBLEMS. 1950: John Day.

Carl Friedrich et al., ed. AMERICAN EXPERIENCES IN MILITARY GOVERNMENT IN WORLD WAR II. 1948: Holt.

Mark Gayn. JAPAN DIARY. 1948: William Sloane.

John Gunther. THE RIDDLE OF MACARTHUR. 1950: Harper.

Robert King Hall. EDUCATION FOR A NEW JAPAN. 1949: Yale University Press.

Douglas G. Haring, ed. JAPAN'S PROSPECT. 1946: Harvard University Press.

Institute of Pacific Relations. SECURITY IN THE PACIFIC. 1945: Institute of Pacific Relations.

_____. PROBLEMS OF ECONOMIC RECONSTRUCTION IN THE FAR EAST. 1949: Inst. of Pacific Relations.

Harold Issacs. NEW CYCLE IN ASIA: SELECTED DOCUMENTS ON MAJOR INTERNATIONAL DEVELOPMENTS IN THE FAR EAST. 1947: Macmillan.

W. C. Johnstone. THE FUTURE OF JAPAN. 1945: Oxford University Press.

Frank Kelley & Cornelius Ryan. STAR SPANGLED MIKADO. 1947: McBride.

Owen Lattimore. SOLUTION IN ASIA. 1945: Little, Brown.

_____. THE SITUATION IN ASIA. 1949: Little, Brown.

John LaCerda. THE CONQUEROR COMES TO TEA: JAPAN UNDER MACARTHUR. 1946: Rutgers Univ. Press.

Helen Mears. MIRROR FOR AMERICANS: JAPAN. 1948: Houghton Mifflin.

Harold B. Moulton & Louis Marlio. THE CONTROL OF GERMANY AND JAPAN. 1944: Brookings Institution.

Andrew Roth. DILEMMA IN JAPAN. 1945: Little, Brown.

Royal Institute of International Affairs, ed. JAPAN IN DEFEAT: A REPORT BY A CHATHAM HOUSE STUDY GROUP. 1945: Oxford University Press.

A. Frank Reel. THE CASE OF GENERAL YAMASHITA. 1949: University of Chicago Press

Robert B. Textor. FAILURE IN JAPAN. 1951: John Day.

Harold Wakefield. NEW PATHS FOR JAPAN. 1948: Royal Institute of International Affairs.

205

MEMOIRS

Dean Acheson. PRESENT AT THE CREATION: MY YEARS IN THE STATE DEPARTMENT. 1969: W. W. Norton.

John Allison. AMBASSADOR FROM THE PRAIRIE, OR ALLISON WONDERLAND. 1973: Houghton Mifflin.

James F. Byrnes. SPEAKING FRANKLY. 1947: Harper.

W. Averell Harriman & Ellie Abel. SPECIAL ENVOY TO CHURCHILL AND STALIN, 1941-1946. 1975: Random House.

George F. Kennan. MEMOIRS, 1925-1950. 1967: Little, Brown.

Douglas MacArthur. REMINISCENCES. 1964: McGraw-Hill.

Alfred C. Oppler. LEGAL REFORM IN OCCUPIED JAPAN: A PARTICIPANT LOOKS BACK. 1976: Princeton University Press.

Matthew B. Ridgway. SOLDIER: THE MEMOIRS OF MATTHEW B. RIDGWAY. 1956: Harper.

Harry S. Truman. MEMOIRS. 2 volumes. 1955: Doubleday.

Tatsuro Uchino. JAPAN'S POSTWAR ECONOMY: AN INSIDER'S VIEW OF ITS HISTORY AND ITS FUTURE. 1983: Kodansha International.

Courtney Whitney. MACARTHUR: HIS RENDEZVOUS WITH HISTORY. 1956: Knopf.

Justin Williams. JAPAN'S POLITICAL REVOLUTION UNDER MACARTHUR: A PARTICIPANT'S ACCOUNT. 1979: University of Georgia Press.

Charles A. Willoughby & John Chamberlain. MACARTHUR, 1941-1951: VICTORY IN THE PACIFIC. 1954: McGraw-Hill.

Shigeru Yoshida. THE YOSHIDA MEMOIRS: THE STORY OF JAPAN IN CRISIS. Kenichi Yoshida, transl. 1962: Houghton Mifflin.

HISTORY OF NON-MILITARY ASPECTS OF THE OCCUPATION OF JAPAN

This series comprises a total of 55 monographs, all of which contain appendices of documents. All but a few of the monographs have been declassified and are available on microfilm from the U.S. National Archives. This is the basic, and by far most comprehensive, official account of the occupation, but should be used with recognition of the fact that (1) it is a house history, which seeks to present the occupation in its most favorable light; (2) most of the monographs cover only the period up to 1950, and thus this is not an adequate source for the crucial 1950-1952 period; (3) the authors of the series (SCAP's Civil Historical Section) relied primarily on public statements and internal SCAP memoranda, and were not privileged with access to materials at the highest and most classified levels; (4) attention is devoted primarily to the formal policy process, rather than to critical analysis of the actual effects and implications of policy application and policy revisions; (5) the monographic approach adopted tends to convey a fragmented and compartmentalized impression of the occupation, rather than the broader overview which was held by key decision-makers then, and which the scholar must also recreate; (6) the approach is essentially unilinear, that is, focused on American policy and initiative, and neglects the crucial dimension of US-Japanese interaction. The series nonetheless remains of central importance to scholars of the period. The individual monographs, in their officially designated order, are as follows:

1. Introduction
2. Administration of the Occupation
3. Logistic Support
4. Population
5. Trials of Class 'B' and Class 'C' War Criminals
6. Local Government Reform
7. The Purge
8. Constitutional Revision
9. National Administrative Reorganization
10. Election Reform
11. Development of Political Parties
12. Development of Legislative Responsibilities
13. Reorganization of Civil Services
14. Legal and Judicial Reform
15. Freedom of the Press
16. Theater and Motion Pictures
17. Treatment of Foreign Nationals
18. Public Welfare
19. Public Health
20. Social Security
21. Foreign Property Administration
22. Reparations
23. Japanese Property Administration
24. Elimination of Zaibatsu Control
25. Deconcentration of Economic Power
26. Promotion of Fair Trade Practices
27. The Rural Land Reform Program
28. Development of the Trade Union Movement
29. Working Conditions
30. Agriculture Cooperatives
31. Education
32. Religion
33. Radio Broadcasting
34. Price and Distribution Stabilization: Non-Food Program
35. Price and Distribution Stabilization: Food Program
36. Agriculture
37. National Government Finance
38. Local Government Finance
39. Money and Banking

ECONOMIC ISSUES

Martin Bronfenbrenner. "Occupation Period Economy (1945-1952)," KODANSHA ENCYCLOPEDIA OF JAPAN 2: 154-158.

_____. "Four Positions on Japanese Finance," *Journal of Political Economy* 58.4 (1950), 281-288.

_____. "Inflation Theories of the SCAP Period," *History of Political Economy* 7.2 (1975), 137-155.

Takafusa Nakamura. THE POSTWAR JAPANESE ECONOMY: ITS DEVELOPMENT AND STRUCTURE. 1981: University of Tokyo Press.

MacArthur Memorial. THE OCCUPATION OF JAPAN: ECONOMIC POLICY AND REFORM (proceedings of the 1978 symposium). Includes papers on the Dodge Line, land reform and labor policy, zaibatsu dissolution, economic deconcentration, banking, and trade recovery.

Hyoe Ouchi. FINANCIAL AND MONETARY SITUATION IN POST-WAR JAPAN. 1947: Institute of Pacific Relations.

Jerome B. Cohen. JAPAN'S ECONOMY IN WAR AND RECONSTRUCTION. 1949: University of Minnesota Press.

_____. JAPAN'S POSTWAR ECONOMY. 1958: Indiana University Press.

Leon Hollerman. "International Economic Controls in Occupied Japan," *Journal of Asian Studies* 38.4 (1979), 707-719.

T. A. Bisson. ZAIBATSU DISSOLUTION IN JAPAN. 1954: University of California Press.

Eleanor M. Hadley. ANTI-TRUST IN JAPAN. 1970: Princeton University Press.

_____. "Zaibatsu" and "Zaibatsu Dissolution," KODANSHA ENCYCLOPEDIA OF JAPAN 8: 361-366.

_____. "From Deconcentration to Reverse Course," in Robert Wolfe, ed. AMERICANS AS PROCONSULS (1984: Southern Illinois University Press), 138-154.

Howard Schonberger. "Zaibatsu Dissolution and the American Restoration of Japan," *Bulletin of Concerned Asian Scholars* 5.2 (September 1973), 16-31.

_____. "The Japan Lobby in American Diplomacy, 1947-1952," *Pacific Historical Review* 46 (1977), 327-359.

John Roberts. "The 'Japan Crowd' and the Zaibatsu Restoration," *Japan Interpreter* 12.3-4 (1979), 384-415.

Kozo Yamamura. ECONOMIC POLICY IN POSTWAR JAPAN: GROWTH VERSUS ECONOMIC DEMOCRACY. 1967: University of California Press.

William S. Borden. THE PACIFIC ALLIANCE: UNITED STATES FOREIGN ECONOMIC POLICY AND JAPANESE TRADE RECOVERY, 1947-1955. 1984: University of Wisconsin Press.

Michael Schaller. THE AMERICAN OCCUPATION OF JAPAN: THE ORIGINS OF THE COLD WAR IN ASIA. 1985: Oxford University Press.

Soong H. Kil. "The Dodge Line and the Japanese Conservative Party." 1977: Ph.D. dissertation in Political Science, University of Michigan.

Chitoshi Yanaga. BIG BUSINESS IN JAPANESE POLITICS. 1968: Yale University Press.

Saburo Shiomi. JAPAN'S FINANCE AND TAXATION, 1940-1956. 1957: Columbia University Press.

ECONOMIC ISSUES--II

Robert S. Ozaki. THE CONTROL OF IMPORTS AND FOREIGN CAPITAL IN JAPAN. 1972: Praeger.

Warren Hunsberger. JAPAN AND THE UNITED STATES IN WORLD TRADE. 1964: Harper & Row.

Sherwood M. Fine. JAPAN'S POSTWAR INDUSTRIAL RECOVERY. 1953: Foreign Affairs Association of Japan.

Chalmers Johnson. MITI AND THE JAPANESE MIRACLE: THE GROWTH OF INDUSTRIAL POLICY, 1925-1975. 1982: Stanford University Press.

Edwin W. Pauley. REPORT ON JAPANESE REPARATIONS TO THE PRESIDENT OF THE UNITED STATES, NOVEMBER 1945 TO APRIL 1946. Department of State Publication 3174, Far Eastern Series 25. 1946. The Pauley Report.

U. S. Department of State. REPORT OF THE MISSION ON JAPANESE COMBINES, PART I, ANALYTICAL AND TECHNICAL DATA. Department of State Publication 2628, Far Eastern Series 14. 1946. The Edwards Report. Part II of this report, formerly classified Top Secret, is now also available.

U. S. Department of the Army. REPORT ON THE ECONOMIC POSITION AND PROSPECTS OF JAPAN AND KOREA AND THE MEASURES REQUIRED TO IMPROVE THEM. 1948. The Johnston Report.

Japanese Ministry of Foreign Affairs. BASIC PROBLEMS FOR POSTWAR RECONSTRUCTION OF JAPANESE ECONOMY: TRANSLATION OF A REPORT OF MINISTRY OF FOREIGN AFFAIRS' SPECIAL SURVEY COMMITTEE, SEPTEMBER 1946. An important internal Japanese study, translated and published in 1977 by the Japan Economic Research Center.

Okurasho Zaiseishishitsu (Ministry of Finance, Financial History Section), ed. SHOWA ZAISEI SHI: SHUSEN KARA KOWA MADE (The Financial History of Japan: The Allied Occupation Period, 1945-1952). Two volumes of this important 20-volume Japanese-language history of Occupation economic and financial policy are of particular interest. Volume 19 (*Tokei*), published in 1978, contains the most comprehensive and authoritative statistical data pertaining to the economy; unfortunately the tables do not include English headings. Volume 20 (*Eibun Shiryo*), published in 1982, is an 851-page collection of basic U.S. documents on economic policy toward Japan, many of them drawn from formerly classified archives.

LAND & LABOR

Ronald P. Dore. LAND REFORM IN JAPAN. 1959: Oxford University Press.

Lawrence I. Hewes. JAPAN: LAND AND MEN. AN ACCOUNT OF THE JAPANESE LAND REFORM PROGRAM, 1945-1951. 1955: Iowa State College Press.

Tsutomu Ouchi. "The Japanese Land Reform: Its Efficacy and Limitations," *Developing Economies* 4.2 (1966), 129-150. This issue of *Developing Economies* is devoted to a general reassessment of the land reform.

MacArthur Memorial. THE OCCUPATION OF JAPAN: ECONOMIC POLICY AND REFORM (proceedings of the 1978 symposium). Includes papers by Frank Sackton and Hiromitsu Kaneda on land reform, and Theodore Cohen and Koji Taira on labor policy.

Solomon Levine. "Labor," KODANSHA ENCYCLOPEDIA OF JAPAN 4: 343-349, esp. 345-347.

_____. INDUSTRIAL RELATIONS IN POSTWAR JAPAN. 1958: University of Illinois Press.

Joe B. Moore. JAPANESE WORKERS AND THE STRUGGLE FOR POWER, 1945-1947. 1983: University of Wisconsin Press.

Miriam S. Farley. ASPECTS OF JAPAN'S LABOR PROBLEMS. 1950: John Day.

I. F. Ayusawa. A HISTORY OF LABOR IN MODERN JAPAN. 1966: University of Hawaii Press.

Kazuo Okochi. LABOR IN MODERN JAPAN. 1958: Science Council of Japan.

Koji Taira. ECONOMIC DEVELOPMENT AND THE LABOR MARKET IN JAPAN. 1970: Columbia University Press.

Robert Scalapino. "Japan," in Walter Galenson, ed. LABOR AND ECONOMIC DEVELOPMENT (1959: Wiley), 75-145.

Andrew Gordon. THE EVOLUTION OF LABOR RELATIONS IN JAPAN: HEAVY INDUSTRY, 1853-1955. 1985: Harvard East Asian Monographs.

Sheldon M. Garon. "The Imperial Bureaucracy and Labor Policy in Postwar Japan," *Journal of Asian Studies* 43.3 (1984), 441-457.

Howard Schonberger. "American Labor's Cold War in Occupied Japan," *Diplomatic History* 5 (1977), 327-359.

Taishiro Shirai, ed. CONTEMPORARY INDUSTRIAL RELATIONS IN JAPAN. 1983: University of Wisconsin Press.

211

POLITICAL ACTIVITY

Supreme Commander Allied Powers, Government Section. POLITICAL REORIENTATION OF JAPAN: SEPTEMBER, 1945 TO SEPTEMBER, 1948. 2 volumes. 1949: Government Printing Office. The basic and most often cited official documentary source. As its title indicates, however, this is restricted to political matters (with a few exceptions) during the first three years of occupation only.

Justin Willliams. JAPAN'S POLITICAL REVOLUTION UNDER MACARTHUR: A PARTICIPANT'S ACCOUNT. 1979: University of Georgia Press.

John W. Dower. EMPIRE AND AFTERMATH: YOSHIDA SHIGERU AND THE JAPANESE EXPERIENCE, 1878-1954. 1979: Harvard East Asian Monographs.

Harold S. Quigley & John E. Turner. THE NEW JAPAN: GOVERNMENT AND POLITICS. 1956: University of Minnesota Press.

Paul Linebarger, Chu Djang & Ardath Burks. FAR EASTERN GOVERNMENTS AND POLITICS. 1954: Van Nostrand.

Haruhiro Fukui. PARTY IN POWER: THE JAPANESE LIBERAL DEMOCRATS AND POLICY MAKING. 1970: University of California Press.

Robert A. Scalapino & Junnosuke Masumi. PARTIES AND POLITICS IN CONTEMPORARY JAPAN. 1962: University of California Press.

Junnosuke Masumi. POSTWAR POLITICS IN JAPAN. 1985: Institute of East Asian Studies, University of California, Berkeley.

Kurt Steiner. LOCAL GOVERNMENT IN JAPAN. 1965: Stanford University Press.

Evelyn Colbert. THE LEFT WING IN JAPANESE POLITICS. 1952: Institute of Pacific Relations.

A. Cole, G. Totten & C. Uyehara. SOCIALIST PARTIES IN POSTWAR JAPAN. 1966: Yale University Press.

J. A. A. Stockwin. JAPAN: DIVIDED POLITICS IN A GROWTH ECONOMY. 1975: Weidenfeld & Nicholson.

Joe B. Moore. JAPANESE WORKERS AND THE STRUGGLE FOR POWER, 1945-1947. 1983: University of Wisconsin Press.

Roger Swearingen & Paul Langer. RED FLAG IN JAPAN: INTERNATIONAL COMMUNISM IN ACTION, 1919-1951. 1952: Harvard University Press.

Robert A. Scalapino. THE JAPANESE COMMUNIST MOVEMENT, 1920-1966. 1966: Univ. of California Press.

Toshio G. Tsukahira. THE POSTWAR EVOLUTION OF COMMUNIST STRATEGY IN JAPAN. 1954: Massachusetts Institute of Technology Press.

Richard L-G. Deverall. RED STAR OVER JAPAN. 1952: Temple Press, Calcutta.

George Beckmann & Genji Okubo. THE JAPANESE COMMUNIST PARTY, 1922-1945. 1969: Stanford Univ. Press.

Chalmers Johnson. CONSPIRACY AT MATSUKAWA. 1972: University of California Press.

Benjamin C. Duke. JAPAN'S MILITANT TEACHERS: A HISTORY OF THE LEFT-WING TEACHERS' MOVEMENT. 1973: University of Hawaii Press.

Ivan Morris. NATIONALISM AND THE RIGHT WING IN POSTWAR JAPAN. 1960: Oxford University Press.

OTHER SPECIAL SUBJECTS

Wartime Thinking & Presurrender Planning

Marlene J. Mayo. "American Wartime Planning for Occupied Japan: The Role of the Experts," in Robert Wolfe, ed. AMERICANS AS PROCONSULS (1984: Southern Illinois University Press), 3-51, 447-474.

_____. "American Economic Planning for Occupied Japan: The Issue of *Zaibatsu* Dissolution, 1942-1945," in the MacArthur Memorial's THE OCCUPATION OF JAPAN: ECONOMIC POLICY AND REFORM (1980: MacArthur Memorial), 205-228, 252-262.

Hugh Borton. "Preparation for the Occupation of Japan," *Journal of Asian Studies* 25.2 (1966), 203-212.

_____. AMERICAN PRESURRENDER PLANNING FOR POSTWAR JAPAN. 1967: Occasional Papers of the East Asian Institute, Columbia University.

Akira Iriye. POWER AND CULTURE: THE JAPANESE-AMERICAN WAR, 1941-1945. 1981: Harvard University Press.

Christopher Thorne. ALLIES OF A KIND: THE UNITED STATES, BRITAIN, AND THE WAR AGAINST JAPAN, 1941-1945. 1978: Oxford University Press.

The Purge

Hans H. Baerwald. THE PURGE OF JAPANESE LEADERS UNDER THE OCCUPATION. 1959: Univ. of California Press.

John D. Montgomery. THE PURGE IN OCCUPIED JAPAN: A STUDY IN THE USE OF CIVILIAN AGENCIES UNDER MILITARY GOVERNMENT. 1953: Johns Hopkins.

War Crimes

See pages 173-174 above for the published proceedings of the International Military Tribunal for the Far East and key sources on the general issue of war crimes—including the I.M.T.F.E. judgment, Justice Pal's famous lengthy dissent, the transcript of the 1949 U.S.S.R. Khabarovsk trial of Japanese accused of biological-warfare experiments, and pertinent writings by Richard Minear, Philip Piccigallo, John Powell, and Frank Reel.

Legal Reform & Constitutional Revision

MacArthur Memorial. THE OCCUPATION OF JAPAN: IMPACT OF LEGAL REFORM (proceedings of the 1977 symposium). Papers and discussions deal with local government, election reform, constitutional revision, the supreme court, and women's rights.

Alfred C. Oppler. LEGAL REFORM IN OCCUPIED JAPAN: A PARTICIPANT LOOKS BACK. 1976: Princeton University Press.

University of Washington School of Law, ed. LEGAL REFORMS IN JAPAN DURING THE ALLIED OCCUPATION. 1977: University of Washington. A special issue of the *Washington Law Review* , reprinting 7 articles on the subject published between 1949 and 1951.

OTHER SPECIAL SUBJECTS--II

John M. Maki, transl. and ed. JAPAN'S COMMISSION ON THE CONSTITUTION: THE FINAL REPORT. 1980: University of Washington Press.

Kenzo Takayanagi. "Some Reminiscences of Japan's Commission on the Constitution," *Washington Law Review* 43 (1968), 961-978.

Justin Williams. "Making the Japanese Constitution: A Further Look," *American Political Science Review* 59 (1965), 665-679.

_____. "Completing Japan's Political Reorientation, 1947-1952: Crucial Phase of the Allied Occupation," *American Historical Review* 73 (1968), 1454-1469.

Theodore McNelly. "The Japanese Constitution: Child of the Cold War," *Political Science Quarterly* 74 (1958), 176-195.

_____. "The Renunciation of War in the Japanese Constitution," *Political Science Quarterly* 77 (1962), 350-378.

Tatsuo Sato. "The Origin and Development of the Draft Constitution of Japan," *Contemporary Japan* 24. 4-6, 7-9 (1956), 175-187, 371-387.

H. Fukui. "Twenty Years of Revisionism," *Washington Law Review* 43 (1968), 931-960.

Dan Fenno Henderson, ed. THE CONSTITUTION OF JAPAN: THE FIRST TWENTY YEARS, 1947-1967. 1968: University of Washington Press.

Kenzo Takayanagi, Ichiro Ohtomo & Hideo Tanaka, eds. NIHONKOKU KEMPO SEITEI NO KATEI (The Making of the Constitution of Japan). 2 volumes. 1972: Yuhikaku. Includes English memoranda from the papers of Milo Rowell.

Bureaucracy

Akira Kubota. HIGHER CIVIL SERVANTS IN POSTWAR JAPAN. 1969: Princeton University Press.

Chalmers Johnson. MITI AND THE JAPANESE MIRACLE: THE GROWTH OF INDUSTRIAL POLICY, 1925-1975. 1982: Stanford University Press.

The Emperor & Emperor System

Genji Okubo. THE PROBLEMS OF THE EMPEROR SYSTEM IN POSTWAR JAPAN. 1948: Japan Institute of Pacific Studies.

Kiyoko Takeda Cho. "The Dual Image of the Japanese Tenno: Conflicting Foreign Ideas About the Remoulding of the *Tenno sei* at the End of the War," *Proceedings of the British Association for Japanese Studies* 1 (1976), 110-130.

214

OTHER SPECIAL SUBJECTS--III

Education

Supreme Commander for the Allied Powers, Civil Information and Education Section. POST-WAR DEVELOPMENTS IN JAPANESE EDUCATION. 1952: Civil Information and Education Section.

Toshio Nishi. UNCONDITIONAL DEMOCRACY: EDUCATION AND POLITICS IN OCCUPIED JAPAN, 1945-1952. 1982: Hoover Institution Press.

MacArthur Memorial. THE OCCUPATION OF JAPAN: EDUCATIONAL AND SOCIAL REFORM (proceedings of the 1980 symposium). Includes papers on various aspects of educational reform, welfare policy, and the civil service.

Robert K. Hall. EDUCATION FOR A NEW JAPAN. 1949: Yale University Press.

_____. "Education in the Development of Postwar Japan," in MacArthur Memorial, THE OCCUPATION OF JAPAN AND ITS LEGACY TO THE POSTWAR WORLD (proceedings of the 1975 symposium), 117-148.

Victor N. Kobayashi. "Japan Under American Occupation," in Edward R. Beauchamp, ed. LEARNING TO BE JAPANESE (1978: Linnet), 181-207.

Miscellaneous Subjects

William P. Woodard. THE ALLIED OCCUPATION OF JAPAN AND JAPANESE RELIGIONS. 1972: Brill.

William J. Coughlin. CONQUERED PRESS: THE MACARTHUR ERA IN JAPANESE JOURNALISM. 1952: Pacific.

Jay Rubin. "From Wholesomeness to Decadence: The Censorship of Literature Under the Allied Occupation," Journal of Japanese Studies 11.1 (1985), 71-103.

Akira Iwasaki. "The Occupied Screen," Japan Quarterly 25.3 (1978), 302-322.

THE OCCUPATION IN GLOBAL PERSPECTIVE

John W. Dower. EMPIRE AND AFTERMATH: YOSHIDA SHIGERU AND THE JAPANESE EXPERIENCE, 1878-1954. 1979: Harvard East Asian Monographs.

_____. "The Eye of the Beholder: Background Notes on the U.S.-Japan Military Relationship," *Bulletin of Concerned Asian Scholars* 2.1 (October 1969), 15-30.

_____. "Occupied Japan in the American Lake, 1945-1950," in Edward Friedman & Mark Selden, eds. AMERICA'S ASIA: DISSENTING ESSAYS ON ASIAN-AMERICAN RELATIONS (1971: Pantheon), 146-206.

_____. "The Superdomino in Postwar Asia: Japan In and Out of the Pentagon Papers," in Noam Chomsky & Howard Zinn, eds. THE SENATOR GRAVEL EDITION OF THE PENTAGON PAPERS. Volume 5 (1972: Beacon), 101-142.

Michael Schaller. "Securing the Great Crescent: Occupied Japan and the Origins of Containment in South East Asia," *Journal of American History* 69 (1982), 392-414.

_____. THE AMERICAN OCCUPATION OF JAPAN: THE ORIGINS OF THE COLD WAR IN ASIA. 1985: Oxford University Press.

William S. Borden. THE PACIFIC ALLIANCE: UNITED STATES FOREIGN ECONOMIC POLICY AND JAPANESE TRADE RECOVERY, 1947-1955. 1984: University of Wisconsin Press.

Gabriel Kolko. THE POLITICS OF WAR: THE WORLD AND UNITED STATES FOREIGN POLICY, 1943-1945. 1968: Random House.

Joyce & Gabriel Kolko. THE LIMITS OF POWER: THE WORLD AND UNITED STATES FOREIGN POLICY, 1945-1954. 1972: Harper & Row.

MacArthur Memorial. THE OCCUPATION OF JAPAN: THE INTERNATIONAL CONTEXT (proceedings of the 1982 symposium). Includes papers on the Allied Council, the peace settlement, Japan and Southeast Asia, and the Occupation as seen from Great Britain, Australia, and Canada.

Herbert Feis. CONTEST OVER JAPAN. 1967: Norton.

Roger Dingman. "Strategic Planning and the Policy Process: American Plans for War in East Asia, 1945-50," *Naval War College Review* 32 (1979), 4-21.

Frederick S. Dunn. PEACE-MAKING AND THE SETTLEMENT WITH JAPAN. 1963: Princeton University Press.

Michael M. Yoshitsu. JAPAN AND THE SAN FRANCISCO PEACE SETTLEMENT. 1982: Columbia University Press.

Bernard C. Cohen. THE POLITICAL PROCESS AND FOREIGN POLICY: THE MAKING OF THE JAPANESE PEACE SETTLEMENT. 1957: Princeton University Press.

Martin E. Weinstein. JAPAN'S POSTWAR DEFENSE POLICY, 1947-1968. 1971: Columbia University Press.

James E. Auer. THE POSTWAR REARMAMENT OF JAPANESE MARITIME FORCES, 1945-1971. 1973: Praeger.

Takeshi Igarashi. "Peace-Making and Party Politics: The Formation of the Domestic Foreign-Policy System in Postwar Japan," *Journal of Japanese Studies* 11.2 (1985), 323-356.

R. K. Jain. JAPAN'S POSTWAR PEACE SETTLEMENTS. 1979: Radiant.

George H. Blakeslee. THE FAR EASTERN COMMISSION: A STUDY IN INTERNATIONAL COOPERATION, 1945-1952. Department of State Publication 5138, Far Eastern Series 60. 1953.

U. S. Department of State. TREATY OF PEACE WITH JAPAN. SIGNED AT SAN FRANCISCO, SEPTEMBER 8, 1951. Department of State Publication 4613. 1952.

U. S. Congress, Senate, Committee on Armed Services. MILITARY SITUTATION IN THE FAR EAST. 82nd Congress, 1st Session. 5 parts. The 1951 Congressional hearings upon the recall of General MacArthur.

Robin Kay, ed. THE SURRENDER AND OCCUPATION OF JAPAN, volume 2 of DOCUMENTS ON NEW ZEALAND EXTERNAL RELATIONS. 1982: Government Printer, Wellington, N.Z. A huge official collection of almost 1,800 pages.

Roger W. Buckley. OCCUPATION DIPLOMACY: BRITAIN, THE UNITED STATES, AND JAPAN, 1945-1952. 1982: Cambridge University Press.

Richard N. Rosecrance. AUSTRALIAN DIPLOMACY AND JAPAN, 1945-1951. 1962: Melbourne University Press.

Ben-Ami Shillony, ed. JAPAN THIRTY YEARS AFTER THE END OF OCCUPATION: POLITICAL, ECONOMIC AND CULTURAL TRENDS. 1984. Special Issue in volume 18 of *Asian and African Studies*.

Diplomatic History 10.1 (1986). Special issue focusing on post-1945 U.S. policy toward Asia. Articles include Michael Schaller on "MacArthur's Japan"; David McLean on China policy in 1949-1950; Rosemary Foot on "Anglo-American Relations in the Korean Crisis"; Howard Schonberger on Japanese recognition of Nationalist China in 1951-1952; and Yoko Yasuhara on "Japan, Communist China, and Export Controls in Asia, 1948-52."

217

BASIC DOCUMENTARY COLLECTIONS & OFFICIAL PUBLICATIONS

Supreme Commander Allied Powers. Government Section. POLITICAL REORIENTATION OF JAPAN: SEPTEMBER, 1945 TO SEPTEMBER, 1948. 2 volumes. 1949.

_____. INSTRUCTIONS TO THE JAPANESE GOVERNMENT FROM 4 SEPTEMBER 1945 TO 8 MARCH 1952. 1952. The complete collection of SCAP instructions on political, economic, and social matters.

_____. SUMMATION OF NON-MILITARY ACTIVITIES IN JAPAN. 35 volumes. Useful week-by-week coverage of activities from September 1945 through August 1948.

[For the gamut of SCAP publications, see Robert Ward & Frank Joseph Shulman, THE ALLIED OCCUPATION OF JAPAN, 114-123]

Okurasho Zaiseishishitsu (Ministry of Finance, Financial History Section), ed. SHOWA ZAISEI SHI: SHUSEN KARA KOWA MADE. The 20th and last volume of this official history (which bears the English title *The Financial History of Japan: The Allied Occupation Period, 1945-1952*), published in 1982, is an 851-page collection of official U.S. documents pertaining to the Occupation, beginning with presurrender planning and extending to the immediate post-Occupation period. Many of these documents come from declassified U. S. archives. This is the most important single documentary source for basic economic policies.

U. S. Department of the Army. REPORTS OF GENERAL MACARTHUR. 1966. "Volume 1: Supplement" of this 4-volume publication deals with such military aspects of the occupation as repatriation, demobilization, and destruction of Japanese military stocks.

Gaimusho Tokubetsu Shiryoka, ed. NIHON SENRYO OYOBI KANRI JUYO BUNSHO SHU. 4 volumes. Basic documents in English with Japanese translations, to December 1949.

Far Eastern Commission. ACTIVITIES OF THE FAR EASTERN COMMISSION, REPORT BY THE SECRETARY-GENERAL, FEBRUARY 26, 1946 - JULY 10, 1947. Department of State Publication 2888, Far Eastern Series 24. 1947.

_____. THE FAR EASTERN COMMISSION, SECOND REPORT BY THE SECRETARY-GENERAL, JULY 10, 1947 - DECEMBER 23, 1948. Department of State Publication 3420, Far Eastern Series 29. 1949.

_____. THE FAR EASTERN COMMISSION, THIRD REPORT BY THE SECRETARY-GENERAL, DECEMBER 24, 1948 - JUNE 30, 1950. Department of State Publication 3925, Far Eastern Series 35. 1950.

George Blakeslee. THE FAR EASTERN COMMISSION: A STUDY IN INTERNATIONAL COOPERATION, 1945-1952. Department of State Publication 5138, Far Eastern Series 60. 1953.

Japanese Diet. OFFICIAL GAZETTE and OFFICIAL GAZETTE EXTRA. Basic English-language sources for activities in both houses of the Japanese legislature. The OFFICIAL GAZETTE contains texts of laws, ordinances, and government announcements from April 1946. The OFFICIAL GAZETTE EXTRA contains translations of discussions on the Diet floor from May 1946, including policy speeches by cabinet members and the ensuing interpellations by Diet members.

U. S. Department of State. FOREIGN RELATIONS OF THE UNITED STATES. See especially the annual volumes on Japan and the Far East in this basic State Department archival series.

Thomas H. Etzold & John Lewis Gaddis, eds. CONTAINMENT: DOCUMENTS ON AMERICAN POLICY AND STRATEGY, 1945-1950. 1978: Columbia University Press.

Robin Kay, ed. THE SURRENDER AND OCCUPATION OF JAPAN, volume 2 of DOCUMENTS ON NEW ZEALAND EXTERNAL RELATIONS. 1982: Government Printer, Wellington, N.Z. An official collection of almost 1,800 pages.

A substantial portion of the many official U. S. documents declassified since the 1960s is accessible in commercial microfilm collections. See especially the following:

From Scholarly Resources, Inc.:

SWNCC (State-War-Navy Coordinating Committee) / SANACC (State-Army-Navy-Air Force Coordinating Committee) Case Files, 1944-1949. 32 reels.

From University Publications of America:

Documents of the National Security Council, 1947-1977. 14 reels.

Minutes of the National Security Council, with Special Advisory Reports. 3 reels.

Records of the Joint Chiefs of Staff :

> *Pacific Theater, 1942-1945.* 14 reels.
> *The Far East, 1946-1953.* 14 reels.

Confidential U. S. State Department Central Files:

> *Japan: Internal Affairs, 1945-1949.* 42 reels.
> *Japan: Internal Affairs, 1950-1954.* 62 reels.

CIA Research Reports:

> *China, 1946-1976.* 6 reels.
> *Japan, Korea, and the Security of Asia, 1946-1976.* 5 reels.
> *Vietnam and Southeast Asia, 1946-1976.* 7 reels.

OSS/ State Department Intelligence and Research Reports:

> *Japan and Its Occupied Territories During World War II.* 16 reels.
> *Postwar Japan, Korea and Southeast Asia.* 6 reels.
> *Japan, Korea, Southeast Asia, and the Far East Generally: 1950-1961 Supplement.* 7 reels.

ACCESSIBLE DECLASSIFIED ARCHIVES--II

Formerly secret executive sessions of Congressional hearings pertinent to Japan and Asia began to be declassified as a "Historical Series" and published in the 1970s. See especially the following:

U. S. Congress. Senate Foreign Relations Committee. *Executive Sessions of the Senate Foreign Relations Committee (Historical Series)*. Multi-volume, beginning with the 80th Congress of 1947-48 and including:

_____. *Legislative Origins of the Truman Doctrine*. 1947.

_____. *Foreign Relief Aid*. 1947.

_____. *Foreign Relief Assistance Act*. 1948.

_____. *Vandenberg Resolution and NATO*. 1948-1949.

_____. *Economic Assistance to China and Korea*. 1949-1950.

_____. *Reviews of the World Situation*. 1949-1950.

_____. *Military Assistance Program*. 1949.

_____. *Extension of European Recovery Program*. 1949.

U. S. Congress. House Committee on International Relations. *Selected Executive Session Hearings of the Committee, 1943-1950*. 8 volumes; see especially volume 7 on "Policy in the Far East" and volume 8 on "Mutual Defense Assistance Program."

THE COLD WAR IN ASIA: COUNTRY & REGIONAL STUDIES

Harold R. Issacs. NEW CYCLE IN ASIA: SELECTED DOCUMENTS ON MAJOR INTERNATIONAL DEVEOPMENTS IN THE FAR EAST. 1947: Macmillan.

Akira Iriye. THE COLD WAR IN ASIA: A HISTORICAL INTRODUCTION. 1974: Prentice-Hall.

_____ & Yonosuke Nagai, eds. THE ORIGINS OF THE COLD WAR IN ASIA. 1977: Columbia University Press.

Edward Friedman & Mark Selden, eds. AMERICA'S ASIA: DISSENTING ESSAYS ON ASIAN-AMERICAN RELATIONS. 1969: Pantheon.

Noam Chomsky & Howard Zinn, eds. THE SENATOR GRAVEL EDITION OF THE PENTAGON PAPERS, volume 5: "Critical Essays." 1972: Beacon.

Japanese Association for American Studies. UNITED STATES POLICY TOWARD EAST ASIA, 1945-1950. Six essays by Japanese scholars in the maiden issue of the English-language *Japanese Journal of American Studies* (1980).

Tang Tsou. AMERICA'S FAILURE IN CHINA, 1941-1950. 1963: University of Chicago Press.

Dorothy Borg & Waldo Heinrichs, eds. UNCERTAIN YEARS: CHINESE-AMERICAN RELATIONS, 1947-1950. 1980: Columbia University Press.

Robert M. Blum. DRAWING THE LINE: THE ORIGIN OF THE AMERICAN CONTAINMENT POLICY IN EAST ASIA. 1982: Norton.

Nancy Bernkopf Tucker. PATTERNS IN THE DUST: CHINESE-AMERICAN RELATIONS AND THE RECOGNITION CONTROVERSY, 1949-1950. 1983: Columbia University Press.

_____. "American Policy Toward Sino-Japanese Trade in the Postwar Years: Politics and Prosperity," *Diplomatic History* 8.3 (1984), 183-208.

Bruce Cumings. "The Origins and Development of the Northeast Asian Political Economy: Industrial Sectors, Product Cycles, and Political Consequences," *International Organization* 38.1 (1984), 1-40.

_____, ed. CHILD OF CONFLICT: THE KOREAN-AMERICAN RELATIONSHIP, 1943-1953. 1983: University of Washington Press.

_____. THE ORIGINS OF THE KOREAN WAR: LIBERATION AND THE EMERGENCE OF SEPARATE REGIMES, 1945-1947. 1981: Princeton University Press.

James I. Matray. THE RELUCTANT CRUSADE: AMERICAN FOREIGN POLICY IN KOREA, 1941-1950. 1985: University of Hawaii Press.

Frank Baldwin, ed. WITHOUT PARALLEL: THE AMERICAN-KOREAN RELATIONSHIP SINCE 1945. 1974: Pantheon.

Soon Chung Cho. KOREA IN WORLD POLITICS, 1940-1950: AN EVALUATION OF AMERICAN RESPONSIBILITY. 1967: University of California Press.

William W. Stueck, Jr. THE ROAD TO CONFRONTATION: AMERICAN POLICY TOWARD CHINA AND KOREA, 1947-1950. 1981: University of North Carolina Press.

THE COLD WAR IN ASIA: COUNTRY & REGIONAL STUDIES--II

Samuel P. Hayes. THE BEGINNING OF AMERICAN AID TO SOUTHEAST ASIA: THE GRIFFIN MISSION OF 1950 1971: Heath.

David Wightman. TOWARD ECONOMIC COOPERATION IN ASIA: THE ECONOMIC COMMISSION FOR ASIA AND THE FAR EAST. 1963: Yale University Press.

Russell Fifield. AMERICANS IN SOUTHEAST ASIA: THE ROOTS OF COMMITMENT. 1973: Crowell.

George M. Kahin & John W. Lewis. THE UNITED STATES IN VIETNAM. Revised edition. 1967: Dial.

William Appleman Williams, Thomas McCormick, Lloyd Gardner & Walter LaFeber, eds. AMERICA IN VIETNAM: A DOCUMENTARY HISTORY. 1985: Anchor-Doubleday.

Robert J. McMahon. COLONIALISM AND COLD WAR: THE UNITED STATES AND THE STRUGGLE FOR INDONESIAN INDEPENDENCE, 1945-1949. 1981: Cornell University Press.

Max Beloff. SOVIET POLICY IN THE FAR EAST, 1944-1951. 1953: Oxford University Press.

Russell D. Buhite. SOVIET-AMERICAN RELATIONS IN ASIA, 1945-1954. 1981: University of Oklahoma Press.

Rodger Swearingen. THE SOVIET UNION AND POSTWAR JAPAN: ESCALATING CHALLENGE AND RESPONSE. 1978: Hoover Institution.

Bibliographies & Research Guides

ternational Secretariat, Institute of Pacific Relations. IPR PUBLICATIONS ON THE PACIFIC, 1925-1952. 1953: Institute of Pacific Relations. 1,408 entries.

brary of Congress. THE JAPANESE EMPIRE: INDUSTRIES AND TRANSPORTATION--A SELECTED LIST OF REFERENCES. 1943. 598 entries.

____. JAPAN: ECONOMIC DEVELOPMENT AND FOREIGN POLICY--A SELECTED LIST OF REFERENCES. 1940. 403 entries.

Raymond Nunn. JAPANESE PERIODICALS AND NEWSPAPERS IN WESTERN LANGUAGES. 1979: Mansell. Lists 3,500 titles, dating from the 1860s to 1978.

ugh Borton, Serge Elisseeff, William Lockwood & John C. Pelzel. A SELECTED LIST OF BOOKS AND ARTICLES ON JAPAN IN ENGLISH, FRENCH, AND GERMAN. 1954: Harvard-Yenching Institute. 1,781 entries.

ernard S. Silberman. JAPAN AND KOREA: A CRITICAL BIBLIOGRAPHY. 1962: University of Arizona Press. 1,933 entries.

okusai Bunka Kaikan (Naomi Fukuda, ed). UNION CATALOG OF BOOKS ON JAPAN IN WESTERN LANGUAGES. 1968. 543 pages.

ssociation for Asian Studies. CUMULATIVE BIBLIOGRAPHY OF ASIAN STUDIES, 1941-1965 (1969). Covers both books and articles, and consists of a 4-volume *Author Bibliography* and 4-volume *Subject Bibliography*.

____. CUMULATIVE BIBLIOGRAPY OF ASIAN STUDIES, 1966-1970 (1973). Consists of a 3-volume *Author Bibliography* and 4-volume *Subject Bibliography*.

____. BIBLIOGRAPHY OF ASIAN STUDIES. Annual, beginning in 1970 with books and articles published in 1969. The annual bibliographies are published as separate volumes accompanying the *Journal of Asian Studies*.

ank J. Shulman, comp. & ed. JAPAN AND KOREA: AN ANNOTATED BIBLIOGRAPHY OF DOCTORAL DISSERTATIONS IN WESTERN LANGUAGES, 1877-1969. 1970: American Library Association.

____. DOCTORAL DISSERTATIONS ON JAPAN AND KOREA, 1969-1979: AN ANNOTATED BIBLIOGRAPHY OF STUDIES IN WESTERN LANGUAGES . 1982: University of Washington Press.

____. DOCTORAL DISSERTATIONS ON ASIA: AN ANNOTATED BIBLIOGRAPHICAL JOURNAL OF CURRENT INTERNATIONAL RESEARCH. Published periodically for the Association for Asian Studies by Xerox University Microfilms, beginning with volume 1, number 1 in Winter 1975.

erbert Passin, comp. JAPANESE EDUCATION: A BIBLIOGRAPHY OF MATERIALS IN THE ENGLISH LANGUAGE. 1970: Teachers College, Columbia University. Contains 1,524 entries.

mes William Morley, ed. JAPAN'S FOREIGN POLICY, 1868-1941: A RESEARCH GUIDE. 1974: Columbia University Press. Contains both critical essays and bibliographies, with strong emphasis on Japanese materials up to 1970-1971.

nest R. May & James C. Thomson Jr., eds. AMERICAN-EAST ASIAN RELATIONS: A SURVEY. 1972: Harvard University Press. Bibliographic essays organized by chronology rather than topical focus.

ernd Martin. "Japan und der Krieg in Ostasien: Kommentierender Bericht uber das Schrifttum," Sonderheft 8, *Historische Zeitschrift* (1980), 79-228. A detailed bibliographic essay on World War Two in Asia.

GUIDES TO WESTERN-LANGUAGE MATERIALS--II

R. John Pritchard & Sonia Zaide Pritchard, eds. GUIDE TO THE INTERNATIONAL MILITARY TRIBUNAL FOR THE FAR EAST, 5 volumes. Included in the 27-volume Garland reprint of the records of the International Military Tribunal for the Far East, under the series title THE TOKYO WAR CRIMES TRIAL.

Robert E. Ward & Frank J. Shulman. THE ALLIED OCCUPATION OF JAPAN, 1945-1952: AN ANNOTATED BIBLIOGRAPHY OF WESTERN-LANGUAGE MATERIALS. 1974: American Library Association. An indispensible 867-page guide.

Frank J. Shulman, comp. & ed. DOCTORAL DISSERTATIONS ON THE ALLIED OCCUPATION OF JAPAN, 1945-1952. 1978: prepared for a symposium at the MacArthur Memorial, Norfolk, Virginia.

Institute of Developing Economies. A SELECTED BIBLIOGRAPHY ON THE ECONOMIC DEVELOPMENT OF JAPAN. 1970. 1,780 entries.

Rex Coleman & John Owen Haley. AN INDEX TO JAPANESE LAW: A BIBLIOGRAPHY OF WESTERN LANGUAGE MATERIALS, 1867-1973. 1975. Special issue of *Law in Japan: An Annual.*

Roberta Abraham. BIBLIOGRAPHY ON TECHNOLOGY AND SOCIAL CHANGE IN CHINA AND JAPAN. 1974: Committee on Technology and Social Change in Foreign Cultures, Iowa State University. 252 pages.

Hesung Chun Koh et al. KOREAN AND JAPANESE WOMEN: AN ANALYTIC BIBLIOGRAPHIC GUIDE. 1982: Greenwood.

International House of Japan Library. MODERN JAPANESE LITERATURE IN TRANSLATION. 1979. Nearly 9,000 citations, covering some 1,500 authors from 1868 to 1978.

Yasuhiro Yoshizaki. STUDIES IN JAPANESE LITERATURE AND LANGUAGE: A BIBLIOGRAPHY OF ENGLISH MATERIALS. 1979: Nichigai.

Latin American Studies Center, California State University, Los Angeles. LATIN AMERICA AND JAPAN: A BIBLIOGRAPHY. 1975. 25 pages.

G. Raymond Nunn. ASIA: REFERENCE WORKS--A SELECT ANNOTATED GUIDE. 1980: Mansell.

Asia / North America Communications Center [Hong Kong]. AMERICA IN ASIA: RESEARCH GUIDES ON UNITED STATES ECONOMICS IN PACIFIC ASIA. 1979

Peter Grilli, ed. JAPAN IN FILM: A COMPREHENSIVE CATALOGUE OF DOCUMENTARY AND THEATRICAL FILMS ON JAPAN AVAILABLE IN THE UNITED STATES. 1984: Japan Society of New York. An excellent annotated guide to Japan-related films.

ENGLISH GUIDES TO JAPANESE MATERIALS

The Japan Foundation. AN INTRODUCTORY BIBLIOGRAPHY FOR JAPANESE STUDIES. Ongoing series from 1974. Includes bibliographic surveys of various disciplines by leading Japanese scholars.

Herschel Webb. RESEARCH IN JAPANESE SOURCES: A GUIDE. 1965: Columbia University Press.

American Library Association. GUIDE TO JAPANESE REFERENCE BOOKS. 1966. English version of *Nihon no Sanko Tosho*, 1965.

Library of Congress. GUIDE TO JAPANESE REFERENCE BOOKS: SUPPLEMENT. 1979.

Naomi Fukuda, ed. BIBLIOGRAPHY OF REFERENCE WORKS FOR JAPANESE STUDIES. 1979: Center for Japanese Studies, University of Michigan. Covers Japanese materials published up to 1977, excluding education, law, science and technology.

Kokusai Bunka Shinkokai. K.B.S. BIBLIOGRAPHY OF STANDARD REFERENCE BOOKS FOR JAPANESE STUDIES, WITH DESCRIPTIVE NOTES. 1971 for "Generalia." Other volumes cover specific areas of study.

Naomi Fukuda, ed. JAPANESE HISTORY: A GUIDE TO SURVEY HISTORIES--PART 1, BY PERIOD. 1984: Center for Japanese Studies, University of Michigan.

_____, ed. JAPANESE HISTORY: A GUIDE TO SURVEY HISTORIES--PART 2, LITERATURE. 1986: Center for Japanese Studies, University of Michigan.

James William Morley, ed. JAPAN'S FOREIGN POLICY, 1868-1941: A RESEARCH GUIDE. 1974: Columbia University Press. Includes detailed discussion of Japanese materials up to 1970-1971.

Cecil H. Uyehara. CHECK LIST OF ARCHIVES IN THE JAPANESE MINISTRY OF FOREIGN AFFAIRS, TOKYO, JAPAN, 1868-1945. 1954: Photoduplication Service, Library of Congress. The basic guide to archives seized after the Pacific War and microfilmed for the Library of Congress. Pages 112-146 deal with materials from the International Military Tribunal for the Far East.

John Young. CHECKLIST OF MICROFILM REPRODUCTIONS OF SELECTED ARCHIVES OF THE JAPANESE ARMY, NAVY, AND OTHER GOVERNMENTAL AGENCIES, 1868-1945. 1959: Georgetown Univ. Press.

_____. THE RESEARCH ACTIVITIES OF THE SOUTH MANCHURIAN RAILWAY COMPANY, 1907-1945: A HISTORY AND BIBLIOGRAPHY. 1966: East Asian Institute, Columbia University.

Wayne Lammers & Osamu Masaoka, comp. JAPANESE A-BOMB LITERATURE: AN ANNOTATED BIBLIOGRAPHY. 1977: Wilmington College Peace Resource Center. 132 pages. Followed by later updates.

Naomi Fukuda, ed. SURVEY OF JAPANESE COLLECTIONS IN THE UNITED STATES, 1979-1980. 1981: Center for Japanese Studies, University of Michigan. Surveys 29 collections.

Japan-U.S. Friendship Commission. CURRENT JAPANESE SERIALS IN THE HUMANITIES AND SOCIAL SCIENCES RECEIVED IN AMERICAN LIBRARIES. 1980. Published by East Asia Collection, Indiana University Library, and itemizing 4,389 serials.

Thaddeus Y. Ohta. JAPANESE NATIONAL GOVERNMENT PUBLICATIONS IN THE LIBRARY OF CONGRESS. 1981: Library of Congress.

Basic guides to current Japanese publications:

* *Nihon Zenkoku Shoshi* (Japan National Bibliography Weekly List). Weekly publication of the National Diet Library.
* *Shuppan Nyusu* (Publishing News). Published 3 times per month by Shuppan News, Ltd.

Journals & Other
Serial Publications

Acta Asiatica (1961-)

Amerasia (1937-1947)

Ampo: Japan-Asia Quarterly Review (1969-)

Asia (1898-1946; from November 1942, title becomes *Asia and the Americas*)

Asian Folklore Studies (1963- ; succeeds *Folklore Studies*, 1942-1962)

Asian Survey (1961- ; successor to *Far Eastern Survey*)

Bulletin of Concerned Asian Scholars (1968-)

China Today (1932-1942; merges with *Amerasia*)

Contemporary Japan (1932-)

Daily Summary of Japanese Press (U.S. Embassy, Japan, from 1954; title varies)

The Developing Economies (1962-)

The East (1964-)

Economic Survey of Japan (Annual from 1950/1951 by the Economic Planning Agency and predecessor agencies of the Japanese Government)

Far Eastern Economic Review (1946-)

Far Eastern Survey (1932-1961; succeeded by *Asian Survey*)

Far Eastern Quarterly (1941-1956; succeeded by *Journal of Asian Studies*)

Folklore Studies (1942-1962; succeeded by *Asian Folklore Studies*)

Harvard Journal of Asiatic Studies (1936-)

History of Religions (1961-)

Hitotsubashi Journal of Economics (1960-)

Hitotsubashi Journal of Law and Politics (1960-)

Hitotsubashi Journal of Social Studies (1960-)

Japan Annual of Law and Politics (1952-)

Japan Christian Quarterly (1925-)

Japan Christian Yearbook (1903-)

Japan Echo (1974-)

Japan Interpreter (1970- ; succeeds *Journal of Social and Political Ideas in Japan*, 1963-1967)

Japan Quarterly (1954-)

Japan Socialist Review (1961-)

Japan Times (newspaper, 1897-)

Japanese Economic Studies (1972-)

Japanese Journal of Religious Studies (1974- ; replaces *Contemporary Religions in Japan*, 1960-1970)

Japanese Studies in the History of Science (1962-1979)

Journal of Asian History (1967-)

Journal of Asian Studies (1956- ; succeeds *Far Eastern Quarterly*, 1941-1956)

Journal of Contemporary Asia (1970-)

Journal of Japanese Studies (1974-)

Journal of Northeast Asian Studies (1982-)

Journal of Social and Political Ideas in Japan (1963-1967; succeeded by *Japan Interpreter*)

Kyoto University Economic Review (1926-)

Law in Japan (1967-)

Memoirs of the Research Department of the Toyo Bunko (1920s-)

Modern Asian Studies (1967-)

Monumenta Nipponica (1938-)

Occasional Papers (Center for Japanese Studies, University of Michigan, 1951-1969)

Oriental Economist (1934-)

Pacific Affairs (1928-)

Pacific Historical Review (1932-)

Papers on Japan (East Asian Research Center, Harvard University, 1961-1972)

Philosophical Studies of Japan (1959-1970)

Summaries of Selected Japanese Magazines (U.S. Embassy, Japan, from 1954; title varies)

Transactions, Asiatic Society of Japan ("Series 1" from 1872; "Series 2" from 1924; "Series 3" from 1948)

Transactions, Japan Society of London (1892-)

Trans-Pacific (newspaper, 1919-1940)

ABOUT THE AUTHOR

John W. Dower, born in 1938, holds the Joseph Naiman Endowed Chair in Japanese Studies at the University of California, San Diego. He is the author of *War Without Mercy: Race and Power in the Pacific War*, *Empire and Aftermath: Yoshida Shigeru and the Japanese Experience, 1878-1954* and *The Elements of Japanese Design*, and is the editor of *The Origins of the Japanese State: Selected Writings of E. H. Norman* and coeditor of *The Hiroshima Murals: The Art of Iri Maruki and Toshi Maruki*.